Getting Started with Google BERT

Build and train state-of-the-art natural language processing models using BERT

Sudharsan Ravichandiran

BIRMINGHAM - MUMBAI

Getting Started with Google BERT

Copyright © 2021 Packt Publishing

Group Product Manager: Kunal Parikh
Publishing Product Manager: Devika Battike
Content Development Editor: Sean Lobo
Senior Editor: Roshan Kumar
Technical Editor: Manikandan Kurup
Copy Editor: Safis Editing
Project Coordinator: Aishwarya Mohan
Proofreader: Safis Editing
Indexer: Priyanka Dhadke
Production Designer: Prashant Ghare

First published: January 2021

Production reference: 2211021

Published by Packt Publishing Ltd.
Livery Place
35 Livery Street
Birmingham
B3 2PB, UK.

ISBN 978-1-83882-159-3

www.packt.com

To my adorable mom, Kasthuri, and to my beloved dad, Ravichandiran.

- Sudharsan Ravichandiran

Subscribe to our online digital library for full access to over 7,000 books and videos, as well as industry leading tools to help you plan your personal development and advance your career. For more information, please visit our website.

Why subscribe?

- Spend less time learning and more time coding with practical eBooks and Videos from over 4,000 industry professionals

- Improve your learning with Skill Plans built especially for you

- Get a free eBook or video every month

- Fully searchable for easy access to vital information

- Copy and paste, print, and bookmark content

Did you know that Packt offers eBook versions of every book published, with PDF and ePub files available? You can upgrade to the eBook version at www.packt.com and as a print book customer, you are entitled to a discount on the eBook copy. Get in touch with us at customercare@packtpub.com for more details.

At www.packt.com, you can also read a collection of free technical articles, sign up for a range of free newsletters, and receive exclusive discounts and offers on Packt books and eBooks.

About the author

Sudharsan Ravichandiran is a data scientist, researcher, and bestselling author. He completed his bachelor's in information technology at Anna University. His area of research focuses on practical implementations of deep learning and reinforcement learning, including natural language processing and computer vision. He is an open source contributor and loves answering questions on Stack Overflow. He also authored a best seller, *Hands-On Reinforcement Learning with Python*, published by Packt Publishing.

I would like to thank my most amazing parents and my brother, Karthikeyan, for inspiring and motivating me. I would like to thank the Packt team, Devika, Sean, and Kirti, for their great help. Without all of their support, it would have been impossible to complete this book.

About the reviewers

Dr. Armando Fandango creates AI-empowered products by leveraging reinforcement learning, deep learning, and distributed computing. Armando has provided thought leadership in diverse roles at small and large enterprises, including Accenture, Nike, Sonobi, and IBM, along with advising high-tech AI-based start-ups. Armando has authored several books, including *Mastering TensorFlow, TensorFlow Machine Learning Projects*, and *Python Data Analysis*, and has published research in international journals and presented his research at conferences. Dr. Armando's current research and product development interests lie in the areas of reinforcement learning, deep learning, edge AI, and AI in simulated and real environments (VR/XR/AR).

Ashwin Sreenivas is the cofounder and chief technology officer of Helia AI, a computer vision company that structures and understands the world's video. Prior to this, he was a deployment strategist at Palantir Technologies. Ashwin graduated in Phi Beta Kappa from Stanford University with a master's degree in artificial intelligence and a bachelor's degree in computer science.

Gabriel Bianconi is the founder of Scalar Research, an artificial intelligence and data science consulting firm. Past clients include start-ups backed by YCombinator and leading venture capital firms (for example, Scale AI, and Fandom), investment firms, and their portfolio companies (for example, the Two Sigma-backed insurance firm MGA), and large enterprises (for example, an industrial conglomerate in Asia, and a leading strategy consulting firm). Beyond consulting, Gabriel is a frequent speaker at major technology conferences and a reviewer on top academic conferences (for example, ICML) and AI textbooks. Previously, he received B.S. and M.S. degrees in computer science from Stanford University, where he conducted award-winning research in computer vision and deep learning.

Mani Kanteswara has a bachelor's and a master's in finance (tech) from BITS Pilani with over 10 years of strong technical expertise and statistical knowledge of analytics. He is currently working as a lead strategist with Google and has previously worked as a senior data scientist at WalmartLabs. He has worked in deep learning, computer vision, machine learning, and the natural language processing space building solutions/frameworks capable of solving different business problems and building algorithmic products. He has extensive expertise in solving problems in IoT, telematics, social media, the web, and the e-commerce space. He strongly believes that learning concepts with a practical implementation of the subject and exploring its application areas leads to a great foundation.

Packt is searching for authors like you

If you're interested in becoming an author for Packt, please visit `authors.packtpub.com` and apply today. We have worked with thousands of developers and tech professionals, just like you, to help them share their insight with the global tech community. You can make a general application, apply for a specific hot topic that we are recruiting an author for, or submit your own idea.

Table of Contents

Section 2: Section 2 - Exploring BERT Variants

Section 3: Section 3 - Applications of BERT

Preface

Bidirectional Encoder Representations from Transformers (**BERT**) has revolutionized the world of **natural language processing** (**NLP**) with promising results. This book is an introductory guide that will help you get to grips with Google's BERT architecture.

The book begins by giving you a detailed explanation of the transformer architecture and helps you understand how the encoder and decoder of the transformer work.

You'll get to grips with BERT and explore its architecture, along with discovering how the BERT model is pre-trained and how to use pre-trained BERT for downstream tasks by fine-tuning it. As you advance, you'll find out about different variants of BERT such as ALBERT, RoBERTa, ELECTRA, and SpanBERT, as well as look into BERT variants based on knowledge distillation, such as DistilBERT and TinyBERT. The book also teaches you about M-BERT, XLM, and XLM-R in detail. You'll then learn about Sentence-BERT, which is used for obtaining sentence representation. You will also see some domain-specific BERT models such as BioBERT and ClinicalBERT. At the end of the book, you will learn about an interesting variant of BERT called VideoBERT.

By the end of this BERT book, you'll be well versed in using BERT and its variants for performing practical NLP tasks.

Who this book is for

This book is for NLP professionals and data scientists looking to simplify NLP tasks to enable efficient language understanding using BERT. A basic understanding of NLP concepts and deep learning is required to get the most out of this book.

What this book covers

Chapter 1, *A Primer on Transformers*, explains the transformer model in detail. We will understand how the encoder and decoder of transformer work by looking at their components in detail.

Chapter 2, *Understanding the BERT model*, helps us to understand the BERT model. We will learn how the BERT model is pre-trained using **Masked Language Model** (**MLM**) and **Next Sentence Prediction** (**NSP**) tasks. We will also learn several interesting subword tokenization algorithms.

Chapter 3, *Getting Hands-On with BERT*, explains how to use the pre-trained BERT model. We will learn how to extract contextual sentences and word embeddings using the pre-trained BERT model. We will also learn how to fine-tune the pre-trained BERT for downstream tasks such as question-answering, text classification, and more.

Chapter 4, *BERT Variants I – ALBERT, RoBERTa, ELECTRA, and SpanBERT*, explains several variants of BERT. We will learn how BERT variants differ from BERT and how they are useful in detail.

Chapter 5, *BERT Variants II – Based on Knowledge Distillation*, deals with BERT models based on distillation, such as DistilBERT and TinyBERT. We will also learn how to transfer knowledge from a pre-trained BERT model to a simple neural network.

Chapter 6, *Exploring BERTSUM for Text Summarization*, explains how to fine-tune the pre-trained BERT model for a text summarization task. We will understand how to fine-tune BERT for extractive summarization and abstractive summarization in detail.

Chapter 7, *Applying BERT to Other Languages*, deals with applying BERT to languages other than English. We will learn about the effectiveness of multilingual BERT in detail. We will also explore several cross-lingual models such as XLM and XLM-R.

Chapter 8, *Exploring Sentence and Domain-Specific BERT*, explains Sentence-BERT, which is used to obtain the sentence representation. We will also learn how to use the pre-trained Sentence-BERT model. Along with this, we will also explore domain-specific BERT models such as ClinicalBERT and BioBERT.

Chapter 9, *Working with VideoBERT, BART, and More*, deals with an interesting type of BERT called VideoBERT. We will also learn about a model called BART in detail. We will also explore two popular libraries known as ktrain and bert-as-service.

To get the most out of this book

To get the most out of the book, run all the code provided in the book using Google Colab.

Software/Hardware requirements	Operating System
Google Colab / Python 3.x	Windows/macOS/Linux

Download the example code files

You can download the example code files for this book from GitHub at https://github.com/PacktPublishing/Getting-Started-with-Google-BERT. In case there's an update to the code, it will be updated on the existing GitHub repository.

We also have other code bundles from our rich catalog of books and videos available at https://github.com/PacktPublishing/. Check them out!

Download the color images

We also provide a PDF file that has color images of the screenshots/diagrams used in this book. You can download it here: https://static.packt-cdn.com/downloads/9781838821593_ColorImages.pdf.

Conventions used

There are a number of text conventions used throughout this book.

CodeInText: Indicates code words in text, database table names, folder names, filenames, file extensions, pathnames, dummy URLs, user input, and Twitter handles. Here is an example: "We will set maxlen to 100 and max_features to 100000."

A block of code is set as follows:

```
(x_train, y_train), (x_test, y_test), preproc = \
text.texts_from_df(train_df = df,
                   text_column = 'reviewText',
                   label_columns=['sentiment'],
                   maxlen=100,
                   max_features=100000,
                   preprocess_mode='bert',
                   val_pct=0.1)
```

Bold: Indicates a new term, an important word, or words that you see onscreen. For example, words in menus or dialog boxes appear in the text like this. Here is an example: "Select **System info** from the **Administration** panel."

Warnings or important notes appear like this.

Tips and tricks appear like this.

Get in touch

Feedback from our readers is always welcome.

General feedback: If you have questions about any aspect of this book, mention the book title in the subject of your message and email us at `customercare@packtpub.com`.

Errata: Although we have taken every care to ensure the accuracy of our content, mistakes do happen. If you have found a mistake in this book, we would be grateful if you would report this to us. Please visit `www.packtpub.com/support/errata`, selecting your book, clicking on the Errata Submission Form link, and entering the details.

Piracy: If you come across any illegal copies of our works in any form on the Internet, we would be grateful if you would provide us with the location address or website name. Please contact us at `copyright@packt.com` with a link to the material.

If you are interested in becoming an author: If there is a topic that you have expertise in and you are interested in either writing or contributing to a book, please visit `authors.packtpub.com`.

Reviews

Please leave a review. Once you have read and used this book, why not leave a review on the site that you purchased it from? Potential readers can then see and use your unbiased opinion to make purchase decisions, we at Packt can understand what you think about our products, and our authors can see your feedback on their book. Thank you!

For more information about Packt, please visit `packt.com`.

Section 1 - Starting Off with BERT

In this section, we will familiarize ourselves with BERT. First, we will understand how the transformer works, and then we will explore BERT in detail. We will also get hands-on with BERT and learn how to use the pre-trained BERT model.

The following chapters are included in this section:

- Chapter 1, *A Primer on Transformers*
- Chapter 2, *Understanding the BERT Model*
- Chapter 3, *Getting Hands–On with BERT*

To overcome this limitation of RNNs, a new architecture called Transformer was introduced in the paper *Attention Is All You Need*. The transformer is currently the state-of-the-art model for several NLP tasks. The advent of the transformer created a major breakthrough in the field of NLP and also paved the way for new revolutionary architectures such as BERT, GPT-3, T5, and more.

The transformer model is based entirely on the attention mechanism and completely gets rid of recurrence. The transformer uses a special type of attention mechanism called **self-attention**. We will learn about this in detail in the upcoming sections.

Let's understand how the transformer works with a language translation task. The transformer consists of an encoder-decoder architecture. We feed the input sentence (source sentence) to the encoder. The encoder learns the representation of the input sentence and sends the representation to the decoder. The decoder receives the representation learned by the encoder as input and generates the output sentence (target sentence).

Suppose we need to convert a sentence from English to French. As shown in the following figure, we feed the English sentence as input to the encoder. The encoder learns the representation of the given English sentence and feeds the representation to the decoder. The decoder takes the encoder's representation as input and generates the French sentence as output:

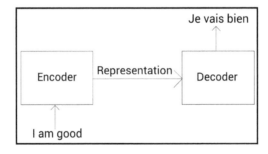

Figure 1.1 – Encoder and decoder of the transformer

Okay, but what's exactly going on here? How does the encoder and decoder in the transformer convert the English sentence (source sentence) to the French sentence (target sentence)? What's going on inside the encoder and decoder? Let's find this out in the next sections. First, we will look into the encoder in detail, and then we will see the decoder.

Understanding the encoder of the transformer

The transformer consists of a stack of N number of encoders. The output of one encoder is sent as input to the encoder above it. As shown in the following figure, we have a stack of N number of encoders. Each encoder sends its output to the encoder above it. The final encoder returns the representation of the given source sentence as output. We feed the source sentence as input to the encoder and get the representation of the source sentence as output:

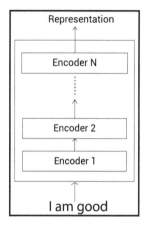

Figure 1.2 – A stack of N number of encoders

Note that in the transformer paper *Attention Is All You Need*, the authors have used $N=6$, meaning that they stacked up six encoders one above the another. However, we can try out different values of N. For simplicity and better understanding, let's keep $N=2$:

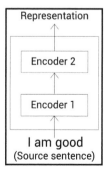

Figure 1.3 – A stack of encoders

Okay, the question is how exactly does the encoder work? How is it generating the representation for the given source sentence (input sentence)? To understand this, let's tap into the encoder and see its components. The following figure shows the components of the encoder:

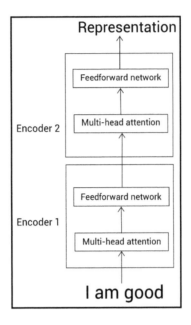

Figure 1.4 – Encoder with its components

From the preceding figure, we can understand that all the encoder blocks are identical. We can also observe that each encoder block consists of two sublayers:

- Multi-head attention
- Feedforward network

Now, let's get into the details and learn how exactly these two sublayers works. To understand how multi-head attention works, first we need to understand the self-attention mechanism. So, in the next section, we will learn how the self-attention mechanism works.

Self-attention mechanism

Let's understand the self-attention mechanism with an example. Consider the following sentence:

```
A dog ate the food because it was hungry
```

In the preceding sentence, the pronoun *it* could mean either *dog* or *food*. By reading the sentence, we can easily understand that the pronoun *it* implies the *dog* and not *food*. But how does our model understand that in the given sentence, the pronoun *it* implies the *dog* and not *food*? Here is where the self-attention mechanism helps us.

In the given sentence, *A dog ate the food because it was hungry*, first, our model computes the representation of the word *A*, next it computes the representation of the word *dog*, then it computes the representation of the word *ate*, and so on. While computing the representation of each word, it relates each word to all other words in the sentence to understand more about the word.

For instance, while computing the representation of the word *it*, our model relates the word *it* to all the words in the sentence to understand more about the word *it*.

As shown in the following figure, in order to compute the representation of the word *it*, our model relates the word *it* to all the words in the sentence. By relating the word *it* to all the words in the sentence, our model can understand that the word *it* is related to the word *dog* and not *food*. As we can observe, the line connecting the word *it* to *dog* is thicker compared to the other lines, which indicates that the word *it* is related to the word *dog* and not *food* in the given sentence:

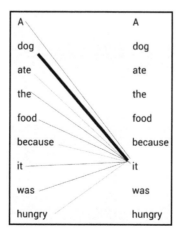

Figure 1.5 – Self-attention example

Okay, but how exactly does this work? Now that we have a basic idea of what the self-attention mechanism is, let's understand more about it in detail.

Suppose our input sentence (source sentence) is *I am good*. First, we get the embeddings for each word in our sentence. Note that the embeddings are just the vector representation of the word and the values of the embeddings will be learned during training.

Let x_1 be the embedding of the word *I*, x_2 be the embedding of the word *am*, and x_3 be the embedding of the word *good*. Consider the following:

- The embedding of the word *I* is $x_1 = [1.76, 2.22, \ldots, 6.66]$.
- The embedding of the word *am* is $x_2 = [7.77, 0.631, \ldots, 5.35]$.
- The embedding of the word *good* is $x_3 = [11.44, 10.10, \ldots, 3.33]$.

Then, we can represent our input sentence *I am good* using the input matrix X (embedding matrix or input embedding) as shown here:

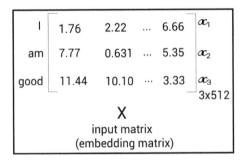

Figure 1.6 – Input matrix

Note that the values used in the preceding matrix are arbitrary just to give us a better understanding.

From the preceding input matrix, X, we can understand that the first row of the matrix implies the embedding of the word *I*, the second row implies the embedding of the word *am*, and the third row implies the embedding of the word *good*. Thus, the dimension of the input matrix X will be [*sentence length* x *embedding dimension*]. The number of words in our sentence (sentence length) is 3. Let the embedding dimension be **512**; then, our input matrix (input embedding) dimension will be [3 x 512].

Now, from the input matrix, *X*, we create three new matrices: a query matrix, *Q*, key matrix, *K*, and value matrix, *V*. Wait. What are these three new matrices? And why do we need them? They are used in the self-attention mechanism. We will see how exactly these three matrices are used in a while.

Okay, how we can create the query, key, and value matrices? To create these, we introduce three new weight matrices, called W^Q, W^K, W^V. We create the query, *Q*, key, *K*, and value, *V*, matrices by multiplying the input matrix, *X*, by W^Q, W^K, and W^V, respectively.

Note that the weight matrices, W^Q, W^K, and W^V, are randomly initialized and their optimal values will be learned during training. As we learn the optimal weights, we will obtain more accurate query, key, and value matrices.

As shown in the following figure, multiplying the input matrix, *X*, by the weight matrices, W^Q, W^K, and W^V, we obtain the query, key, and value matrices:

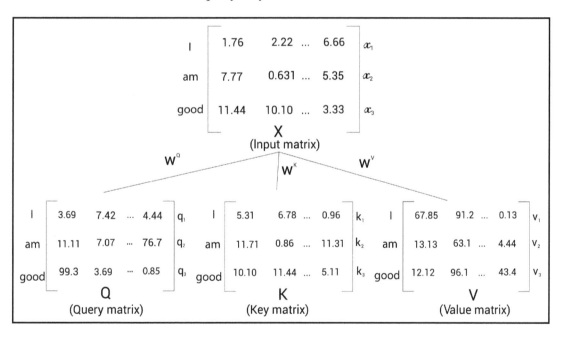

Figure 1.7 – Creating query, key, and value matrices

From the preceding figure, we can understand the following:

- The first row in the query, key, and value matrices – q_1 , k_1 , and v_1– implies the query, key, and value vectors of the word *I*.
- The second row in the query, key, and value matrices – q_2 , k_2 , and v_2 – implies the query, key, and value vectors of the word *am*.
- The third row in the query, key, and value matrices – q_3 , k_3 , and v_3 – implies the query, key, and value vectors of the word *good*.

Note that the dimensionality of the query, key, value vectors are 64. Thus, the dimension of our query, key, and value matrices is [*sentence length* x *64*]. Since we have three words in the sentence, the dimensions of the query, key, and value matrices are [3 x 64].

But still, the ultimate question is why are we computing this? What is the use of query, key, and value matrices? How is this going to help us? This is exactly what we will discuss in detail in the next section.

Understanding the self-attention mechanism

We learned how to compute query, Q, key, K, and value, V, matrices and we also learned that they are obtained from the input matrix, X. Now, let's see how the query, key, and value matrices are used in the self-attention mechanism.

We learned that in order to compute a representation of a word, the self-attention mechanism relates the word to all the words in the given sentence. Consider the sentence *I am good*. To compute the representation of the word *I*, we relate the word *I* to all the words in the sentence, as shown in the following figure:

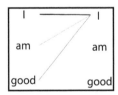

Figure 1.8 – Self-attention example

But why do we need to do this? Understanding how a word is related to all the words in the sentence helps us to learn better representation. Now, let's learn how the self-attention mechanism relates a word to all the words in the sentence using the query, key, and value matrices. The self-attention mechanism includes four steps; let's take a look at them one by one.

Step 1

The first step in the self-attention mechanism is to compute the dot product between the query matrix, Q, and the key matrix, K^T:

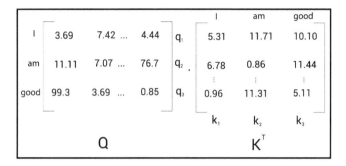

Figure 1.9 – Query and key matrices

The following shows the result of the dot product between the query matrix, Q, and the key matrix, K^T:

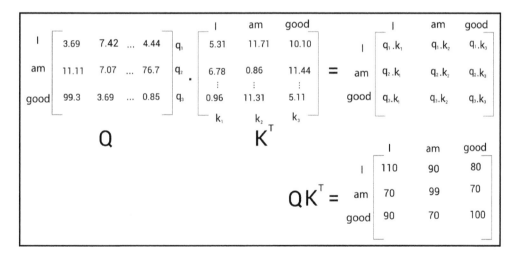

Figure 1.10 – Computing the dot product between the query and key matrices

But what is the use of computing the dot product between the query and key matrices? What exactly does $Q.K^T$ signify? Let's understand this by looking at the result of $Q.K^T$ in detail.

Let's look into the first row of the $Q.K^T$ matrix as shown in the following figure. We can observe that we are computing the dot product between the query vector q_1 (*I*), and all the key vectors – k_1 (*I*), k_2(*am*), and k_3 (*good*). Computing the dot product between two vectors tells us how similar they are.

Thus, computing the dot product between the query vector (q_1) and the key vectors (k_1, k_2, k_3) tells us how similar the query vector q_1 (*I*) is to all the key vectors – k_1 (*I*), k_2(*am*), and k_3 (*good*). By looking at the first row of the $Q.K^T$ matrix, we can understand that the word *I* is more related to itself than the words *am* and *good* since the dot product value is higher for $q_1.k_1$ compared to $q_1.k_2$ and $q_1.k_3$:

		I	am	good
	I	110 $q_1.k_1$	90 $q_1.k_2$	80 $q_1.k_3$
QK^T =	am	70	99	70
	good	90	70	100

Figure 1.11 – Computing the dot product between the query vector (q_1) and the key vectors (k_1, k_2, and k_3)

Note that the values used in this chapter are arbitrary just to give us a better understanding.

Now, let's look into the second row of the $Q.K^T$ matrix . As shown in the following figure, we can observe that we are computing the dot product between the query vector, q_2 (*am*), and all the key vectors – k_1(*I*), k_2(*am*), and k_3 (*good*). This tells us how similar the query vector q_2 (*am*) is to the key vectors – k_1 (*I*), k_2(*am*), and k_3 (*good*).

By looking at the second row of the $Q.K^T$ matrix, we can understand that the word *am* is more related to itself than the words *I* and *good* since the dot product value is higher for $q_2.k_2$ compared to $q_2.k_1$ and $q_2.k_3$:

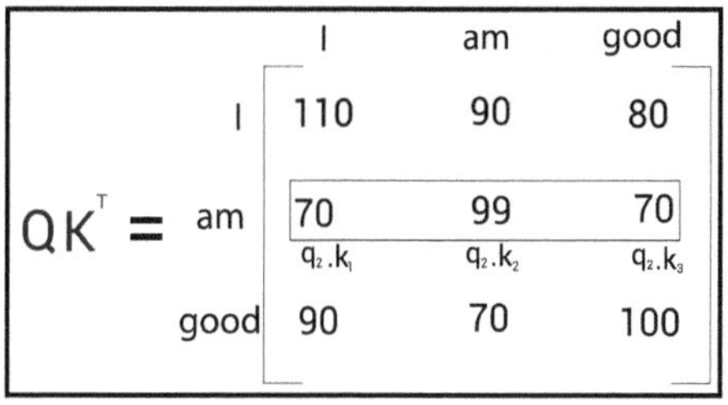

Figure 1.12 – Computing dot product between the query vector (q_2) and the key vectors (k_1, k_2, and k_3)

Similarly, let's look into the third row of the $Q.K^T$ matrix. As shown in the following figure, we can observe that we are computing the dot product between the query vector $q_3(good)$ and all the key vectors – $k_1(I)$, $k_2(am)$, and $k_3(good)$. This tells us how similar the query vector q_3 (*good*) is to all the key vectors – k_1 (*I*), $k_2(am)$, and k_3 (*good*).

By looking at the third row of the $Q.K^T$ matrix, we can understand that the word *good* is more related to itself than the words *I* and *am* in the sentence since the dot product value is higher for $q_3.k_3$ compared to $q_3.k_1$ and $q_3.k_2$:

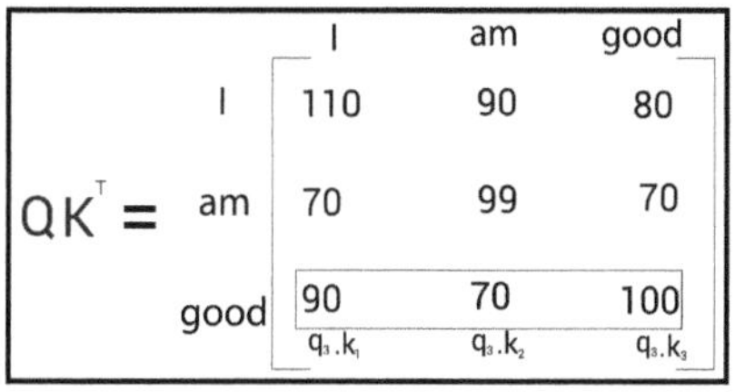

Figure 1.13 – Computing the dot product between the query vector (q_3) and the key vectors (k_1, k_2, and k_3)

Thus, we can say that computing the dot product between the query matrix, Q, and the key matrix, K^T, essentially gives us the similarity score, which helps us to understand how similar each word in the sentence is to all other words.

Step 2

The next step in the self-attention mechanism is to divide the $Q.K^T$ matrix by the square root of the dimension of the key vector. But why do we have to do that? This is useful in obtaining stable gradients.

Let d_k be the dimension of the key vector. Then, we divide $Q.K^T$ by $\sqrt{d_k}$. The dimension of the key vector is 64. So, taking the square root of it, we will obtain 8. Hence, we divide $Q.K^T$ by 8 as shown in the following figure:

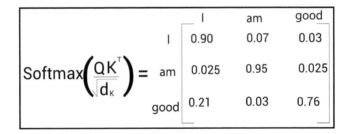

	I	am	good
$\dfrac{QK^T}{\sqrt{d_K}} = \dfrac{QK^T}{8} =$ I	13.75	11.25	10
am	8.75	12.375	8.75
good	11.25	8.75	12.5

Figure 1.14 – Dividing Q.K^T by the square root of d$_k$

Step 3

By looking at the preceding similarity scores, we can understand that they are in the unnormalized form. So, we normalize them using the softmax function. Applying softmax function helps in bringing the score to the range of 0 to 1 and the sum of the scores equals to 1, as shown in the following figure:

	I	am	good
$\text{Softmax}\left(\dfrac{QK^T}{\sqrt{d_K}}\right) =$ I	0.90	0.07	0.03
am	0.025	0.95	0.025
good	0.21	0.03	0.76

Figure 1.15 – Applying the softmax function

We can call the preceding matrix a score matrix. With the help of these scores, we can understand how each word in the sentence is related to all the words in the sentence. For instance, look at the first row in the preceding score matrix; it tells us that the word *I* is related to itself by 90%, to the word *am* by 7%, and to the word *good* by 3%.

Step 4

Okay, what's next? We computed the dot product between the query and key matrices, obtained the scores, and then normalized the scores with the softmax function. Now, the final step in the self-attention mechanism is to compute the attention matrix, Z.

The attention matrix contains the attention values for each word in the sentence. We can compute the attention matrix, Z, by multiplying the score matrix, $\text{softmax}\left(\dfrac{QK^T}{\sqrt{d_k}}\right)$, by the value matrix, V, as shown in the following figure:

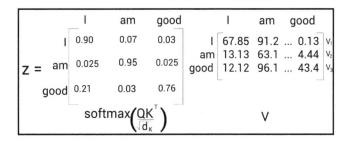

Figure 1.16 – Computing the attention matrix

Say we have the following:

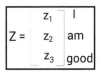

Figure 1.17 – Result of the attention matrix

The attention matrix, Z, is computed by taking the sum of the value vectors weighted by the scores. Let's understand this by looking at it row by row. First, let's see how for the first row, z_1, the self-attention of the word *I* is computed:

$$Z_1 = 0.90 \begin{array}{|c|c|c|} \hline 67.85 & 91.2 & ... \\ \hline \end{array} + 0.07 \begin{array}{|c|c|c|} \hline 13.13 & 63.1 & ... \\ \hline \end{array} + 0.03 \begin{array}{|c|c|c|} \hline 12.12 & 96.1 & ... \\ \hline \end{array}$$

$\qquad\qquad\quad v_1(I) \qquad\qquad\qquad v_2(am) \qquad\qquad\qquad v_3(good)$

Figure 1.18 – Self-attention of the word I

From the preceding figure, we can understand that z_1, the self-attention of the word *I* is computed as the sum of the value vectors weighted by the scores. Thus, the value of z_1 will contain 90% of the values from the value vector v_1 (*I*), 7% of the values from the value vector v_2 (*am*), and 3% of values from the value vector v_3 (*good*).

But how is this useful? To answer this question, let's take a little detour to the example sentence we saw earlier, *A dog ate the food because it was hungry*. Here, the word *it* indicates *dog*. To compute the self-attention of the word *it*, we follow the same preceding steps. Suppose we have the following:

Z_{it} =	0.0	71.1	6.1	...	+ 1.0	31.1	11.1	...	+.....	+0.0	0.9	11.44	...	+.....	+0.0	0.8	12.44	...
		V_1 (A)				V_2 (dog)					V_5 (food)					V_9 (hungry)		

Figure 1.19 – Self-attention of the word it

From the preceding figure, we can understand that the self-attention value of the word *it* contains 100% of the values from the value vector v_2 (*dog*). This helps the model to understand that the word *it* actually refers to *dog* and not *food*. Thus, by using a self-attention mechanism, we can understand how a word is related to all other words in the sentence.

Now, coming back to our example, z_2, the self-attention of the word *am* is computed as the sum of the value vectors weighted by the scores, as shown in the following figure:

Z_2 =	0.025	67.85	91.2	...	+0.95	13.13	63.1	...	+ 0.025	12.12	96.1	...
		v_1 (I)				v_2 (am)				v_3 (good)	

Figure 1.20 – Self-attention of the word am

As we can observe from the preceding figure, the value of z_2 will contain 2.5% of the values from the value vector v_1 (*I*), 95% of the values from the value vector v_2 (*am*), and 2.5% of the values from the value vector v_3 (*good*).

Similarly, z_3, the self-attention of the word *good* is computed as the sum of the value vectors weighted by the scores, as shown in the following figure:

Figure 1.21 – Self-attention of the word good

This implies that the value of z_3 will contain 21% of the values from the value vector $v_1(I)$, 3% of the values from the value vector $v_2(am)$, and 76% of values from the value vector $v_3(good)$.

Thus, the attention matrix, Z, consists of self-attention values of all the words in the sentence and it is computed as follows:

$$Z = \text{softmax}\left(\frac{QK^T}{\sqrt{d_k}}\right)V$$

To get a better understanding of the self-attention mechanism, the steps involved are summarized as follows:

1. First, we compute the dot product between the query matrix and the key matrix, QK^T, and get the similarity scores.
2. Next, we divide QK^T by the square root of the dimension of the key vector, $\sqrt{d_k}$.
3. Then, we apply the softmax function to normalize the scores and obtain the score matrix, $\text{softmax}(QK^T/\sqrt{dk})$.
4. At the end, we compute the attention matrix, Z, by multiplying the score matrix by the value matrix, V.

The self-attention mechanism is graphically shown as follows:

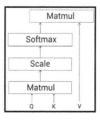

Figure 1.22 – Self-attention mechanism

The self-attention mechanism is also called **scaled dot product attention**, since here we are computing the dot product (between the query and key vectors) and scaling the values (with $\sqrt{d_k}$).

Now that we have understood how the self-attention mechanism works, in the next section, we will learn about the multi-head attention mechanism.

Multi-head attention mechanism

Instead of having a single attention head, we can use multiple attention heads. That is, in the previous section, we learned how to compute the attention matrix, Z. Instead of computing a single attention matrix, Z, we can compute multiple attention matrices. But what is the use of computing multiple attention matrices?

Let's understand this with an example. Consider the phrase *All is well*. Say we need to compute the self-attention of the word *well*. After computing the similarity score, suppose we have the following:

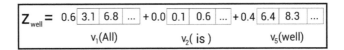

Figure 1.23 – Self-attention of the word well

As we can observe from the preceding figure, the self-attention value of the word *well* is the sum of the value vectors weighted by the scores. If you look at the preceding figure closely, the attention value of the actual word *well* is dominated by the other word *All*. That is, since we are multiplying the value vector of the word *All* by 0.6 and the value vector of the actual word *well* by only 0.4, it implies that Z_{well} will contain 60% of the values from the value vector of the word *All* and only 40% of the values from the value vector of the actual word *well*. Thus, here the attention value of the actual word *well* is dominated by the other word *All*.

This will be useful only in circumstances where the meaning of the actual word is ambiguous. That is, consider the following sentence:

A dog ate the food because it was hungry

Say we are computing the self-attention for the word *it*. After computing the similarity score, suppose we have the following:

Figure 1.24 – Self-attention of the word it

As we can observe from the preceding equation, here the attention value of the word *it* is just the value vector of the word *dog*. Here, the attention value of the actual word *it* is dominated by the word *dog*. But this is fine here since the meaning of the word *it* is ambiguous as it may refer to either *dog* or *food*.

Thus, if the value vector of other words dominates the actual word in cases as shown in the preceding example, where the actual word is ambiguous, then this dominance is useful; otherwise, it will cause an issue in understanding the right meaning of the word. So, in order to make sure that our results are accurate, instead of computing a single attention matrix, we will compute multiple attention matrices and then concatenate their results. The idea behind using multi-head attention is that instead of using a single attention head, if we use multiple attention heads, then our attention matrix will be more accurate. Let's explore this in more detail.

Let's suppose we are computing two attention matrices, Z_1 and Z_2. First, let's compute the attention matrix Z_1.

We learned that to compute the attention matrix, we create three new matrices, called query, key, and value matrices. To create the query, Q_1, key, K_1, and value, V_1, matrices, we introduce three new weight matrices, called W_1^Q, W_1^K, W_1^V. We create the query, key, and value matrices by multiplying the input matrix, X, by W_1^Q, W_1^K, and W_1^V, respectively.

Now, the attention matrix Z_1 can be computed as follows:

$$Z_1 = \text{softmax}\left(\frac{Q_1 K_1^T}{\sqrt{d_k}} \right) V_1$$

Now, let's compute the second attention matrix, Z_2.

To compute the attention matrix Z_2, we create another set of query, Q_2, key, K_2, and value, V_2, matrices. We introduce three new weight matrices, called W_2^Q, W_2^K, W_2^V, and we create the query, key, and value matrices by multiplying the input matrix, X, by W_2^Q, W_2^K, and W_2^V, respectively.

The attention matrix Z_2 can be computed as follows:

$$Z_2 = \text{softmax}\left(\frac{Q_2 K_2^T}{\sqrt{d_k}}\right) V_2$$

Similarly, we can compute h number of attention matrices. Suppose we have eight attention matrices, Z_1 to Z_8; then, we can just concatenate all the attention heads (attention matrices) and multiply the result by a new weight matrix, W^O, and create the final attention matrix as shown:

$$\text{Multi-head attention} = \text{Concatenate}(Z_1, Z_2, \ldots Z_i, \ldots Z_8) W_0$$

Now that we have learned how the multi-attention mechanism works, we will learn about another interesting concept, called positional encoding, in the next section.

Learning position with positional encoding

Consider the input sentence *I am good*. In RNNs, we feed the sentence to the network word by word. That is, first the word *I* is passed as input, next the word *am* is passed, and so on. We feed the sentence word by word so that our network understands the sentence completely. But with the transformer network, we don't follow the recurrence mechanism. So, instead of feeding the sentence word by word, we feed all the words in the sentence parallel to the network. Feeding the words in parallel helps in decreasing the training time and also helps in learning the long-term dependency.

However, the problem is since we feed the words parallel to the transformer, how will it understand the meaning of the sentence if the word order is not retained? To understand the sentence, the word order (position of the words in the sentence) is important, right? Yes, the word order is very important as it helps to understand the position of each word in a sentence, which in turn helps to understand the meaning of the sentence.

So, we should give some information about the word order to the transformer so that it can understand the sentence. How can we do that? Let's explore this in more detail now.

For our given sentence, *I am good*, first, we get the embeddings for each word in our sentence. Let's represent the embedding dimension as d_{model}. Say the embedding dimension, d_{model} is 4. Then, our input matrix dimension will be [*sentence length* x *embedding dimension*] = [3 x 4].

We represent our input sentence *I am good* using the input matrix X(embedding matrix). Let the input matrix X be the following:

$$X = \begin{matrix} & \text{I} & \begin{bmatrix} 1.769 & 2.22 & 3.4 & 5.8 \\ 7.3 & 9.9 & 8.5 & 7.1 \\ 9.1 & 7.1 & 0.85 & 10.1 \end{bmatrix} & \begin{matrix} x_1 \\ x_2 \\ x_3 \end{matrix} \\ & \text{am} & & \\ & \text{good} & & \end{matrix}$$

Input matrix (embedding matrix)

Figure 1.25 – Input matrix

Now, if we pass the preceding input matrix X directly to the transformer, it cannot understand the word order. So, instead of feeding the input matrix directly to the transformer, we need to add some information indicating the word order (position of the word) so that our network can understand the meaning of the sentence. To do this, we introduce a technique called **positional encoding**. Positional encoding, as the name suggests, is an encoding indicating the position of the word in a sentence (word order).

The dimension of the positional encoding matrix, P, is the same dimension as the input matrix X. Now, before feeding the input matrix (embedding matrix) to the transformer directly, we include the positional encoding. So, we simply add the positional encoding matrix P to the embedding matrix X and then feed it as input to the network. So, now our input matrix will have not only the embedding of the word but also the position of the word in the sentence:

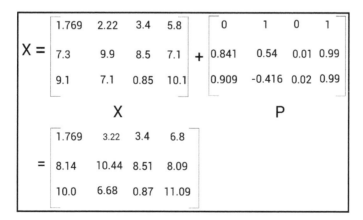

Figure 1.26 – Adding an input matrix and positional encoding matrix

Now, the ultimate question is how exactly is the positional encoding matrix computed? The authors of the transformer paper *Attention Is All You Need* have used the sinusoidal function for computing the positional encoding, as shown:

$$P(\text{pos}, 2i) = \sin\left(\frac{\text{pos}}{10000^{2i/d_{\text{model}}}}\right)$$

$$P(\text{pos}, 2i+1) = \cos\left(\frac{\text{pos}}{10000^{2i/d_{\text{model}}}}\right)$$

In the preceding equation, pos implies the position of the word in a sentence, and *i* implies the position of the embedding. Let's understand the preceding equations with an example. By using the preceding equations, we can write the following:

$$P = \begin{array}{c} \text{I} \\ \text{am} \\ \text{good} \end{array} \begin{bmatrix} \sin\left(\frac{\text{pos}}{10000^0}\right) & \cos\left(\frac{\text{pos}}{10000^0}\right) & \sin\left(\frac{\text{pos}}{10000^{2/4}}\right) & \cos\left(\frac{\text{pos}}{10000^{2/4}}\right) \\ \sin\left(\frac{\text{pos}}{10000^0}\right) & \cos\left(\frac{\text{pos}}{10000^0}\right) & \sin\left(\frac{\text{pos}}{10000^{2/4}}\right) & \cos\left(\frac{\text{pos}}{10000^{2/4}}\right) \\ \sin\left(\frac{\text{pos}}{10000^0}\right) & \cos\left(\frac{\text{pos}}{10000^0}\right) & \sin\left(\frac{\text{pos}}{10000^{2/4}}\right) & \cos\left(\frac{\text{pos}}{10000^{2/4}}\right) \end{bmatrix}$$

Figure 1.27 – Computing the positional encoding matrix

As we can observe from the preceding matrix, in the positional encoding, we use the sin function when *i* is even and the cos function when *i* is odd. Simplifying the preceding matrix, we can write the following:

$$P = \begin{array}{c} \text{I} \\ \text{am} \\ \text{good} \end{array} \begin{bmatrix} \sin(\text{pos}) & \cos(\text{pos}) & \sin\left(\frac{\text{pos}}{100}\right) & \cos\left(\frac{\text{pos}}{100}\right) \\ \sin(\text{pos}) & \cos(\text{pos}) & \sin\left(\frac{\text{pos}}{100}\right) & \cos\left(\frac{\text{pos}}{100}\right) \\ \sin(\text{pos}) & \cos(\text{pos}) & \sin\left(\frac{\text{pos}}{100}\right) & \cos\left(\frac{\text{pos}}{100}\right) \end{bmatrix}$$

Figure 1.28 – Computing the positional encoding matrix

We know that in our input sentence, the word *I* is at the 0th position, *am* is at the 1st position, and *good* is at the 2nd position. Substituting the pos value, we can write the following:

$$P = \begin{array}{c} I \\ am \\ good \end{array} \begin{bmatrix} \sin(0) & \cos(0) & \sin(0/100) & \cos(0/100) \\ \sin(1) & \cos(1) & \sin(1/100) & \cos(1/100) \\ \sin(2) & \cos(2) & \sin(2/100) & \cos(2/100) \end{bmatrix}$$

Figure 1.29 – Computing the positional encoding matrix

Thus, our final positional encoding matrix, *P*, is given as follows:

$$P = \begin{array}{c} I \\ am \\ good \end{array} \begin{bmatrix} 0 & 1 & 0 & 1 \\ 0.841 & 0.540 & 0.009 & 0.999 \\ 0.909 & -0.416 & 0.019 & 0.999 \end{bmatrix}$$

Figure 1.30 – Positional encoding matrix

After computing the positional encoding *P* we simply perform element-wise addition with the embedding matrix *X* and feed the modified input matrix to the encoder.

Now, let's revisit our encoder architecture. A single encoder block is shown in the following figure. As we can observe, before feeding the input directly to the encoder, first, we get the input embedding (embedding matrix), and then we add the positional encoding to it, and then we feed it as input to the encoder:

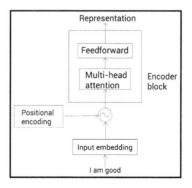

Figure 1.31 – A single encoder block

We learned how the positional encoder works; we also learned how the multi-head attention sublayer works in the previous section. In the next section, we will learn how the feedforward network sublayer works in the encoder.

Feedforward network

The feedforward network sublayer in an encoder block is shown in the following figure:

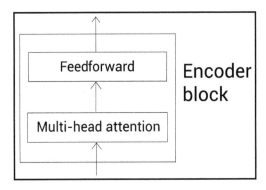

Figure 1.32 – Encoder block

The feedforward network consists of two dense layers with ReLU activations. The parameters of the feedforward network are the same over the different positions of the sentence and different over the encoder blocks. In the next section, we will look into another interesting component of the encoder.

Add and norm component

One more important component in our encoder is the add and norm component. It connects the input and output of a sublayer. That is, as shown in the following figure (dotted lines), we can observe that the add and norm component:

- Connects the input of the multi-head attention sublayer to its output
- Connects the input of the feedforward sublayer to its output:

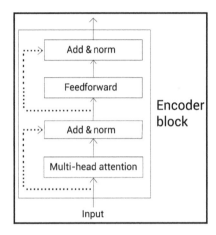

Figure 1.33 – Encoder block with the add and norm component

The add and norm component is basically a residual connection followed by **layer normalization**. Layer normalization promotes faster training by preventing the values in each layer from changing heavily.

Now that we have learned about all the components of the encoder, let's put all of them together and see how the encoder works as a whole in the next section.

Putting all the encoder components together

The following figure shows the stack of two encoders; only encoder 1 is expanded to reduce the clutter:

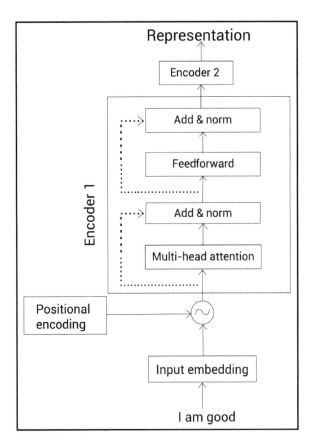

Figure 1.34 – A stack of encoders with encoder 1 expanded

From the preceding figure, we can understand the following:

1. First, we convert our input to an input embedding (embedding matrix), and then add the position encoding to it and feed it as input to the bottom-most encoder (encoder 1).
2. Encoder 1 takes the input and sends it to the multi-head attention sublayer, which returns the attention matrix as output.

3. We take the attention matrix and feed it as input to the next sublayer, which is the feedforward network. The feedforward network takes the attention matrix as input and returns the encoder representation as output.
4. Next, we take the output obtained from encoder 1 and feed it as input to the encoder above it (encoder 2).
5. Encoder 2 carries the same process and returns the encoder representation of the given input sentence as output.

We can stack N number of encoders one above the other; the output (encoder representation) obtained from the final encoder (topmost encoder) will be the representation of the given input sentence. Let's denote the encoder representation obtained from the final encoder (in our example, it is encoder 2) as R.

We take this encoder representation, R, obtained from the final encoder (encoder 2) and feed it as input to the decoder. The decoder takes the encoder representation R as input and tries to generate the target sentence.

Now that we have understood the encoder part of the transformer, in the next section, we will learn how a decoder works in detail.

Understanding the decoder of a transformer

Suppose we want to translate the English sentence (source sentence) *I am good* to the French sentence (target sentence) *Je vais bien*. To perform this translation, we feed the source sentence *I am good* to the encoder. The encoder learns the representation of the source sentence. In the previous section, we learned how exactly the encoder learns the representation of the source sentence. Now, we take this encoder's representation and feed it to the decoder. The decoder takes the encoder representation as input and generates the target sentence *Je vais bien*, as shown in the following figure:

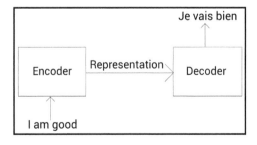

Figure 1.35 – Encoder and decoder of the transformer

In the encoder section, we learned that, instead of having one encoder, we can have a stack of N encoders. Similar to the encoder, we can also have a stack of N decoders. For simplicity, let's set $N=2$. As shown in the following figure, the output of one decoder is sent as the input to the decoder above it. We can also observe that the encoder's representation of the input sentence (encoder's output) is sent to all the decoders. Thus, a decoder receives two inputs: one is from the previous decoder, and the other is the encoder's representation (encoder's output):

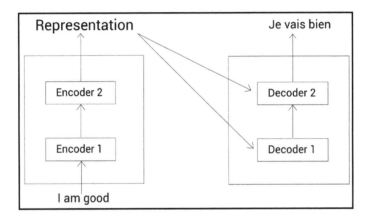

Figure 1.36 – A stack of encoders and decoders

Okay, but how exactly does the decoder generate the target sentence? Let's explore that in more detail. At time step $t=1$, the input to the decoder will be *<sos>*, which indicates the start of the sentence. The decoder takes *<sos>* as input and generates the first word in the target sentence, which is *Je*, as shown in the following figure:

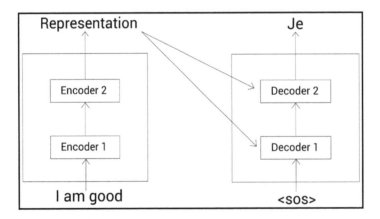

Figure 1.37 – Decoder prediction at time step t = 1

At time step *t*=2, along with the current input, the decoder takes the newly generated word from the previous time step, $t - 1$, and tries to generate the next word in the sentence. Thus, the decoder takes *<sos>* and *Je* (from the previous step) as input and tries to generate the next word in the target sentence, as shown in the following figure:

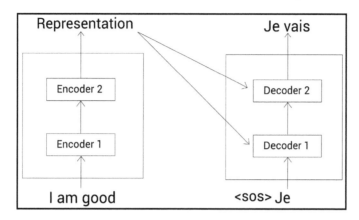

Figure 1.38 – Decoder prediction at time step t = 2

At time step *t*=3, along with the current input, the decoder takes the newly generated word from the previous time step, $t - 1$, and tries to generate the next word in the sentence. Thus, the decoder takes *<sos>*, *Je*, and *vais* (from the previous step) as input and tries to generate the next word in the sentence, as shown in the following figure:

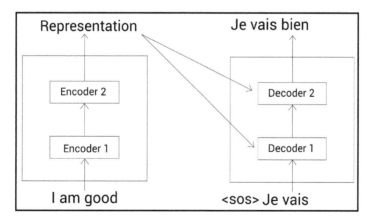

Figure 1.39 – Decoder prediction at time step t = 3

Similarly, on every time step, the decoder combines the newly generated word to the input and predicts the next word. Thus, at time step *t*=4, the decoder takes *<sos>*, *Je*, *vais*, and *bien* as input and tries to generate the next word in the sentence, as shown in the following figure:

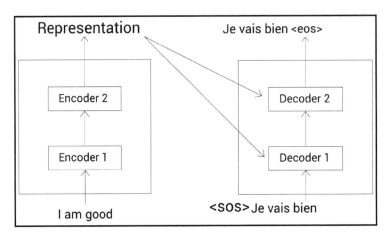

Figure 1.40 – Decoder prediction at time step t = 4

As we can observe from the preceding figure, once the **<eos>** token, which indicates the end of sentence, is generated, it implies that the decoder has completed generating the target sentence.

In the encoder section, we learned that we convert the input into an embedding matrix and add the positional encoding to it, and then feed it as input to the encoder. Similarly, here, instead of feeding the input directly to the decoder, we convert it into an embedding, add the positional encoding to it, and then feed it to the decoder.

For example, as shown in the following figure, say at time step *t*=2 we convert the input into an embedding (we call it an **output embedding** because here we are computing the embedding of the words generated by the decoder in previous time steps), add the positional encoding to it, and then send it to the decoder:

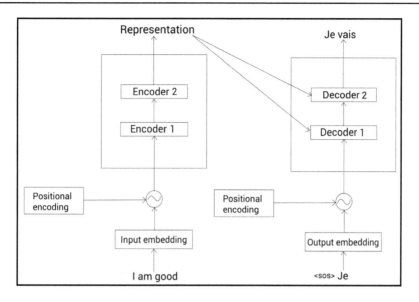

Figure 1.41 – Encoder and decoder with positional encoding

Okay, but the ultimate question is how exactly does the decoder work? What's going on inside the decoder? Let's explore this in detail. A single decoder block with all of its components is shown in the following figure:

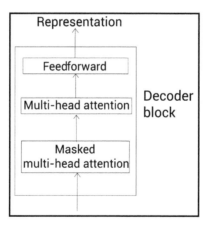

Figure 1.42 – A decoder block

From the preceding figure, we can observe that the decoder block is similar to the encoder and here we have three sublayers:

- Masked multi-head attention
- Multi-head attention
- Feedforward network

Similar to the encoder block, here we have multi-head attention and feedforward network sublayers. However, here we have two multi-head attention sublayers and one of them is masked. Now that we have a basic idea of the decoder, first, let's look into each component of the decoder in detail, and then we will see how the decoder works as a whole.

Masked multi-head attention

In our English-to-French translation task, say our training dataset looks like the one shown here:

Source sentence	Target sentence
I am good	Je vais bien
Good morning	Bonjour
Thank you very much	Merci beaucoup

Figure 1.43 – A sample training set

By looking at the preceding dataset, we can understand that we have source and target sentences. In the previous section, we saw how the decoder predicts the target sentence word by word in each time step and that happens only during testing.

During training, since we have the right target sentence, we can just feed the whole target sentence as input to the decoder but with a small modification. We learned that the decoder takes the input <sos> as the first token, and combines the next predicted word to the input on every time step for predicting the target sentence until the <eos> token is reached. So, we can just add the <sos> token to the beginning of our target sentence and send that as an input to the decoder.

Say we are converting the English sentence *I am good* to the French sentence *Je vais bien*. We can just add the *<sos>* token to the beginning of the target sentence and send *<sos> Je vais bien* as an input to the decoder, and then the decoder predicts the output as *Je vais bien <eos>*, as shown in the following figure:

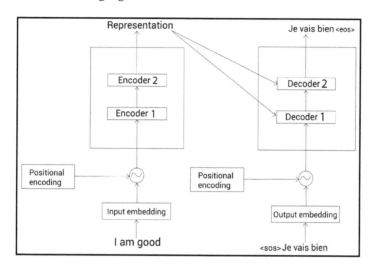

Figure 1.44 – Encoder and decoder of the transformer

But how does this work? Isn't this kind of ambiguous? Why do we need to feed the entire target sentence and let the decoder predict the shifted target sentence as output? Let's explore this in more detail.

We learned that instead of feeding the input directly to the decoder, we convert it into an embedding (output embedding matrix) and add positional encoding, and then feed it to the decoder. Let's suppose the following matrix, X, is obtained as a result of adding the output embedding matrix and positional encoding:

$$
X = \begin{array}{c|cccc|c}
\text{<sos>} & 7.9 & 3.5 & \dots & 16.1 & x_1 \\
\text{Je} & 8.1 & 4.4 & \dots & 83.1 & x_2 \\
\text{vais} & 17 & 0.54 & \dots & 6.12 & x_3 \\
\text{bien} & 11.12 & 11.12 & \dots & 22.1 & x_4 \\
\end{array}
$$

Figure 1.45 – Input matrix

Now, we feed the preceding matrix, X, to the decoder. The first layer in the decoder is the masked-multi head attention. This works similar to the multi-head attention mechanism we learned about with the encoder but in a small difference.

To perform self-attention, we create three new matrices, called query, Q, key, K, and value, V. Since we are computing multi-head attention, we create h number of query, key, and value matrices. Thus, for a head, i, the query, Q_i, key, K_i, and value, V_i, matrices can be created by multiplying X by the weight matrices, W_i^Q, W_i^K, W_i^V, respectively.

Now, let's see how masked multi-head attention works. Our input sentence to the decoder is *<sos> Je vais bien.* We learned that the self-attention mechanism relates a word to all the words in the sentence to understand more about each word. But there is a small catch here. During test time, the decoder will only have the words generated until the previous step as input. For example, during testing, say at time step $t=2$ the decoder will only have the input words as [*<sos>*, *Je*] and it will not have any other words. So, we have to train our model in the same fashion. Thus, our attention mechanism should relate the words only until the word *Je* and not the other words. To do this, we can mask all the words on the right that are not predicted by our model yet.

Say we want to predict the word next to the word *<sos>*. In this case, the model should see only the words up to <sos>, so we mask all the words on the right of <sos>. Say we want to predict the word next to the word *Je*. In this case, the model should see only the words up to *Je*, so we mask all the words to the right of *Je*, and the same applies for other rows, as shown in the following figure:

<sos>	mask	mask	mask
<sos>	Je	mask	mask
<sos>	Je	vais	mask
<sos>	Je	vais	bien

Figure 1.46 – Masking the values

Masking words like this help the self-attention mechanism to attend only to the words that would be available to the model during testing. Okay, but how exactly we can perform this masking? We know that for a head, i, the attention matrix, Z_i, is computed as follows:

$$Z_i = \text{softmax}(\frac{Q_i K_i^T}{\sqrt{d_k}})V_i$$

The first step in computing the attention matrix is computing the dot product between the query and key matrices. The following shows the result of the dot product between the query and the key matrix. Note that the values used here are arbitrary, just to get a good understanding:

	\<sos\>	Je	vais	bien
\<sos\>	73	60	10	45
Je	40	99	25	70
vais	58	40	83	10
bien	12	11	15	80

$Q_i K_i^T =$

Figure 1.47 – Dot product of the query and key matrices

The next is to divide the $Q_i K_i^T$ matrix by the dimension of key vector $\sqrt{d_k}$. Suppose the following is the result of $\frac{Q_i K_i}{\sqrt{d_k}}$:

	\<sos\>	Je	vais	bien
\<sos\>	9.125	7.5	1.25	5.625
Je	5.0	12.37	3.12	8.75
vais	7.25	5.0	10.37	1.25
bien	1.5	1.37	1.87	10.0

$\frac{Q_i K_i^T}{\sqrt{d_k}} =$

Figure 1.48 – Dividing $Q_iK_i^T$ by the square root of d_k

Next, we apply the softmax function to the preceding matrix and normalize the scores. But before applying the softmax function, we need to mask the values. For example, look at the first row of our matrix. To predict the word next to the word *<sos>*, our model should not attend all the words to the right of *<sos>* (as this will not be available during test time). So, we can mask all the words to the right of *<sos>* with $-\infty$:

	<sos>	Je	vais	bien
<sos>	9.125	$-\infty$	$-\infty$	$-\infty$
Je	5.0	12.37	3.12	8.75
vais	7.25	5.0	10.37	1.25
bien	1.5	1.37	1.87	10.0

$$\frac{Q_i K_i^T}{\sqrt{d_k}} =$$

Figure 1.49 – Masking all the words to the right of <sos> with $-\infty$

Now, let's take a look at the second row of the matrix. To predict the word next to the word *Je*, our model should not attend all the words to the right of *Je* (as this will not be available during test time). So, we can mask all the words to the right of *Je* with $-\infty$:

	<sos>	Je	vais	bien
<sos>	9.125	$-\infty$	$-\infty$	$-\infty$
Je	5.0	12.37	$-\infty$	$-\infty$
vais	7.25	5.0	10.37	1.25
bien	1.5	1.37	1.87	10.0

$$\frac{Q_i K_i^T}{\sqrt{d_k}} =$$

Figure 1.50 – Masking all the words to the right of Je with $-\infty$

Similarly, we can mask all the words to the right of vais with $-\infty$ as shown:

$\dfrac{Q_i K_i^T}{\sqrt{d_k}} =$		<sos>	Je	vais	bien
	<sos>	9.125	$-\infty$	$-\infty$	$-\infty$
	Je	5.0	12.37	$-\infty$	$-\infty$
	vais	7.25	5.0	10.37	$-\infty$
	bien	1.5	1.37	1.87	10.0

Figure 1.51 – Masking all the words in the right of vais with $-\infty$

Now, we can apply the softmax function to the preceding matrix and multiply the result by the value matrix, V_i, and obtain the final attention matrix, Z_i. Similarly, we can compute h number of attention matrices, concatenate them, and multiply the result by a new weight matrix, W^O, and create the final attention matrix, M, as shown:

$$M = \text{Concatenate}(Z_1, Z_2, \ldots Z_i, \ldots Z_h)W_0$$

Now, we feed this final attention matrix, M, to the next sublayer in our decoder, which is another multi-head attention layer. Let's see how that works in detail in the next section.

Multi-head attention

The following figure shows the transformer model with both the encoder and decoder. As we can observe, the multi-head attention sublayer in each decoder receives two inputs: one is from the previous sublayer, masked multi-head attention, and the other is the encoder representation:

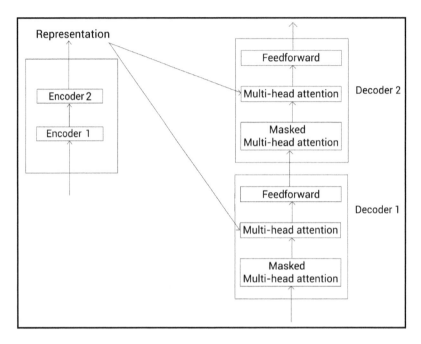

Figure 1.52 – Encoder-decoder interaction

Let's represent the encoder representation by R and the matrix obtained as a result of the masked multi-head attention sublayer by M. Since here we have an interaction between the encoder and decoder, this layer is also called an **encoder-decoder attention layer**.

Now, let's look into the details and learn how exactly this multi-head attention layer works. The first step in the multi-head attention mechanism is creating the query, key, and value matrices. We learned that we can create the query, key, and value matrices by multiplying the input matrix by the weight matrices. But in this layer, we have two input matrices: one is R (the encoder representation) and the other is M (the attention matrix from the previous sublayer). So, which one should we use?

We create the query matrix, Q, using the attention matrix, M, obtained from the previous sublayer and we create the key and value matrices using the encoder representation, R. Since we are performing the multi-head attention mechanism, for head i, we do the following:

- The query matrix, Q_i, is created by multiplying the attention matrix, M, by the weight matrix, W_i^Q.
- The key and value matrices are created by multiplying the encoder representation, R, by the weight matrices, W_i^K and W_i^V, respectively. This is shown in the following figure:

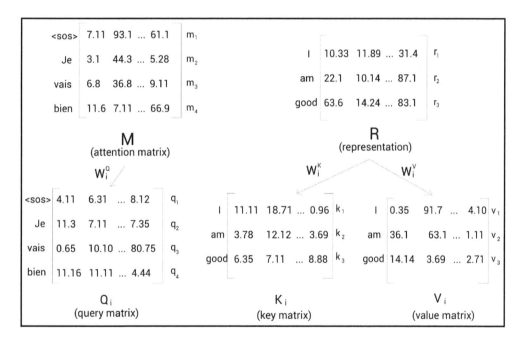

Figure 1.53 – Creating query, key, and value matrices

But why do we have to do this? Why do we obtain the query matrix from M and key and value matrices from R? The query matrix essentially holds the representation of our target sentence since it is obtained from M and the key and value matrices hold the representation of the source sentence since it is obtained from R. But how and why exactly is this useful? Let's understand this by calculating the self-attention step by step.

The first step in self-attention is to compute the dot product between the query and key matrices. The query and key matrices are shown in the following figure. As we can observe, since the query matrix is obtained from M, it holds the representation of the target sentence, and since the key matrix is obtained from R, it holds the representation of the input sentence. Note that the values used here are arbitrary, just to get a good understanding:

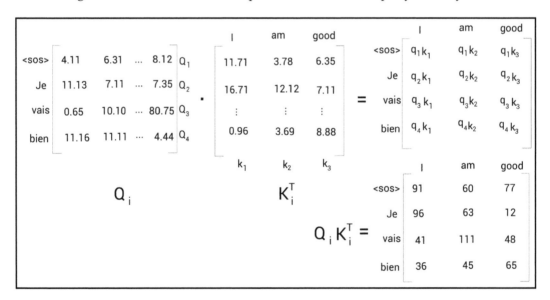

Figure 1.54 – Query and key matrices

The following shows the result of the dot product between the query and key matrices:

Figure 1.55 – Dot product between the query and key matrices

By looking at the preceding matrix, $Q_i \cdot K_i^T$, we can understand the following:

- From the first row of the matrix, we can observe that we are computing the dot product between the query vector q_1 (*<sos>*) and all the key vectors – $k_1(I)$, $k_2(am)$, and $k_3(good)$. Thus, the first row indicates how similar the target word *<sos>* is to all the words in the source sentence (*I*, *am*, and *good*).
- Similarly, from the second row of the matrix, we can observe that we are computing the dot product between the query vector q_2 (*Je*) and all the key vectors – k_1 (*I*), $k_2(am)$, and k_3 (*good*). Thus, the second row indicates how similar the target word *Je* is to all the words in the source sentence (*I*, *am*, and *good*).
- The same applies to all other rows. Thus, computing $Q_i \cdot K_i^T$ helps us to understand how similar our query matrix (target sentence representation) is to the key matrix (source sentence representation).

The next step in the multi-head attention matrix is to divide $Q_i \cdot K_i^T$ by $\sqrt{d_k}$. Then, we apply the softmax function and obtain the score matrix, $\text{softmax}(\dfrac{Q_i K_i^T}{\sqrt{d_k}})$.

Next, we multiply the score matrix by the value matrix, V_i, that is, $\text{softmax}(\dfrac{Q_i K_i^T}{\sqrt{d_k}})V_i$, and obtain the attention matrix, Z_i, as shown:

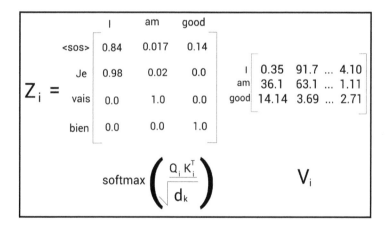

Figure 1.56 – Computing the attention matrix

Say we have the following:

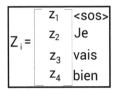

Figure 1.57 – Result of attention matrix

The attention matrix, Z_i, of the target sentence is computed by taking the sum of value vectors weighted by the scores. To get some clarity, let's see how the self-attention value of the word *Je*, z_2, is computed:

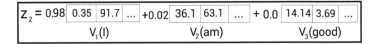

Figure 1.58 – Self-attention of the word Je

As shown, z_2, the self-attention of the word *Je* is computed as the sum of the value vectors weighted by the scores. Thus, the value of z_2 will contain 98% of the values from the value vector v_1 (*I*) and 2% of the values from the value vector v_2 (*am*). This basically helps the model to understand that the target word *Je* means the source word *am*.

Similarly, we can compute h number of attention matrices, concatenate them, and multiply the result by a new weight matrix, W^O, and create the final attention matrix, as shown:

$$\text{Multi-head attention} = \text{Concatenate}(Z_1, Z_2, \dots Z_i, \dots Z_h)W_0$$

Now, we feed this final attention matrix to the next sublayer in our decoder, which is a feedforward network. Let's see how that works in the next section.

Feedforward network

The next sublayer in the decoder is the feedforward network, as shown in the following figure:

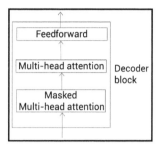

Figure 1.59 – A decoder block

The feedforward layer in the decoder works exactly the same as what we learned in the encoder. Next, we will look into the add and norm component.

Add and norm component

Just like we learned with the encoder, the add and norm component connects the input and output of a sublayer, as shown in the following figure:

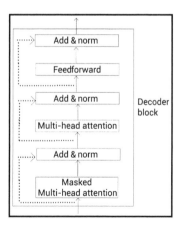

Figure 1.60 – A decoder block with an add and norm component

Next, we will look at the linear and softmax layers.

Linear and softmax layers

Once the decoder learns the representation of the target sentence, we feed the output obtained from the topmost decoder to the linear and softmax layers, as shown in the following figure:

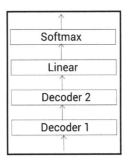

Figure 1.61 – Linear and softmax layers

The linear layer generates the logits whose size is equal to our vocabulary size. Suppose our vocabulary consists of only the following three words:

$$\text{Vocabulary} = [\text{bien}, \text{Je}, \text{vais}]$$

Now, the logits returned by the linear layer will be a vector of size 3. Next, we convert the logits into a probability using the softmax function, and then the decoder outputs the word whose index has a high probability value. Let's understand this with an example.

Suppose the input to the decoder are the words *<sos>* and *Je*. Now, the decoder needs to predict the next word in our target sentence. So, we take the output of the topmost decoder and feed it to the linear layer. The linear layer generates the logits vector whose size is our vocabulary size. Let the logits returned by the linear layer be the following:

$$\text{logits} = [45, 40, 49]$$

Now, we apply the softmax function to the logits generated by the linear layer and obtain the probability:

$$\text{prob} = [0.0179, 0.000, 0.981]$$

From the preceding matrix, we can understand that the probability is high at index 2. So, we look for the word that is at index 2 in our vocabulary. Since the word *vais* is at index 2, our decoder will predict the next word in our target sentence as *vais*. In this way, the decoder predicts the next word in the target sentence.

Now that we have understood all the decoder components, let's put them all together and see how they work as a whole in the next section.

Putting all the decoder components together

The following figure shows the stack of two decoders; only decoder 1 is expanded to reduce the clutter:

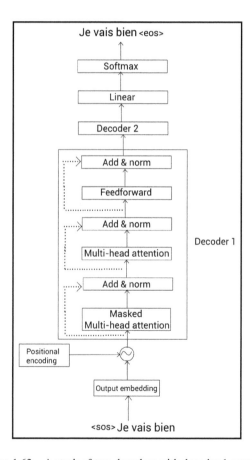

Figure 1.62 – A stack of two decoders with decoder 1 expanded

From the preceding figure, we can understand the following:

1. First, we convert the input to the decoder into an embedding matrix and then add the position encoding to it and feed it as input to the bottom-most decoder (decoder 1).
2. The decoder takes the input and sends it to the masked multi-head attention layer, which returns the attention matrix, M, as output.
3. Now, we take the attention matrix, M, and also the encoder representation, R, and feed them as input to the multi-head attention layer (encoder-decoder attention layer), which again outputs the new attention matrix.
4. We take the attention matrix obtained from the encoder-decoder attention layer and feed it as input to the next sublayer, which is the feedforward network. The feedforward network takes the attention matrix as input and returns the decoder representation as output.
5. Next, we take the output obtained from decoder 1 and feed it as input to the decoder above it (decoder 2).
6. Decoder 2 carries the same process and returns the decoder representation of the target sentence as output.

We can stack N number of decoders one above the other; the output (decoder representation) obtained from the final decoder will be the representation of the target sentence. Next, we feed the decoder representation of the target sentence to the linear and softmax layers and get the predicted word.

Now that we have learned how the encoder and decoder work in detail, let's put the encoder and decoder together and see how the transformer model works as a whole in the next section.

Putting the encoder and decoder together

To give more clarity, the complete transformer architecture with the encoder and decoder is shown in the following figure:

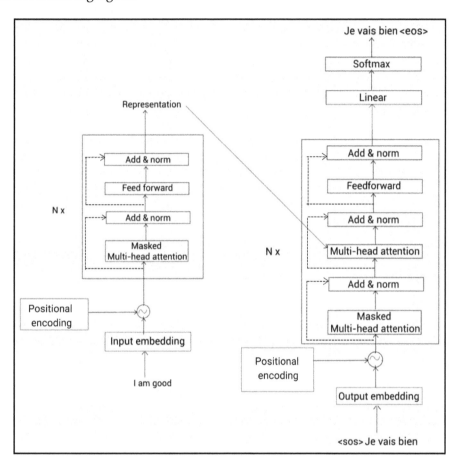

Figure 1.63 – Encoder and decoder of the transformer

In the preceding figure, **Nx** denotes that we can stack N number of encoders and decoders. As we can observe, once we feed the input sentence (source sentence), the encoder learns the representation and sends the representation to the decoder, which in turn generates the output sentence (target sentence).

Training the transformer

We can train the transformer network by minimizing the loss function. Okay, but what loss function should we use? We learned that the decoder predicts the probability distribution over the vocabulary and we select the word that has the highest probability as output. So, we have to minimize the difference between the predicted probability distribution and the actual probability distribution. First, how can we find the difference between the two distributions? We can use cross-entropy for that. Thus, we can define our loss function as a cross-entropy loss and try to minimize the difference between the predicted and actual probability distribution. We train the network by minimizing the loss function and we use Adam as an optimizer.

One additional point we need to note down is that to prevent overfitting, we apply dropout to the output of each sublayer and we also apply dropout to the sum of the embeddings and the positional encoding.

Thus, in this chapter, we learned how the transformer works in detail. In the next chapter, we will get started with BERT.

Summary

We started off the chapter by understanding what the transformer model is and how it uses encoder-decoder architecture. We looked into the encoder section of the transformer and learned about different sublayers used in encoders, such as multi-head attention and feedforward networks.

We learned that the self-attention mechanism relates a word to all the words in the sentence to better understand the word. To compute self-attention, we used three different matrices, called the query, key, and value matrices. Following this, we learned how to compute positional encoding and how it is used to capture the word order in a sentence. Next, we learned how the feedforward network works in the encoder and then we explored the add and norm component.

After understanding the encoder, we understood how the decoder works. We explored three sublayers used in the decoder in detail, which are the masked multi-head attention, encoder-decoder attention, and feedforward network. Following this, we understood how the transformer works with the encoder and decoder, and then at the end of the chapter, we learned how we train the network.

In the next chapter, we will learn what BERT is and how it uses the transformer for learning contextual embeddings in detail.

Questions

Let's put our newly acquired knowledge to the test. Try answering the following questions:

1. What are the steps involved in the self-attention mechanism?
2. What is scaled dot product attention?
3. How do we create the query, key, and value matrices?
4. Why do we need positional encoding?
5. What are the sublayers of the decoder?
6. What are the inputs to the encoder-decoder attention layer of the decoder?

Further reading

To learn more, check out the following resources:

- *Attention Is All You Need* by *Ashish Vaswani, Noam Shazeer*, and *Niki Parmar*, available at *https://papers.nips.cc/paper/7181-attention-is-all-you-need.pdf*
- *The Illustrated Transformer* blog by *Jay Alammar*, at `http://jalammar.github.io/illustrated-transformer`

Understanding the BERT Model 2

In this chapter, we will get started with one of the most popularly used state-of-the-art text embedding models called **BERT**. BERT has revolutionized the world of NLP by providing state-of-the-art results on many NLP tasks. We will begin the chapter by understanding what BERT is and how it differs from the other embedding models. We will then look into the working of BERT and its configuration in detail.

Moving on, we will learn how the BERT model is pre-trained using two tasks, called masked language modeling and next sentence prediction, in detail. We will then look into the pre-training procedure of BERT. At the end of the chapter, we will learn about several interesting subword tokenization algorithms, including byte pair encoding, byte-level byte pair encoding, and WordPiece.

In this chapter, we will cover the following topics:

- Basic idea of BERT
- Working of BERT
- Configurations of BERT
- Pre-training the BERT model
- Pre-training procedure
- Subword tokenization algorithms

Basic idea of BERT

BERT stands for **B**idirectional **E**ncoder **R**epresentation from **T**ransformer. It is the state-of-the-art embedding model published by Google. It has created a major breakthrough in the field of NLP by providing greater results in many NLP tasks, such as question answering, text generation, sentence classification, and many more besides. One of the major reasons for the success of BERT is that it is a context-based embedding model, unlike other popular embedding models, such as word2vec, which are context-free.

First, let's understand the difference between context-based and context-free embedding models. Consider the following two sentences:

Sentence A: He got bit by Python.

Sentence B: Python is my favorite programming language.

By reading the preceding two sentences, we can understand that the meaning of the word *'Python'* is different in both sentences. In sentence A, the word *'Python'* refers to the snake, while in sentence B, the word *'Python'* refers to the programming language.

Now, if we get embeddings for the word *'Python'* in the preceding two sentences using an embedding model such as word2vec, the embedding of the word *'Python'* would be the same in both sentences, and so this renders the meaning of the word *'Python'* the same in both sentences. This is because word2vec is the context-free model, so it will ignore the context and always give the same embedding for the word *'Python'* irrespective of the context.

BERT, on the other hand, is a context-based model. It will understand the context and then generate the embedding for the word based on the context. So, for the preceding two sentences, it will give different embeddings for the word *'Python'* based on the context. But how does this work? How does BERT understand the context? Let's explore this in more depth.

Let's take sentence A: *He got bit by Python*. First, BERT relates each word in the sentence to all the other words in the sentence to understand the contextual meaning of every word. So, to understand the contextual meaning of the word *'Python'*, BERT takes the word *'Python'* and relates it to all the words in the sentence. By doing this, BERT can understand that the word *'Python'* in sentence A denotes the snake through the use of the word *bit*, as shown here:

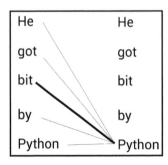

Figure 2.1 – Relating the word 'Python' to all other words

Now, let's take sentence B: *Python is my favorite programming language*. Similarly, here BERT relates each word in the sentence to all the words in the sentence to understand the contextual meaning of every word. So, BERT takes the word '*Python*' and relates it to all the words in the sentence to understand the meaning of the word '*Python*'. By doing this, BERT understands that the word '*Python*' in sentence B is related to a programming language through the use of the word *programming*, as shown here:

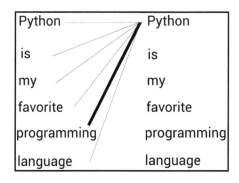

Figure 2.2 – Relating the word 'Python' to all other words

Thus, unlike context-free models such as word2vec, which generate static embeddings irrespective of the context, BERT generates dynamic embeddings based on the context.

Okay, the question is how exactly does BERT work? How does it understand the context? Now that we have a basic idea of BERT, in the next section, we will explore BERT in greater detail and find the answers to these questions.

Working of BERT

Bidirectional Encoder Representation from Transformer (**BERT**), as the name suggests, is based on the transformer model. We can perceive BERT as the transformer, but only with the encoder.

Remember that, in the previous `Chapter 1`, *A Primer on Transformers*, we learned that we feed the sentence as input to the transformer's encoder and it returns the representation for each word in the sentence as an output. Well, that's exactly what BERT is – an **E**ncoder **R**epresentation from **T**ransformer. Okay, so what about the term *Bidirectional*?

The encoder of the transformer is bidirectional in nature since it can read a sentence in both directions. Thus, BERT is basically the **B**idirectional **E**ncoder **R**epresentation obtained from the **T**ransformer.

Let's understand how BERT is bidirectional encoder representation from the transformer with the help of an example. Let's take the same sentences we saw in the previous section.

Say we have a sentence A: *'He got bit by Python'*. Now, we feed this sentence as an input to the transformer's encoder and get the contextual representation (embedding) of each word in the sentence as an output. Once we feed the sentence as an input to the encoder, the encoder understands the context of each word in the sentence using the **multi-head attention mechanism** (relates each word in the sentence to all the words in the sentence to learn the relationship and contextual meaning of words) and returns the contextual representation of each word in the sentence as an output.

As shown in the following diagram, we feed the sentence as an input to the transformer's encoder and get the representation of each word in the sentence as an output. We can stack up **N** number of encoders, as shown in the following diagram. We have only expanded encoder 1 so as to reduce clutter. In the following diagram, R_{He} denotes the representation of the word *'He'*, R_{got} is the representation of the word *'got'*, and so on. The representation size of each token will be the size of the encoder layer. Suppose the size of the encoder layer is 768, then the representation size of each token will be 768:

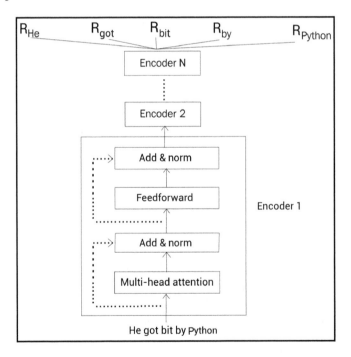

Figure 2.3 – BERT generating the representation of each word in the sentence

Similarly, if we feed sentence B, '*Python is my favorite programming language*', to the transformer's encoder, we get the contextual representation of each word in the sentence as output, as shown in the following diagram:

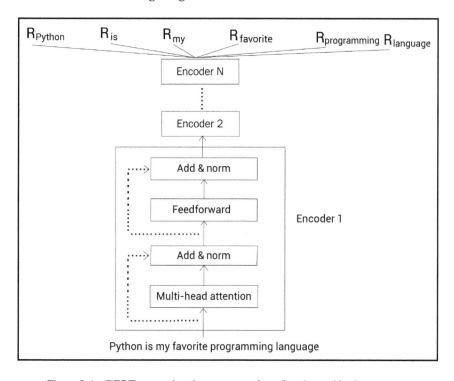

Figure 2.4 – BERT generating the representation of each word in the sentence

Thus, with the BERT model, for a given sentence, we obtain the contextual representation (embedding) of each word in the sentence as an output. Now that we understand how BERT generates contextual representation, in the next section, we will look into different configurations of BERT.

Configurations of BERT

The researchers of BERT have presented the model in two standard configurations:

- BERT-base
- BERT-large

Let's take a look at each of these in detail.

BERT-base

BERT-base consists of **12** encoder layers, each stacked one on top of the other. All the encoders use **12** attention heads. The feedforward network in the encoder consists of **768** hidden units. Thus, the size of the representation obtained from BERT-base will be 768.

We use the following notations:

- The number of encoder layers is denoted by L.
- The attention head is denoted by A.
- The hidden unit is denoted by H.

Thus, in the BERT-base model, we have, $L = 12$, $A = 12$, and $H = 768$. The total number of parameters in BERT-base is **110 million**. The BERT-base model is shown in the following diagram:

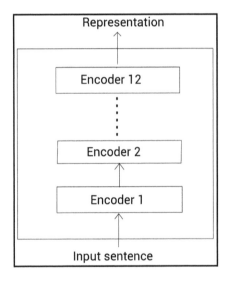

Figure 2.5 – BERT-base

BERT-large

BERT-large consists of **24** encoder layers, each stacked one on top of the other. All the encoders use **16** attention heads. The feedforward network in the encoder consists of **1,024** hidden units. Thus, the size of the representation obtained from BERT-large will be 1,024.

Hence, in the BERT-large model, we have, $L = 24$, $A = 16$, and $H = 1024$. The total number of parameters in BERT-large is **340 million**. The BERT-large model is shown in the following diagram:

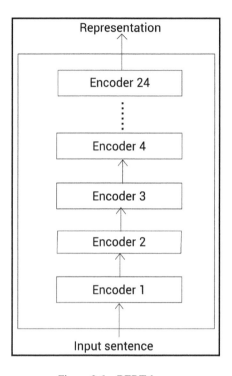

Figure 2.6 – BERT-large

Other configurations of BERT

Apart from the preceding two standard configurations, we can also build the BERT model with other different configurations. Some of the smaller configurations of BERT are shown here:

- Bert-tiny, with $L = 2$, $H = 128$
- Bert-mini, with $L = 4$, $H = 256$
- Bert-small, with $L = 4$, $H = 512$
- Bert-medium, with $L = 8$, $H = 512$

The following diagram shows the different configurations of BERT:

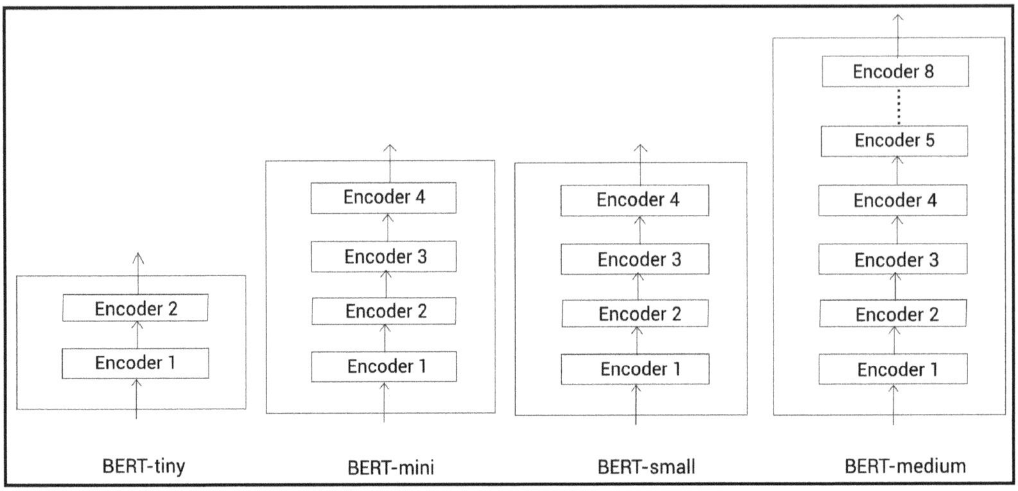

Figure 2.7 – Different configurations of BERT

We can use smaller configurations of BERT in settings where computational resources are limited. However, the standard BERT configurations, such as BERT-base and BERT-large, give more accurate results and they are the most widely used.

Okay, we understand how BERT works and we have also covered the different configurations of BERT. But how can BERT be trained to generate representations? What dataset should we use for training? What is the training strategy we should follow? This is precisely what we will discuss in the next section.

Pre-training the BERT model

In this section, we will learn how to pre-train the BERT model. But what does pre-training mean? Say we have a model, *m*. First, we train the model *m* with a huge dataset for a particular task and save the trained model. Now, for a new task, instead of initializing a new model with random weights, we will initialize the model with the weights of our already trained model, *m* (pre-trained model). That is, since the model *m* is already trained on a huge dataset, instead of training a new model from scratch for a new task, we use the pre-trained model, *m*, and adjust (fine-tune) its weights according to the new task. This is a type of transfer learning.

The BERT model is pre-trained on a huge corpus using two interesting tasks, called masked language modeling and next sentence prediction. Following pre-training, we save the pre-trained BERT model. For a task, say question answering, instead of training BERT from scratch, we will use the pre-trained BERT model. That is, we will use the pre-trained BERT model and adjust (fine-tune) its weights for the new task.

In this section, we will learn how the BERT model is pre-trained in detail. Before diving into pre-training, first, let's take a look into how to structure the input data in a way that BERT accepts.

Input data representation

Before feeding the input to BERT, we convert the input into embeddings using the three embedding layers indicated here:

- Token embedding
- Segment embedding
- Position embedding

Let's understand how each of these embedding layers work one by one.

Token embedding

First, we have a token embedding layer. Let's understand this with an example. Consider the following two sentences:

Sentence A: Paris is a beautiful city.

Sentence B: I love Paris.

First, we tokenize both two sentences and obtain the tokens, as shown here. In our example, we have not lowercased the tokens:

```
tokens  =  [Paris, is, a, beautiful, city, I, love, Paris]
```

Next, we add a new token, called the [CLS] token, only at the beginning of the first sentence:

```
tokens  =  [ [CLS], Paris, is, a, beautiful, city, I, love, Paris]
```

And then we add a new token called [SEP] at the end of every sentence:

```
tokens  =  [ [CLS], Paris, is, a, beautiful, city, [SEP], I, love, Paris,
[SEP]]
```

Note that the [CLS] token is added only at the beginning of the first sentence, while the [SEP] token is added at the end of every sentence. The [CLS] token is used for classification tasks and the [SEP] token is used to indicate the end of every sentence. We will understand how these two tokens, [CLS] and [SEP], are useful in detail as we move forward through the chapter.

Now, before feeding all the tokens to BERT, we convert the tokens into embeddings using an embedding layer called *token embedding*. Note that the value of token embeddings will be learned during training. As shown in the following diagram, we have embeddings for all the tokens, that is, E_{cls} indicates the embedding of the token [CLS], E_{Paris} indicates the embedding of the token *Paris*, and so on:

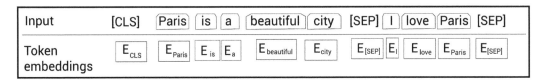

Figure 2.8 – Token embeddings

Segment embedding

Next, we have a segment embedding layer. Segment embedding is used to distinguish between the two given sentences. Let's understand segment embedding with an example. Consider the same two sentences we saw in the previous section:

Sentence A: Paris is a beautiful city.

Sentence B: I love Paris.

After tokenizing the preceding two sentences, we will have the following:

```
tokens  =  [ [CLS], Paris, is, a, beautiful, city, [SEP], I, love, Paris,
[SEP]]
```

Now, apart from the [SEP] token, we have to give some sort of indicator to our model to distinguish between the two sentences. To do this, we feed the input tokens to the segment embedding layer.

The segment embedding layer returns only either of the two embeddings, E_A or E_B, as an output. That is, if the input token belongs to sentence A, then the token will be mapped to the embedding E_A, and if the token belongs to sentence B, then it will be mapped to the embedding E_B.

As shown in the following diagram, all the tokens from sentence A are mapped to the embedding E_A, and all the tokens from the sentence B are mapped to the embedding E_B:

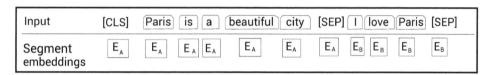

Figure 2.9 – Segment embeddings

Okay, so how does segment embedding work if we have only one sentence? Say we have just the sentence *'Paris is a beautiful city'*. In that case, all the tokens of the sentence will be mapped to embedding E_A, as shown here:

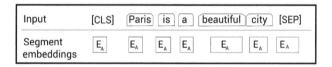

Figure 2.10 – Segment embeddings

Position embedding

Next, we have a position embedding layer. In the previous chapter, we learned that since the transformer does not use any recurrence mechanism and processes all the words in parallel, we need to provide some information relating to word order, so we used positional encoding.

We know that BERT is essentially the transformer's encoder, and so we need to give information about the position of the words (tokens) in our sentence before feeding them directly to BERT. So, we use a layer called the position embedding layer and get the position embedding for each token in our sentence.

As we can observe from the following diagram, E_0 indicates the position embedding of the token [CLS], E_1 indicates the position embedding of the token *Paris*, and so on:

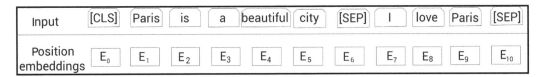

Figure 2.11 – Position embeddings

Final representation

Now, let's take a look at the final input data representation. As shown in the following diagram, first we convert the given input sentences to tokens and feed the tokens to the token embedding, segment embedding, and position embedding layers and obtain the embeddings. Next, we sum up all the embeddings together and feed them as input to BERT:

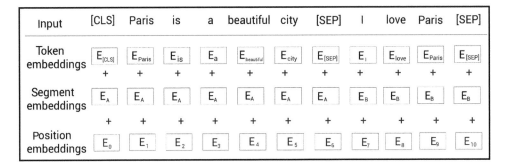

Figure 2.12 – Final representation of the input

Now that we have learned how to convert the input into embeddings using three embedding layers, in the next section, we will learn about the tokenizer used by BERT called a WordPiece tokenizer.

WordPiece tokenizer

BERT uses a special type of tokenizer called a WordPiece tokenizer. The WordPiece tokenizer follows the subword tokenization scheme. Let's understand how the WordPiece tokenizer works with the help of an example. Consider the following sentence:

"Let us start pretraining the model."

Now, if we tokenize the sentence using the WordPiece tokenizer, then we obtain the tokens as shown here:

```
tokens = [let, us, start, pre, ##train, ##ing, the, model]
```

We can observe that while tokenizing the sentence using the WordPiece tokenizer, the word *pertaining* is split into the following subwords – pre, ##train, ##ing. But what does this imply?

When we tokenize using the WordPiece tokenizer, first we check whether the word is present in our vocabulary. If the word is present in the vocabulary, then we use it as a token. If the word is not present in the vocabulary, then we split the word into subwords and we check whether the subword is present in the vocabulary. If the subword is present in the vocabulary, then we use it as a token. But if the subword is not present in the vocabulary, then again we split the subword and check whether it is present in the vocabulary. If it is present in the vocabulary, then we use it as a token, otherwise we split it again. In this way, we keep splitting and check the subword with the vocabulary until we reach individual characters. This is effective in handling the **out-of-vocabulary (OOV)** words.

The size of the BERT vocabulary is 30K tokens. If a word belongs to these 30K tokens, then we use it as a token. Otherwise, we split the word into subwords and check whether the subword belongs to these 30K tokens. We keep splitting and check the subwords with these 30K tokens in the vocabulary until we reach the individual characters.

In our example, the word *pretraining* is not in BERT's vocabulary. Therefore, we split the word *pretraining* into the subwords pre, ##train, and ##ing. The hash signs before the tokens ##train and ##ing indicate that it is a subword and that it is preceded by other words. Now we check whether the subwords ##train and ##ing are present in the vocabulary. Since they are present in the vocabulary, we don't split again and use them as tokens.

Thus, by using a WordPiece tokenizer, we obtain the following tokens:

```
tokens = [let, us, start, pre, ##train, ##ing, the, model]
```

Next, we add a `[CLS]` token at the beginning of the sentence and an `[SEP]` token at the end of the sentence:

```
tokens = [ [CLS], let, us, start, pre, ##train, ##ing, the model, [SEP] ]
```

Now, just like we learned in the previous section, we feed the input tokens to the token, segment, and position embedding layers, obtain the embeddings, sum the embeddings, and then feed them as input to BERT. A more detailed explanation of how the WordPiece tokenizer works and how we build the vocabulary is discussed at the end of the chapter, along with other tokenizers, in the *Subword tokenization algorithms* section.

Now that we have learned how to feed the input to BERT by converting it into embeddings, and also how to tokenize the input using a WordPiece tokenizer, in the next section, we will learn how to pre-train the BERT model.

Pre-training strategies

The BERT model is pre-trained on the following two tasks:

1. Masked language modeling
2. Next sentence prediction

Let's understand how the two aforementioned pre-training strategies work by looking at each in turn. Before diving directly into the masked language modeling task, first, let's understand how a language modeling task works.

Language modeling

In the language modeling task, we train the model to predict the next word given a sequence of words. We can categorize the language modeling into two aspects:

- Auto-regressive language modeling
- Auto-encoding language modeling

Auto-regressive language modeling

We can categorize the auto-regressive language modeling as follows:

- Forward (left-to-right) prediction
- Backward (right-to-left) prediction

Let's understand how these two methods work with the help of an example. Consider the text *'Paris is a beautiful city. I love Paris'*. Let's remove the word *'city'* and add a blank, as shown here:

Paris is a beautiful __. I love Paris

Now, our model has to predict the blank. If we use forward prediction, then our model reads all the words from left to right up to the blank in order to make a prediction, as shown here:

Paris is a beautiful __.

If we use backward prediction, then our model reads all the words from right to left up to the blank in order to make a prediction, as shown here:

__. I love Paris

Thus, auto-regressive models are unidirectional in nature, meaning that they read the sentence in only one direction.

Auto-encoding language modeling

Auto-encoding language modeling takes advantage of both forward (left-to-right) and backward (right-to-left) prediction. That is, it reads the sentence in both directions while making a prediction. Thus, we can say that the auto-encoding language model is bidirectional in nature. As we can observe from the following, to predict the bank, the auto-encoding language model reads the sentence in both directions, that is, left-to-right and right-to-left:

Paris is a beautiful __. I love Paris

The bidirectional model gives better results because if we read the sentence from both directions, it will give us more clarity in terms of understanding the sentence.

Now that we have understood how language modeling works, in the next section, we will look into one of the pre-training strategies of BERT, called masked language modeling.

Masked language modeling

BERT is an auto-encoding language model, meaning that it reads the sentence in both directions to make a prediction. In a masked language modeling task, in a given input sentence, we randomly mask 15% of the words and train the network to predict the masked words. To predict the masked words, our model reads the sentence in both directions and tries to predict the masked words.

Let's understand how masked language modeling works with an example. Let's take the same sentences we saw earlier: *'Paris is a beautiful city', and 'I love Paris'*. First, we tokenize the sentences and get the tokens, as shown here:

```
tokens = [Paris, is, a beautiful, city, I, love, Paris]
```

Now, we add the [CLS] token at the beginning of the first sentence and the [SEP] token at the end of every sentence, as shown here:

```
tokens = [ [CLS], Paris, is, a beautiful, city, [SEP], I, love, Paris,
[SEP] ]
```

Next, we randomly mask 15% of the tokens (words) in our preceding tokens list. Say we mask the word *city*, then we replace the word *city* with a [MASK] token, as shown here:

```
tokens = [ [CLS], Paris, is, a beautiful, [MASK], [SEP], I, love, Paris,
[SEP] ]
```

As we can observe from the preceding tokens list, we have replaced the word *city* with a [MASK] token. Now we train our BERT model to predict the masked token.

There is a small catch here. Masking tokens in this way will create a discrepancy between pre-training and fine-tuning. That is, we learned that we train BERT by predicting the [MASK] token. After training, we can fine-tune the pre-trained BERT model for downstream tasks, such as sentiment analysis. But during fine-tuning, we will not have any [MASK] tokens in the input. So it will cause a mismatch between the way in which BERT is pre-trained and how it is used for fine-tuning.

To overcome this issue, we apply the 80-10-10% rule. We learned that we randomly mask 15% of the tokens in the sentence. Now, for these of 15% tokens, we do the following:

- For 80% of the time, we replace the token (actual word) with the [MASK] token. So, for 80% of the time, the input to the model will be as follows:

```
tokens = [ [CLS], Paris, is, a beautiful, [MASK], [SEP], I, love,
Paris, [SEP] ]
```

- For 10% of the time, we replace the token (actual word) with a random token (random word). So, for 10% of the time, the input to the model will be as follows:

```
tokens = [ [CLS], Paris, is, a beautiful, love, [SEP], I, love,
Paris, [SEP] ]
```

- For 10% of the time, we don't make any changes. So, for 10% of the time, the input to the model will be as follows:

```
tokens = [ [CLS], Paris, is, a beautiful, city, [SEP], I, love,
Paris, [SEP] ]
```

Following tokenization and masking, we feed the input tokens to the token, segment, and position embedding layers and get the input embeddings.

Next, we feed the input embeddings to BERT. As shown in the following diagram, BERT takes the input and returns a representation of each token as an output. R_{CLS} denotes the representation of the token [CLS], R_{Paris} denotes the representation of the token *Paris,* and so on. In this example, we use BERT-base, which has 12 encoder layers, 12 attention heads, and 768 hidden units. Since we are using the BERT-base model, the size of the representation of each token will be 768:

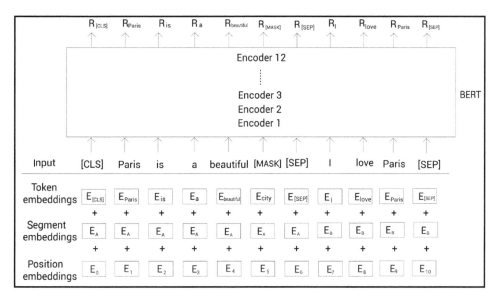

Figure 2.13 – BERT

From the preceding diagram, we observe that we obtained the representation R of each of the tokens. Now, how do we predict the masked token with these representations?

To predict the masked token, we feed the representation of the masked token R_{MASK} returned by BERT to the feedforward network with a softmax activation. Now, the feedforward network takes R_{MASK} as input and returns the probability of all the words in our vocabulary to be the masked word, as shown in the following diagram. Here, input embedding layers (token, segment, and position) are not shown so as to reduce clutter:

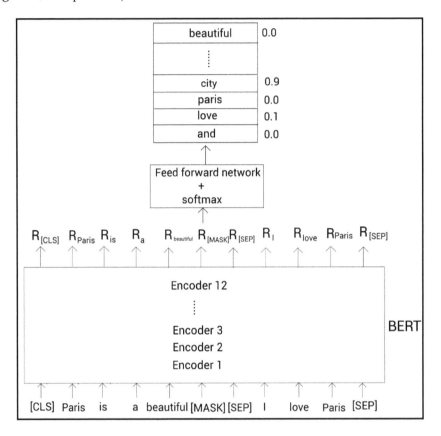

Figure 2.14 – Predicting the masked token

As shown in the preceding diagram, there is a high probability of the word *'city'* being the masked word. So, in this case, the masked word will be predicted as *'city'*.

Note that in the initial iterations, our model will not return the correct probability because the weights of the feedforward network and encoder layers of BERT will not be optimal. However, over a series of iterations, with backpropagation, we update the weights of the feedforward network and encoder layers of BERT and learn the optimal weights.

The masked language modeling task is also known as a **cloze task.** We learned how the masked language modeling task works and how we train the BERT model using the masked language modeling task. While masking the input tokens, we can also use a slightly different method, known as whole word masking. We will learn about whole word masking in the next section.

Whole word masking

Let's understand how **Whole Word Masking** (**WWM**) works with the help of an example. Consider the sentence *"Let us start pretraining the model"*. Remember that BERT uses a WordPiece tokenizer, so, after tokenizing the sentence using the WordPiece tokenizer, we will have the following tokens:

```
tokens  =  [let, us, start, pre, ##train, ##ing, the, model]
```

Next, we add a [CLS] token at the beginning of the sentence and an [SEP] token at the end of the sentence:

```
tokens  =  [[CLS], let, us, start, pre, ##train, ##ing, the, model, [SEP]]
```

Now, we randomly mask 15% of the words. Suppose we have the following:

```
tokens  =  [[CLS], [MASK], us, start, pre, [MASK], ##ing, the, model,
[SEP]]
```

As we can observe from the preceding, we have masked the words let and ##train. Note that the word ##train is actually a subword and is part of the word *pretraining*. In the WWM method, if the subword is masked, then we mask all the words corresponding to that subword. Thus, our tokens now become the following:

```
tokens  =  [[CLS], [MASK], us, start, [MASK], [MASK], [MASK], the, model,
[SEP]]
```

As we can observe from the preceding, all the tokens corresponding to the subword ##train are masked. Thus, in the case of WWM, if a subword is masked, then we mask all the words corresponding to that subword. Note that we also have to retain our mask rate, which is 15%. So, while masking all the words corresponding to subwords, we can ignore masking other words if it exceeds the 15% mask rate. As shown in the following, we have ignored masking the word let *so as* to retain the mask rate:

```
tokens = [[CLS], let, us, start, [MASK], [MASK], [MASK], the, model,
[SEP]]
```

Thus, in this way, we mask tokens using WWM. After masking, we feed the input tokens to BERT and train the model to predict the masked token, just like we learned in the previous section.

Now that we have learned how to train BERT using a masked language modeling task, in the next section, we will look at another interesting task associated with training BERT.

Next sentence prediction

Next sentence prediction (**NSP**) is another interesting strategy used for training the BERT model. NSP is a binary classification task. In the NSP task, we feed two sentences to BERT and it has to predict whether the second sentence is the follow-up (next sentence) of the first sentence. Let's understand the NSP task with the help of an example.

Consider the following two sentences:

Sentence A: She cooked pasta.

Sentence B: It was delicious.

In the preceding pair of sentences, sentence B is a follow-up, that is, the sentence following on from sentence A. So, we label this sentence pair as **isNext**, indicating that sentence B follows on from sentence A.

Now, consider the following two sentences:

Sentence A: Turn the radio on.

Sentence B: She bought a new hat.

In the preceding sentence pair, sentence B is not a follow-up, that is, it does not follow on from sentence A. So, we label this sentence pair as **notNext**, indicating that sentence B does not follow on from sentence A.

In the NSP task, the goal of our model is to predict whether the sentence pair belongs to the isNext or notNext category. We feed the sentence pair (sentences A and B) to BERT and train it to predict whether sentence B follows on from sentence A. The model returns isNext if sentence B follows on from sentence A, otherwise, it will return notNext as an output. Thus, NSP is essentially a binary classification task.

But what is the use of the NSP task? By performing the NSP task, our model can understand the relation between the two sentences. Understanding the relation between two sentences is useful in the case of many downstream tasks, such as question answering and text generation.

Okay, so how can we obtain the dataset for the NSP task? We can generate the dataset from any monolingual corpus. Let's say we have a couple of documents. For the isNext class, we take any two consecutive sentences from one document and label them as isNext, and for the notNext class, we take one sentence from one document and another sentence from a random document and label them as notNext. Note that we need to maintain 50% of data points in the isNext class and 50% of data points in the notNext class.

Now that we have learned what the NSP task is, let's see how to train the BERT model for performing NSP tasks. Suppose our dataset appears as shown in the following table:

Sentence Pair	Label
She cooked pasta It was delicious	isNext
Jack loves songwriting He wrote a new song	isNext
Birds fly in the sky He was reading	NotNext
Turn the radio on She bought a new hat	NotNext

Figure 2.15 – Sample dataset

Let's take the first data point in the preceding sample dataset. First, we will tokenize the sentence pair, as shown here:

```
tokens  =  [She, cooked, pasta, It, was, delicious]
```

Next, we add a `[CLS]` token just at the beginning of the first sentence, and an `[SEP]` token at the end of every sentence, as shown here:

```
tokens  =  [[CLS], She, cooked, pasta, [SEP], It, was, delicious, [SEP]]
```

Now, we feed the input tokens to the token, segment, and position embedding layers and get the input embeddings. Then, we feed the input embeddings to BERT and obtain the representation of each token. As shown in the following diagram, R_{CLS} denotes the representation of the token `[CLS]`, R_{she} denotes the representation of the token *She*, and so on:

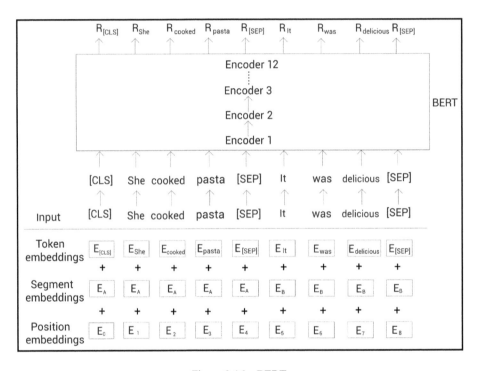

Figure 2.16 – BERT

We learned that NSP is a binary classification task. But now we have just the representation of each token in the sentence pair. How can we classify the sentence pair based on these representations?

To perform classification, we simply take the representation of the [CLS] token and feed it to the feedforward network with the softmax function, which then returns the probability of our sentence pair being isNext and notNext. Wait! Why do we need to take the embedding of the [CLS] token alone? Why not the embeddings of other tokens?

The [CLS] token basically holds the aggregate representation of all the tokens. So, it basically holds the aggregate representation of our sentences. Thus, we can ignore the representation of all the other tokens and simply take the representation of the [CLS] token R_{CLS} and feed it to the feedforward layer with a softmax function, which returns the probability. This is shown in the following diagram. Note that here, the input embedding layers (token, segment, and position embedding layers) are not shown so as to reduce clutter:

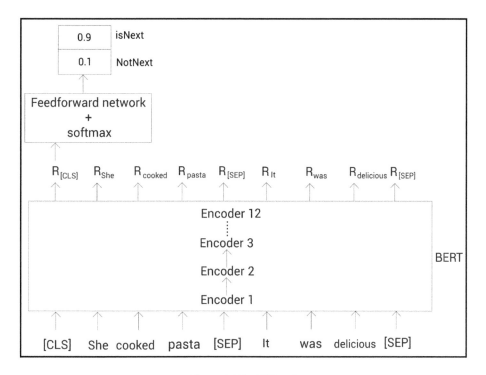

Figure 2.17 – NSP task

From the preceding diagram, we can understand that the feedforward network returns the high probability of our input sentence pair to be in the `isNext` class.

Note that in the initial iterations, our model will not return the correct probability because the weights of the feedforward network and encoder layers of BERT will not be optimal. However, over a series of iterations, with backpropagation, we update the weights of the feedforward network and the encoder layers of BERT and learn the optimal weights.

In this way, we train our BERT model with the NSP task. We learned how to pre-train BERT using masked language modeling and NSP tasks. In the next section, we will look into the pre-training procedure.

Pre-training procedure

BERT is pre-trained using Toronto BookCorpus and the Wikipedia dataset. We learned that BERT is pre-trained using masked language modeling (cloze task) and the NSP task. Now, how do we prepare the dataset to train BERT using these two tasks?

First, we sample two sentences (two text spans) from the corpus. Let's say we sampled two sentences A and B. The sum of the total number of tokens from the two sentences A and B should be less than or equal to 512. While sampling two sentences (two text spans), for 50% of the time, we sample sentence B as the follow-up sentence to sentence A, and for the other 50% of the time, we sample sentence B as not being the follow-up sentence to sentence A.

Suppose we sampled the following two sentences:

Sentence A: We enjoyed the game

Sentence B: Turn the radio on

First, we tokenize the sentence using a WordPiece tokenizer, add the `[CLS]` token to the beginning of the first sentence, and then add the `[SEP]` token to the end of every sentence. So, our tokens become the following:

```
tokens = [[CLS], we, enjoyed, the, game, [SEP], turn, the radio, on,
[SEP]]
```

Next, we randomly mask 15% of tokens according to the 80-10-10% rule. Suppose we masked the token game, then we have the following:

```
tokens   =   [[CLS], we, enjoyed, the, [MASK], [SEP], turn, the radio, on,
[SEP]]
```

Now, we feed the tokens to BERT and train BERT in predicting the masked tokens and also to classify whether sentence B is the follow-up sentence to sentence A. That is, we train BERT with both the masked language modeling and NSP tasks simultaneously.

BERT is trained on 256 sequences per batch of 1,000,000 steps. We use the Adam optimizer for training with a learning rate, $lr = 1e-4$, $\beta_1 = 0.9$, and $\beta_2 = 0.999$, and with a warm-up step set to 10,000. But wait, what is the warm-up step?

During training, we can take large steps in the initial iterations by setting a high learning rate, but we should take smaller steps in the later iterations by setting a low learning rate. This is because, in the initial iteration, we will be far from convergence, so it is okay to take large steps, but in the later iterations, we will be close to convergence and in that case, if we take a larger step, we miss out the convergence. Setting the learning rate value as high in the initial iterations and then decreasing it in later iterations is known as learning rate scheduling.

The warm-up step is used in learning rate scheduling. Say our learning rate is 1e-4 and the warm-up step is 10,000 iterations. This implies that we increase the learning rate linearly from 0 to 1e-4 in the initial 10,000 iterations. After these 10,000 iterations, we decrease the learning rate linearly as we move close to convergence.

We also apply dropout to all layers with a 0.1 dropout probability. BERT uses an activation function called GELU. GELU stands for **Gaussian Error Linear Unit**.

The GELU function is given as follows:

$$\text{GELU}(x) = x\Phi(x)$$

Here, $\Phi(x)$ is the Gaussian cumulative distribution function. The GELU function is approximated, as indicated here:

$$\text{GELU}(x) = 0.5x(1 + \tanh[\sqrt{2/\pi}(x + 0.044715x^3)])$$

The following diagram shows the plot of the GELU function:

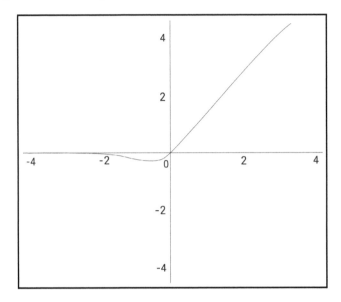

Figure 2.18 – The GELU activation function

That's it. In this way, we can pre-train BERT using masked language modeling and NSP tasks. The pre-trained BERT model can be used for a variety of tasks and we will learn how to use the pre-trained BERT model in detail in the next chapter. In the next section, we will learn several interesting subword tokenization algorithms.

Subword tokenization algorithms

Subword tokenization is popularly used in many state-of-the-art natural language models, including BERT and GPT-3. It is very effective in handling OOV words. In this section, we will understand how subword tokenization works in detail. Before directly looking into subword tokenization, let's first take a look at word-level tokenization.

Let's suppose we have a training dataset. Now, from this training set, we build a vocabulary. To build the vocabulary, we split the text present in the dataset by white space and add all the unique words to the vocabulary. Generally, the vocabulary consists of many words (tokens), but just for the sake of an example, let's suppose our vocabulary consists of just the following words:

```
vocabulary = [game, the, I, played, walked, enjoy]
```

Now that we have created the vocabulary, we use this vocabulary for tokenizing the input. Let's consider an input sentence *"I played the game"*. In order to create tokens from the sentence, first, we split the sentence by white space and obtain all the words in the sentence. So we have - [I, play, the, game]. Now, we check whether we have all the words (I, play, the, game) present in the vocabulary. Since all the words are present in the vocabulary, our final tokens for the given sentence will be as follows:

```
tokens = [I, played, the, game]
```

Let's consider another sentence: *"I enjoyed the game"*. To tokenize the sentence, we split the given sentence by white space and obtain the words. Then we have [I, enjoyed, the, game]. Now, we check whether we have all the words (I, enjoyed, the, game) present in the vocabulary. We can observe that we have all the words present in the vocabulary except for the word enjoyed. Since the word enjoyed is not present in the vocabulary, we replace it with an unknown token, <UNK>. Thus, our final tokens will be as follows:

```
tokens = [ I, <UNK>, the, game]
```

We can observe that although we have the word *enjoy* in our vocabulary, just because we didn't have the exact word enjoyed, it is marked as an unknown word with the <UNK> token. Generally, we build a huge vocabulary with many words, and if a rare word, that is, the word that is not present in the vocabulary, comes in, then it will be marked as an unknown word with an <UNK> token. However, having a huge vocabulary causes memory and performance issues and it still cannot handle the unseen words (words that are not present in the vocabulary).

Is there a better way to handle this? Yes! This is where subword tokenization helps us. Let's see how subword tokenization works with the same preceding example. We learned that our vocabulary consists of the following:

```
vocabulary = [game, the, I, played, walked, enjoy]
```

In subword tokenization, we split the words into subwords. Suppose we split the word played into subwords [play, ed] and the word walked into subwords [walk, ed]. After splitting the subwords, we will add them to the vocabulary. Note that the vocabulary consists of only unique words. So, our vocabulary now consists of the following:

```
vocabulary = [game, the, I, play, walk, ed, enjoy]
```

Let's consider the same sentence we saw earlier: *"I enjoyed the game"*. To tokenize the sentence, we split the given sentence by white space and obtain the words. So we have [I, enjoyed, the, game]. Now, we check whether we have all the words (I, enjoyed, the, game) present in the vocabulary. We can notice that we have all the words present in the vocabulary except for the word enjoyed. Since the word enjoyed is not present in the vocabulary, we split it into subwords, [enjoy, ed]. Now, we check whether we have the subwords enjoy and ed present in the vocabulary, and since they are present in the vocabulary, our tokens become the following:

```
tokens  =  [ I, enjoy, ##ed, the, game]
```

We can observe that the word ed has two hash signs preceding it. This indicates that ##ed is a subword and is preceded by another word. We don't add the ## signs for the subword that is at the start of the word, and that's why there are no ## signs in the subword enjoy. The ## signs are added just to indicate that it is a subword and that it is preceded by another word. In this way, subword tokenization handles the unknown words, that is, words that are not present in the vocabulary.

But the question is, we saw that we split the words played and walked into subwords and added them to the vocabulary. But why we are splitting just those words? Why not other words in the vocabulary? How do we decide which words to split and which not to? This is where we use the subword tokenization algorithm.

Let's learn about several interesting subword tokenization algorithms that are used to create the vocabulary. After creating the vocabulary, we can use it for tokenization. Let's understand the following three popularly used subword tokenization algorithms:

- Byte pair encoding
- Byte-level byte pair encoding
- WordPiece

Byte pair encoding

Let's understand how **Byte Pair Encoding** (BPE) works with the help of an example. Let's suppose we have a dataset. First, we extract all the words from the dataset along with their count. Suppose the words extracted from the dataset along with the count are *(cost, 2)*, *(best, 2)*, *(menu, 1)*, *(men, 1)*, and *(camel, 1)*.

Now, we split all the words into characters and create a character sequence. The following table shows the character sequence along with the wordcount:

Character sequence	Cost
C o s t	2
b e s t	2
m e n u	1
m e n	1
c a me l	1

Figure 2.19 – Character sequence with count

Next, we define a vocabulary size. Let's suppose we build a vocabulary of size 14. This implies that we create a vocabulary with 14 tokens. Now, let's understand how to create the vocabulary using BPE.

First, we add all the unique characters present in the character sequence to the vocabulary, as shown here:

Character sequence	Cost	Vocabulary
C o s t	2	a, b, c, e, l, m, n, o, s, t, u
b e s t	2	
m e n u	1	
m e n	1	
c a me l	1	

Figure 2.20 – Creating a vocabulary with all unique characters

As we can observe, our vocabulary size is 11. Now, let's see how to add new tokens to the vocabulary.

To add a new token to the vocabulary, first, we identify the most frequent symbol pair. Then we merge that most frequent symbol pair and add it to the vocabulary. We repeat this step iteratively until we reach the vocabulary size. Let's understand this in detail.

By looking at the following character sequence, we can observe that the most frequent symbol pair we have is **s** and **t** since the symbol pair **s** and **t** has occurred four times (two times in *cost* and two times in *best*):

Character sequence	Cost	Vocabulary
C o <u>s t</u>	2	a, b, c, e, l, m, n, o, s, t, u
b e <u>s t</u>	2	
m e n u	1	
m e n	1	
c a m e l	1	

Figure 2.21 – Finding the most frequent symbol pair

So, we merge the symbols **s** and **t** and add it to the vocabulary, as shown here:

Character sequence	Cost	Vocabulary
C o **st**	2	a, b, c, e, l, m, n, o, s, t, u ,**st**
b e **st**	2	
m e n u	1	
m e n	1	
c a m e l	1	

Figure 2.22 – Merging the symbols s and t

Now, we repeat the same step. That is, we again check for the most frequent symbol pair. We can observe that the most frequent symbol pair we now have is **m** and **e**, since they have occurred three times (one time in *menu*, one time in *men*, and one time in *camel*):

Character sequence	Cost	Vocabulary
C o st	2	a, b, c, e, l, m, n, o, s, t, u ,st
b e st	2	
me n u	1	
me n	1	
c a **me** l	1	

Figure 2.23 – Finding the most frequent symbol pair

So, we merge the symbols **m** and **e** and add it to the vocabulary, as shown here:

Character sequence	Cost	Vocabulary
C o st	2	a, b, c, e, l, m, n, o, s ,t , u, st, **me**
b e st	2	
me n u	1	
me n	1	
c a me l	1	

Figure 2.24 – Merging the symbols m and e

Again, we check for the most frequent symbol pair. We can observe that the most frequent symbol pair we now have is **me** and **n**, since they have occurred two times (once in *menu* and once in *men*):

Character sequence	Cost	Vocabulary
C o st	2	a, b, c, e, l, m, n, o, s ,t , u, st, me
b e st	2	
me n u	1	
me n	1	
c a me l	1	

Figure 2.25 – Finding the most frequent symbol pair

So, we merge the symbols **me** and **n** and add it to the vocabulary, as shown here:

Character sequence	Cost	Vocabulary
C o st	2	a, b, c, e, l, m, n, o, s, t, u, st, me, **men**
b e st	2	
men u	1	
men	1	
c a me l	1	

Figure 2.26 – Merging the symbols me and n

In this way, we repeat this step several times until we reach the vocabulary size. From the preceding diagram, we can observe that now our vocabulary has 14 tokens. Since, in this example, we are creating a vocabulary of size 14, we stop at this step.

Thus, from the given dataset, we built a vocabulary containing 14 tokens:

```
vocabulary = {a,b,c,e,l,m,n,o,s,t,u,st,me,men}
```

The steps involved in BPE are provided here:

1. Extract the words from the given dataset along with their count.
2. Define the vocabulary size.
3. Split the words into a character sequence.
4. Add all the unique characters in our character sequence to the vocabulary.
5. Select and merge the symbol pair that has a high frequency.
6. Repeat step 5 until the vocabulary size is reached.

We learned how to build the vocabulary using BPE. Okay, but how can this vocabulary be used? We use the vocabulary to tokenize the given input. Let's understand this concept with the help of a few examples in the next section.

Tokenizing with BPE

In the previous section, we learned that with the given dataset, we created the following vocabulary:

```
vocabulary  =  {a,b,c,e,l,m,n,o,s,t,u,st,me,men}
```

Now, let's see how this vocabulary can be used. Let's suppose our input text consists of only one word – mean. Now we check whether the word mean is present in our vocabulary. We can observe that it is not present in the vocabulary. So we split the word mean into subwords [me, an]. Now, we check whether the subwords are present in the vocabulary. We can observe that the subword me is present in the vocabulary, but the subword an is not present in our vocabulary. Therefore, we split the subword an, so now our subwords consist of [me, a,n]. Now we check whether the characters a and n are present in our vocabulary. Since they are present in our vocabulary, our final tokens will be as follows:

```
tokens  =  [me,a,n]
```

Let's consider one more input word: bear. We can observe that the word bear is not present in our vocabulary. So now we split it into subwords [be, ar]. Now we check whether the subwords be and ar are present in the vocabulary. The subword be is present, but ar is not present in the vocabulary. Therefore, we split the subword ar, and now subwords consist of [be, a,r]. Now we check whether the characters a and r are present in the vocabulary. We can observe that a is present in the vocabulary, but r is not present in the vocabulary. We are unable to effect another split since now we have only individual characters. Now we replace r with a <UNK> token. Thus, our final tokens will be as follows:

```
tokens  =  [be,a,<UNK>]
```

Wait. We learned that BPE handles rare words well, but now we have a <UNK> token. This is because since this is a small example, the character r is not present in our vocabulary. But when we create a vocabulary with a huge corpus, our vocabulary will have all the characters.

Let's consider one more input word: men. Now we check whether the word men is present in our vocabulary. Since the word men is present in our vocabulary, we can return it directly as a token. Thus, our final token will be as follows:

```
tokens = [men]
```

In this way, we tokenize the input sentence using BPE. Now that we have understood how BPE works, in the next section, we will look into byte-level byte pair encoding.

Byte-level byte pair encoding

Byte-level byte pair encoding (**BBPE**) is another popularly used algorithm. It works very similar to BPE, but instead of using a character-level sequence, it uses a byte-level sequence. Let's understand how BBPE works with the help of an example.

Let's suppose our input text consists of just the word '*best*'. We know that in BPE, we convert the word into a character sequence, so we will have the following:

Character sequence: b e s t

Whereas in BBPE, instead of converting the word to a character sequence, we convert it to a byte-level sequence. Hence, we convert the word '*best*' into a byte sequence:

Byte sequence: 62 65 73 74

In this way, we convert the given input into a byte-level sequence instead of a character-level sequence. Each Unicode character is converted into a byte. A single character can have 1 to 4 bytes.

Let's consider one more example. Let's suppose that our input consists of a Chinese word, 你好. Now, instead of converting the word into a character sequence, we will convert the word into a byte-level sequence. Hence, we have the following:

Byte sequence: e4 bd a0 e5 a5 bd

As we can observe, we converted the input word into a byte sequence. In this manner, we convert the given text to a byte-level sequence, and then we apply the BPE algorithm and build a vocabulary using byte-level frequent pairs. But what is the purpose of doing byte-level BPE instead of character-level BPE? Well, byte-level BPE will be very useful in a multilingual setting. It is very effective in handling OOV words and it is great at sharing vocabulary across multiple languages.

WordPiece

WordPiece works similar to BPE, with one minor difference. We learned that in BPE, from a given dataset, first we extract the words with their count. Then we split the words into character sequences. Next, we merge the symbol pair that has a high frequency. We then keep merging symbol pairs with a high frequency iteratively until we reach the vocabulary size. We do the same in WordPiece, with one difference being that here we don't merge symbol pairs based on frequency. Instead, we merge symbol pairs based on likelihood. So, we merge the symbol pair that has a high likelihood of the language model, which is trained on the given training data. Let's understand this with the help of an example.

Consider the same example we used in the BPE section:

Character sequence	Cost	Vocabulary
C o s t	2	a, b, c, e, l, m, n, o, s, t, u
b e s t	2	
m e n u	1	
m e n	1	
c a m e l	1	

Figure 2.27 – Character sequence and count

We learned that in BPE, we merge the most frequent symbol pair. In BPE, we merged the symbol pair **s** and **t** since they occurred four times. But now, in this method, we don't merge symbol pairs based on frequency; instead, we merge them based on likelihood. First, we check the likelihood of the language model (which is trained on a given training set) for every symbol pair. Then we merge the symbol pair that has the highest likelihood. The likelihood of the symbol pair **s** and **t** is computed, as shown here:

$$\frac{p(st)}{p(s)p(t)}$$

If the likelihood is high, we simply merge the symbol pair and add them to the vocabulary. In this way, we compute the likelihood of all symbol pairs and merge the one that has the maximum likelihood and add it to the vocabulary. The following steps help us to understand the algorithm better:

1. Extract the words from the given dataset along with their count.
2. Define the vocabulary size.
3. Split the words into a character sequence.
4. Add all the unique characters in our character sequence to the vocabulary.
5. Build the language model on the given dataset (training set).
6. Select and merge the symbol pair that has the maximum likelihood of the language model trained on the training set.
7. Repeat *step 6* until the vocabulary size is reached.

After building the vocabulary, we use it for tokenization. Let's suppose the following is the vocabulary we built using the WordPiece method:

```
vocabulary  =  {a,b,c,e,l,m,n,o,s,t,u,st,me}
```

Let's now suppose that our input text consists of just one word -stem. We can observe that the word stem is not present in our vocabulary. So now we split it into subwords [st, ##em]. Now we check whether the subwords st and em are present in the vocabulary. The subword st is present, but em is not. Therefore, we split the subword em, and now the subwords consist of [be, ##e,##m]. Now we check whether the characters e and m are present in the vocabulary. Since they are present in the vocabulary, our final tokens will be as follows:

```
tokens  =  [st, ##e, ##m]
```

In this way, we can create a vocabulary using the WordPiece subword tokenization algorithm and use the vocabulary for tokenization.

In this chapter, we covered in detail how BERT is pre-trained and we also looked into the different subword tokenization algorithms. In the next chapter, let's understand how to apply the pre-trained BERT in detail.

Summary

We began this chapter by understanding the basic idea of BERT. We learned that BERT can understand the contextual meaning of words and generate embeddings according to context, unlike context-free models such as word2vec, which generate embeddings irrespective of the context.

Next, we looked into the workings of BERT. We understood that **B**idirectional **E**ncoder **R**epresentation from **T**ransformer (**BERT**), as the name suggests, is basically the transformer model.

Following on from this, we looked into the different configurations of BERT. We learned that the BERT-base consists of 12 encoder layers, 12 attention heads, and 768 hidden units, while BERT-large consists of 24 encoder layers, 16 attention heads, and 1,024 hidden units.

Moving on, we learned how the BERT model is pre-trained using two interesting tasks, called masked language modeling and NSP. We learned that in masked language modeling, we mask 15% of the tokens and train BERT to predict the masked tokens, while, in the NSP task, we train BERT to classify whether the second sentence is a follow-on sentence from the first sentence.

Then, we learned about the pre-training procedure of BERT. At the end of the chapter, we learned about three popularly used subword tokenization algorithms – BPE, BBPE, and WordPiece. In this next chapter, let's get hands-on with BERT.

Questions

Let's evaluate our understanding of BERT by trying to answer the following questions:

1. How does BERT differ from other embedding models?
2. What are the differences between the BERT-base and BERT-large models?
3. Define segment embedding.
4. How is BERT pre-trained?

5. How does the masked language modeling task work?
6. What is the 80-10-10% rule?
7. How does the NSP task work?

Further reading

To learn more, check out the following papers:

- **BERT: Pre-training of Deep Bidirectional Transformers for Language Understanding,** by *Jacob Devlin, Ming-Wei Chang, Kenton Lee,* and *Kristina Toutanova,* available at `https://arxiv.org/pdf/1810.04805.pdf`.

- **Gaussian Error Linear Units (GELUs),** by *Dan Hendrycks* and *Kevin Gimpel,* available at `https://arxiv.org/pdf/1606.08415.pdf`.

- **Neural Machine Translation of Rare Words with Subword Units,** by *Rico Sennrich, Barry Haddow,* and *Alexandra Birch,* available at `https://arxiv.org/pdf/1508.07909.pdf`.

- **Neural Machine Translation with Byte-Level Subwords,** by *Changhan Wang, Kyunghyun Cho,* and *Jiatao Gu,* available at `https://arxiv.org/pdf/1909.03341.pdf`.

- **Japanese and Korean Voice Search**, by *Mike Schuster* and *Kaisuke Nakajima,* available at `https://static.googleusercontent.com/media/research.google.com/en//pubs/archive/37842.pdf`.

Getting Hands-On with BERT

3

In this chapter, we will learn how to use the pre-trained BERT model in detail. First, we will look at the different configurations of the pre-trained BERT model open sourced by Google. Then, we will learn how to use the pre-trained BERT model as a feature extractor. We will also explore Hugging Face's transformers library and learn how to use it to extract embeddings from the pre-trained BERT.

Moving on, we will understand how to extract embeddings from all encoder layers of BERT. Next, we will learn how to fine-tune the pre-trained BERT model for the downstream tasks. First, we will learn to fine-tune the pre-trained BERT model for a text classification task. Next, we will learn to fine-tune BERT for sentiment analysis tasks using the `transformers` library. Then, we will look into fine-tuning the pre-trained BERT model for natural language inference, question answering tasks, and named entity recognition tasks.

In this chapter, we will learn the following topics:

- Exploring the pre-trained BERT model
- Extracting embeddings from pre-trained BERT
- Extracting embeddings from all encoder layers of BERT
- Fine-tuning BERT for downstream tasks

Exploring the pre-trained BERT model

In Chapter 2, *Understanding the BERT Model*, we learned how to pre-train BERT using masked language modeling and next-sentence prediction tasks. But pre-training BERT from scratch is computationally expensive. So, we can download the pre-trained BERT model and use it. Google has open sourced the pre-trained BERT model and we can download it from Google Research's GitHub repository – https://github.com/google-research/bert. They have released the pre-trained BERT model with various configurations, shown in the following figure. *L* denotes the number of encoder layers and *H* denotes the size of the hidden unit (representation size):

	H=128	H=256	H=512	H=768
L=2	2/128 (BERT-tiny)	2/256	2/512	2/768
L=4	4/128	4/256 (BERT-mini)	4/512 (BERT-small)	4/768
L=6	6/128	6/256	6/512	6/768
L=8	8/128	8/256	8/512 (BERT-medium)	8/768
L=10	10/128	10/256	10/512	10/768
L=12	12/128	12/256	12/512	12/768 (BERT-base)

Figure 3.1 – Different configurations of pre-trained BERT as provided by Google (https://github.com/google-research/bert)

The pre-trained model is also available in the BERT-uncased and BERT-cased formats. In BERT-uncased, all the tokens are lowercased, but in BERT-cased, the tokens are not lowercased and are used directly for training. Okay, which pre-trained BERT model we should use? BERT-cased or BERT-uncased? The BERT-uncased model is the one that is most commonly used, but if we are working on certain tasks such as **Named Entity Recognition** (**NER**) where we have to preserve the case, then we should use the BERT-cased model. Along with these, Google also released pre-trained BERT models trained using the whole word masking method. Okay, but how exactly we can use the pre-trained BERT model?

We can use the pre-trained model in the following two ways:

- As a feature extractor by extracting embeddings
- By fine-tuning the pre-trained BERT model on downstream tasks such as text classification, question-answering, and more

In the upcoming sections, we will learn how to use the pre-trained BERT model as a feature extractor by extracting embeddings, and we will also learn how to fine-tune the pre-trained BERT model for downstream tasks in detail.

Extracting embeddings from pre-trained BERT

Let's learn how to extract embeddings from pre-trained BERT with an example. Consider a sentence – *I love Paris*. Say we need to extract the contextual embedding of each word in the sentence. To do this, first, we tokenize the sentence and feed the tokens to the pre-trained BERT model, which will return the embeddings for each of the tokens. Apart from obtaining the token-level (word-level) representation, we can also obtain the sentence-level representation.

In this section, let's learn how exactly we can extract the word-level and sentence-level embedding from the pre-trained BERT model in detail.

Let's suppose we want to perform a sentiment analysis task, and say we have the dataset shown in the following figure:

Sentence	Label
I love paris	1
Sam hated the movie	0
It was a great day	1
The song is not good	0
⋮	⋮
We loved the game	1

Figure 3.2 – Sample dataset

As we can observe from the preceding table, we have sentences and their corresponding labels, where 1 indicates positive sentiment and 0 indicates negative sentiment. We can train a classifier to classify the sentiment of a sentence using the given dataset.

But we can't feed the given dataset directly to a classifier, since it has text. So first, we need to vectorize the text. We can vectorize the text using methods such as TF-IDF, word2vec, and others. In the previous chapter, we learned that BERT learns the contextual embedding, unlike other context-free embedding models such as word2vec. Now, we will see how to use the pre-trained BERT model to vectorize the sentences in our dataset.

Let's take the first sentence in our dataset – *I love Paris*. First, we tokenize the sentence using the WordPiece tokenizer and get the tokens (words). After tokenizing the sentence, we have the following:

```
tokens = [I, love, Paris]
```

Now, we add the [CLS] token at the beginning and the [SEP] token at the end. Thus, our tokens list becomes this:

```
tokens = [ [CLS], I, love, Paris, [SEP] ]
```

Similarly, we can tokenize all the sentences in our training set. But the length of each sentence varies, right? Yes, and so does the length of the tokens. We need to keep the length of all the tokens the same. Say we keep the length of the tokens to 7 for all the sentences in our dataset. If we look at our preceding tokens list, the tokens length is 5. To make the tokens length 7, we add a new token called [PAD]. Thus, now our tokens are as follows:

```
tokens = [ [CLS], I, love, Paris, [SEP], [PAD], [PAD] ]
```

As we can observe, now our tokens length is 7, as we have added two [PAD] tokens. The next step is to make our model understand that the [PAD] token is added only to match the tokens length and it is not part of the actual tokens. To do this, we introduce an attention mask. We set the attention mask value to 1 in all positions and 0 to the position where we have a [PAD] token, as shown here:

```
attention_mask = [ 1,1,1,1,1,0,0]
```

Next, we map all the tokens to a unique token ID. Suppose the following is the mapped token ID:

```
token_ids = [101, 1045, 2293, 3000, 102, 0, 0]
```

It implies that ID 101 indicates the token [CLS], 1045 indicates the token *I*, 2293 indicates the token Paris, and so on.

Now, we feed `token_ids` along with `attention_mask` as input to the pre-trained BERT model and obtain the vector representation (embedding) of each of the tokens. This will be made more clear once we look into the code.

The following figure shows how we use the pre-trained BERT model to obtain the embedding. For clarity, the tokens are shown instead of token IDs. As we can see, once we feed the tokens as the input, encoder 1 computes the representation of all the tokens and sends it to the next encoder, which is encoder 2. Encoder 2 takes the representation computed by encoder 1 as input, computes its representation, and sends it to the next encoder, which is encoder 3. In this way, each encoder sends its representation to the next encoder above it. The final encoder, which is encoder 12, returns the final representation (embedding) of all the tokens in our sentence:

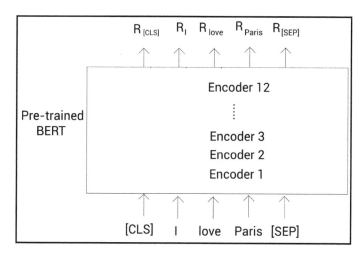

Figure 3.3 – Pre-trained BERT

As shown in the preceding figure, $R_{[CLS]}$ is the embedding of the token [CLS], R_I is the embedding of the token *I*, R_{love} is the embedding of the token *love*, and so on. Thus, in this way, we can obtain the representation of each of the tokens. These representations are basically the contextualized word (token) embeddings. Say we are using the pre-trained BERT-base model; in that case, the representation size of each token is 768.

We learned how to obtain the representation for each word in the sentence *I love Paris*. But how do we obtain the representation of the complete sentence?

We learned that we have prepended the [CLS] token to the beginning of our sentence. The representation of the [CLS] token will hold the aggregate representation of the complete sentence. So, we can ignore the embeddings of all other tokens and take the embedding of the [CLS] token and assign it as a representation of our sentence. Thus, the representation of our sentence *I love Paris* is just the representation of the [CLS] token $R_{[CLS]}$.

In a very similar fashion, we can compute the vector representation of all the sentences in our training set. Once we have the sentence representation of all the sentences in our training set, we can feed those representations as input and train a classifier to perform a sentiment analysis task.

Note that using the representation of the [CLS] token as a sentence representation is not always a good idea. The efficient way to obtain the representation of a sentence is either averaging or pooling the representation of all the tokens. We will learn more about this in the upcoming chapters.

Now that we have learned how to use the pre-trained BERT model to extract an embedding (representation), in the next section, we will learn how to do this using a library known as **transformers**.

Hugging Face transformers

Hugging Face is an organization that is on the path of democratizing AI through natural language. Their open source transformers library is very popular among the **Natural Language Processing** (NLP) community. It is very useful and powerful for several NLP and **Natural Language Understanding** (NLU) tasks. It includes thousands of pre-trained models in more than 100 languages. One of the many advantages of the transformer's library is that it is compatible with both PyTorch and TensorFlow.

We can install transformers directly using pip as shown here:

```
pip install transformers==3.5.1
```

As we can see, in this book, we use transformers version 3.5.1. Now that we have installed transformers, let's get started.

Generating BERT embeddings

In this section, we will learn how to extract embeddings from the pre-trained BERT model. Consider the sentence *I love Paris*. Let's see how to obtain the contextualized word embedding of all the words in the sentence using the pre-trained BERT model with Hugging Face's transformers library. We can also access the complete code from the GitHub repository of the book. In order to run the code smoothly, clone the GitHub repository of the book and run the code using Google Colab.

First, let's import the necessary modules:

```
from transformers import BertModel, BertTokenizer
import torch
```

Next, we download the pre-trained BERT model. We can check all the available pre-trained BERT models here – https://huggingface.co/transformers/pre-trained_models.html. We use the `'bert-base-uncased'` model. As the name suggests, it is the BERT-base model with 12 encoders and it is trained with uncased tokens. Since we are using BERT-base, the representation size will be 768.

Download and load the pre-trained `bert-base-uncased` model:

```
model = BertModel.from_pretrained('bert-base-uncased')
```

Next, we download and load the tokenizer that was used to pre-train the `bert-base-uncased` model:

```
tokenizer = BertTokenizer.from_pretrained('bert-base-uncased')
```

Now, let's see how to preprocess the input before feeding it to BERT.

Preprocessing the input

Define the sentence:

```
sentence = 'I love Paris'
```

Tokenize the sentence and obtain the tokens:

```
tokens = tokenizer.tokenize(sentence)
```

Let's print the tokens:

```
print(tokens)
```

The preceding code will print the following:

```
['i', 'love', 'paris']
```

Now, we will add the [CLS] token at the beginning and the [SEP] token at the end of the tokens list:

```
tokens = ['[CLS]'] + tokens + ['[SEP]']
```

Let's look at our updated tokens list:

```
print(tokens)
```

The previous code will print the following:

```
['[CLS]', 'i', 'love', 'paris', '[SEP]']
```

As we can observe, we have a [CLS] token at the beginning and an [SEP] token at the end of our tokens list. We can also see that length of our tokens list is 5.

Say we need to keep the length of our tokens list to 7; in that case, we add two [PAD] tokens at the end as shown in the following snippet:

```
tokens = tokens + ['[PAD]'] + ['[PAD]']
```

Let's print our updated tokens list:

```
print(tokens)
```

The preceding code will print the following:

```
['[CLS]', 'i', 'love', 'paris', '[SEP]', '[PAD]', '[PAD]']
```

As we can see, now we have the tokens list with [PAD] tokens and the length of our tokens list is 7.

Next, we create the attention mask. We set the attention mask value to 1 if the token is not a [PAD] token, else we set the attention mask to 0, as shown here:

```
attention_mask = [1 if i!= '[PAD]' else 0 for i in tokens]
```

Let's print attention_mask:

```
print(attention_mask)
```

The preceding code will print this:

```
[1, 1, 1, 1, 1, 0, 0]
```

As we can see, we have attention mask values 0 at positions where have a [PAD] token and 1 at other positions.

Next, we convert all the tokens to their token IDs as follows:

```
token_ids = tokenizer.convert_tokens_to_ids(tokens)
```

Let's have a look at token_ids:

```
print(token_ids)
```

The preceding code will print the following:

```
[101, 1045, 2293, 3000, 102, 0, 0]
```

From the output, we can observe that each token is mapped to a unique token ID.

Now, we convert token_ids and attention_mask to tensors as shown in the following code:

```
token_ids = torch.tensor(token_ids).unsqueeze(0)
attention_mask = torch.tensor(attention_mask).unsqueeze(0)
```

That's it. Next, we feed token_ids and attention_mask to the pre-trained BERT model and get the embedding.

Getting the embedding

As shown in the following code, we feed token_ids and attention_mask to model and get the embeddings. Note that model returns the output as a tuple with two values. The first value indicates the hidden state representation, hidden_rep, and it consists of the representation of all the tokens obtained from the final encoder (encoder 12), and the second value, cls_head, consists of the representation of the [CLS] token:

```
hidden_rep, cls_head = model(token_ids, attention_mask = attention_mask)
```

In the preceding code, hidden_rep contains the embedding (representation) of all the tokens in our input. Let's print the shape of hidden_rep:

```
print(hidden_rep.shape)
```

The preceding code will print the following:

```
torch.Size([1, 7, 768])
```

The size [1,7,768] indicates [batch_size, sequence_length, hidden_size].

Our batch size is 1. The sequence length is the token length. Since we have 7 tokens, the sequence length is 7. The hidden size is the representation (embedding) size and it is 768 for the BERT-base model.

We can obtain the representation of each token as follows:

- `hidden_rep[0][0]` gives the representation of the first token, which is `[CLS]`.
- `hidden_rep[0][1]` gives the representation of the second token, which is `I`.
- `hidden_repo[0][2]` gives the representation of the third token, which is `love`.

In this way, we can obtain the contextual representation of all the tokens. This is basically the contextualized word embeddings of all the words in the given sentence.

Now, let's take a look at `cls_head`. It contains the representation of the [CLS] token. Let's print the shape of `cls_head`:

```
print(cls_head.shape)
```

The preceding code will print the following:

```
torch.Size([1, 768])
```

The size `[1,768]` indicates `[batch_size, hidden_size]`.

We learned that `cls_head` holds the aggregate representation of the sentence, so we can use `cls_head` as the representation of the sentence *I love Paris*.

We learned how to extract embeddings from the pre-trained BERT model. But these are the embeddings obtained only from the topmost encoder layer of BERT, which is encoder 12. Can we also extract the embeddings from all the encoder layers of BERT? Yes! We will find out how to do that in the next section.

Extracting embeddings from all encoder layers of BERT

We learned how to extract the embedding from the pre-trained BERT model in the previous section. We learned that they are the embeddings obtained from the final encoder layer. Now the question is, should we consider the embeddings obtained only from the final encoder layer (final hidden state), or should we also consider the embeddings obtained from all the encoder layers (all hidden states)? Let's explore this.

Let's represent the input embedding layer with h_0, the first encoder layer (first hidden layer) with h_1, the second encoder layer (second hidden layer) with h_2, and so on to the final twelfth encoder layer, h_{12}, as shown in the following figure:

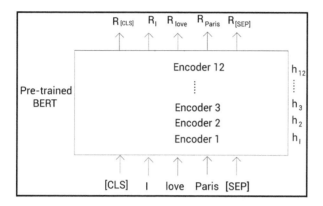

Figure 3.4 – Pre-trained BERT

Instead of taking the embeddings (representations) only from the final encoder layer, the researchers of BERT have experimented with taking embeddings from different encoder layers.

For instance, for NER task, the researchers have used the pre-trained BERT model to extract features. Instead of using the embedding only from the final encoder layer (final hidden layer) as a feature, they have experimented with using embeddings from other encoder layers (other hidden layers) as features and obtained the following F1 score:

Feature	Notation	F1 score
Embeddings	h_0	91.0
Second to last hidden	h_{11}	95.6
Last hidden	h_{12}	94.9
Weighted sum of last four hidden	$h_{9\,to}\,h_{12}$	95.9
Concat last four hidden	$h_{9\,to}\,h_{12}$	96.1
Weighted sum of all 12 layer	$h_{1\,to}\,h_{12}$	95.5

Figure 3.5 – F1 score of using embeddings from different layers

As we can observe from the preceding table, concatenating the embeddings of the last four encoder layers (last four hidden layers) gives us a greater F1 score of 96.1%. Thus, instead of taking embeddings only from the final encoder layer (final hidden layer), we can also use embeddings from the other encoder layers.

Now, we will learn how to extract the embeddings from all the encoder layers using the transformers library.

Extracting the embeddings

First, let's import the necessary modules:

```
from transformers import BertModel, BertTokenizer
import torch
```

Next, download the pre-trained BERT model and tokenizer. As we can see, while downloading the pre-trained BERT model, we need to set `output_hidden_states = True`. Setting this to `True` helps us to obtain embeddings from all the encoder layers:

```
model = BertModel.from_pretrained('bert-base-uncased',
                                  output_hidden_states = True)
tokenizer = BertTokenizer.from_pretrained('bert-base-uncased')
```

Next, we preprocess the input before feeding it to the model.

Preprocessing the input

Let's consider the sentence we saw in the previous section. First, we tokenize the sentence and add a `[CLS]` token at the beginning and an `[SEP]` token at the end:

```
sentence = 'I love Paris'
tokens = tokenizer.tokenize(sentence)
tokens = ['[CLS]'] + tokens + ['[SEP]']
```

Suppose we need to keep the token length to 7. So, we add the `[PAD]` tokens and also define the attention mask:

```
tokens = tokens + ['[PAD]'] + ['[PAD]']
attention_mask = [1 if i!= '[PAD]' else 0 for i in tokens]
```

Next, we convert `tokens` to their token IDs:

```
token_ids = tokenizer.convert_tokens_to_ids(tokens)
```

Now, we convert `token_ids` and `attention_mask` to tensors:

```
token_ids = torch.tensor(token_ids).unsqueeze(0)
attention_mask = torch.tensor(attention_mask).unsqueeze(0)
```

Now that we have preprocessed the input, let's get the embeddings.

Getting the embeddings

Since we set `output_hidden_states = True` while defining the model to get the embeddings from all the encoder layers, now the model returns an output tuple with three values, as shown in the following code:

```
last_hidden_state, pooler_output, hidden_states = \
model(token_ids, attention_mask = attention_mask)
```

In the preceding code, the following applies:

- The first value, `last_hidden_state`, contains the representation of all the tokens obtained only from the final encoder layer (encoder 12).
- Next, `pooler_output` indicates the representation of the [CLS] token from the final encoder layer, which is further processed by a linear and tanh activation function.
- `hidden_states` contains the representation of all the tokens obtained from all the encoder layers.

Now, let's take a look at each of these values and understand them in more detail.

First, let's look at `last_hidden_state`. As we learned, it holds the representation of all the tokens obtained only from the final encoder layer (encoder 12). Let's print the shape of `last_hidden_state`:

```
last_hidden_state.shape
```

The preceding code will print the following:

```
torch.Size([1, 7, 768])
```

The size `[1,7,768]` indicates `[batch_size, sequence_length, hidden_size]`.

Our batch size is 1. The sequence length is the token length. Since we have 7 tokens, the sequence length is 7. The hidden size is the representation (embedding) size and it is 768 for the BERT-base model.

We can obtain the embedding of each token as follows:

- `last_hidden[0][0]` gives the representation of the first token, which is `[CLS]`.
- `last_hidden[0][1]` gives the representation of the second token, which is `I`.
- `last_hidden[0][2]` gives the representation of the third token, which is `love`.

Similarly, we can obtain the representation of all the tokens from the final encoder layer.

Next, we have `pooler_output`, which contains the representation of the [CLS] token from the final encoder layer, which is further processed by a linear and tanh activation function. Let's print the shape of `pooler_output`:

```
pooler_output.shape
```

The size `[1,768]` indicates `[batch_size, hidden_size]`.

We learned that the [CLS] token holds the aggregate representation of the sentence. Thus, we can use `pooler_output` as the representation of the sentence *I love Paris*.

Finally, we have `hidden_states`, which contains the representation of all the tokens obtained from all the encoder layers. It is a tuple containing 13 values holding the representation of all encoder layers (hidden layers), from the input embedding layer h_0 to the final encoder layer h_{12}

```
len(hidden_states)
```

The preceding code will print the following:

```
13
```

As we can see, it contains 13 values holding the representation of all layers:

- `hidden_states[0]` contains the representation of all the tokens obtained from the input embedding layer h_0.
- `hidden_states[1]` contains the representation of all the tokens obtained from the first encoder layer h_1.
- `hidden_states[2]` contains the representation of all the tokens obtained from the second encoder layer h_2.
- `hidden_states[12]` contains the representation of all the tokens obtained from the final encoder layer h_{12}.

Let's explore this more. First, let's print the shape of `hidden_states[0]`, which contains the representation of all the tokens obtained from the input embedding layer h_0:

```
hidden_states[0].shape
```

The preceding code will print the following:

```
torch.Size([1, 7, 768])
```

The size `[1, 7, 768]` indicates `[batch_size, sequence_length, hidden_size]`.

Now, let's print the shape of `hidden_states[1]`, which contains the representation of all tokens obtained from the first encoder layer h_1:

```
hidden_states[1].shape
```

The preceding code will print the following:

```
torch.Size([1, 7, 768])
```

Thus, in this way, we can obtain the embedding of tokens from all the encoder layers. We learned how to use the pre-trained BERT model to extract embeddings; can we also use pre-trained BERT for a downstream task such as sentiment analysis? Yes! We will learn about this in the next section.

Fine-tuning BERT for downstream tasks

So far, we have learned how to use the pre-trained BERT model. Now, let's learn how to fine-tune the pre-trained BERT model for downstream tasks. Note that fine-tuning implies that we are not training BERT from scratch; instead, we are using the pre-trained BERT and updating its weights according to our task.

In this section, we will learn how to fine-tune the pre-trained BERT model for the following downstream tasks:

- Text classification
- Natural language inference
- NER
- Question-answering

Text classification

Let's learn how to fine-tune the pre-trained BERT model for a text classification task. Say we are performing sentiment analysis. In the sentiment analysis task, our goal is to classify whether a sentence is positive or negative. Suppose we have a dataset containing sentences along with their labels.

Consider a sentence: *I love Paris*. First, we tokenize the sentence, add the [CLS] token at the beginning, and add the [SEP] token at the end of the sentence. Then, we feed the tokens as an input to the pre-trained BERT model and get the embeddings of all the tokens.

Next, we ignore the embedding of all other tokens and take only the embedding of [CLS] token, which is $R_{[CLS]}$. The embedding of the [CLS] token will hold the aggregate representation of the sentence. We feed $R_{[CLS]}$ to a classifier (feed-forward network with softmax function) and train the classifier to perform sentiment analysis.

Wait! How does this differ from what we saw at the beginning of the section? How does fine-tuning the pre-trained BERT model differ from using the pre-trained BERT model as a feature extractor?

In the *Extracting embeddings from pre-trained BERT* section, we learned that after extracting the embedding $R_{[CLS]}$ of a sentence, we feed $R_{[CLS]}$ to a classifier and train the classifier to perform classification. Similarly, during fine-tuning, we feed the embedding of $R_{[CLS]}$ to a classifier and train the classifier to perform classification.

The difference is that when we fine-tune the pre-trained BERT model, we update the weights of the model along with a classifier. But when we use the pre-trained BERT model as a feature extractor, we update only the weights of the classifier and not the pre-trained BERT model.

During fine-tuning, we can adjust the weights of the model in the following two ways:

- Update the weights of the pre-trained BERT model along with the classification layer.
- Update only the weights of the classification layer and not the pre-trained BERT model. When we do this, it becomes the same as using the pre-trained BERT model as a feature extractor.

The following figure shows how we fine-tune the pre-trained BERT model for a sentiment analysis task:

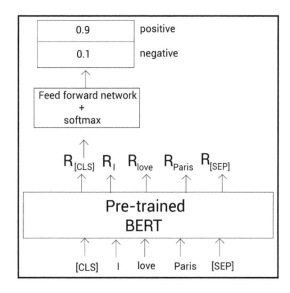

Figure 3.6 – Fine-tuning the pre-trained BERT model for text classification

As we can observe from the preceding figure, we feed the tokens to the pre-trained BERT model and get the embeddings of all the tokens. We take the embedding of the [CLS] token and feed it to a feedforward network with a softmax function and perform classification.

Let's get a better understanding of how fine-tuning works by getting hands-on with fine-tuning the pre-trained BERT model for sentiment analysis task in the next section.

Fine-tuning BERT for sentiment analysis

Let's explore how to fine-tune the pre-trained BERT model for a sentiment analysis task with the IMDB dataset. The IMDB dataset consists of movie reviews along with the respective sentiment of the review. We can also access the complete code from the GitHub repository of the book. In order to run the code smoothly, clone the GitHub repository of the book and run the code using Google Colab.

Importing the dependencies

First, let's install the necessary libraries:

```
!pip install nlp==0.4.0
!pip install transformers==3.5.1
```

Import the necessary modules:

```
from transformers import BertForSequenceClassification, BertTokenizerFast,
Trainer, TrainingArguments
from nlp import load_dataset
import torch
import numpy as np
```

Loading the model and dataset

Load the model and dataset. First, let's download and load the dataset using the `nlp` library:

```
!gdown https://drive.google.com/uc?id=11_M4ootuT7I1G0RlihcC0cA3Elqotlc-
dataset = load_dataset('csv', data_files='./imdbs.csv', split='train')
```

Let's check the datatype:

```
type(dataset)
```

Here is the output:

```
nlp.arrow_dataset.Dataset
```

Next, let's split the dataset into train and test sets:

```
dataset = dataset.train_test_split(test_size=0.3)
```

Let's print the dataset:

```
dataset
```

The preceding code will print the following:

```
{
'test': Dataset(features: {'text': Value(dtype='string', id=None), 'label':
Value(dtype='int64', id=None)}, num_rows: 30),
 'train': Dataset(features: {'text': Value(dtype='string', id=None),
'label': Value(dtype='int64', id=None)}, num_rows: 70)
}
```

Now, we create the train and test sets:

```
train_set = dataset['train']
test_set = dataset['test']
```

Next, let's download and load the pre-trained BERT model. In this example, we use the pre-trained `bert-base-uncased` model. As we can see, since we are performing sequence classification, we use the `BertForSequenceClassification` class:

```
model = BertForSequenceClassification.from_pretrained('bert-base-uncased')
```

Next, we download and load the tokenizer that was used to pre-train the `bert-base-uncased` model.

As we can see, we create the tokenizer using the `BertTokenizerFast` class instead of `BertTokenizer`. The `BertTokenizerFast` class has many advantages compared to `BertTokenizer`. We will learn about this in the next section:

```
tokenizer = BertTokenizerFast.from_pretrained('bert-base-uncased')
```

Now that we have loaded the dataset and model, let's preprocess the dataset.

Preprocessing the dataset

We can preprocess the dataset quickly using our tokenizer. For example, consider the sentence *I love Paris.*

First, we tokenize the sentence and add a `[CLS]` token at the beginning and a `[SEP]` token at the end, as shown here:

```
tokens = [ [CLS], I, love, Paris, [SEP] ]
```

Next, we map the tokens to the unique input IDs (token IDs). Suppose the following are the unique input IDs (token IDs):

```
input_ids = [101, 1045, 2293, 3000, 102]
```

Then, we need to add the segment IDs (token type IDs). Wait, what are segment IDs? Suppose we have two sentences in the input. In that case, segment IDs are used to distinguish one sentence from the other. All the tokens from the first sentence will be mapped to 0 and all the tokens from the second sentence will be mapped to 1. Since here we have only one sentence, all the tokens will be mapped to 0 as shown here:

```
token_type_ids = [0, 0, 0, 0, 0]
```

Now, we need to create the attention mask. We know that an attention mask is used to differentiate the actual tokens and `[PAD]` tokens. It will map all the actual tokens to `1` and the `[PAD]` tokens to `0`. Suppose our `tokens` length should be 5. Our `tokens` list already has five tokens, so we don't have to add a `[PAD]` token. Our attention mask will become the following:

```
attention_mask = [1, 1, 1, 1, 1]
```

That's it. But instead of doing all the aforementioned steps manually, our tokenizer will do these steps for us. We just need to pass the sentence to the tokenizer as shown in the following code:

```
tokenizer('I love Paris')
```

The preceding code will return the following. As we can see, our input sentence is tokenized and mapped to `input_ids`, `token_type_ids`, and also `attention_mask`:

```
{
'input_ids': [101, 1045, 2293, 3000, 102],
'token_type_ids': [0, 0, 0, 0, 0],
'attention_mask': [1, 1, 1, 1, 1]
}
```

With the tokenizer, we can also pass any number of sentences and perform padding dynamically. To do that, we need to set `padding` to `True` and also the maximum sequence length. For instance, as shown in the following code, we pass three sentences and we set the maximum sequence length, `max_length`, to 5:

```
tokenizer(['I love Paris', 'birds fly','snow fall'], padding = True,
          max_length=5)
```

The preceding code will return the following. As we can see, all the sentences are mapped to `input_ids`, `token_type_ids`, and `attention_mask`. The second and third sentences have only two tokens, and after adding `[CLS]` and `[SEP]`, they will have four tokens. Since we set `padding` to `True` and `max_length` to 5, an additional `[PAD]` token is added to the second and third sentences, and that's why we have `0` in the attention mask of the second and third sentences:

```
{
'input_ids': [[101, 1045, 2293, 3000, 102], [101, 5055, 4875, 102, 0],
[101, 4586, 2991, 102, 0]],
'token_type_ids': [[0, 0, 0, 0, 0], [0, 0, 0, 0, 0], [0, 0, 0, 0, 0]],
'attention_mask': [[1, 1, 1, 1, 1], [1, 1, 1, 1, 0], [1, 1, 1, 1, 0]]
}
```

That's it – with the tokenizer, we can easily preprocess our dataset. So, we define a function called `preprocess` to process the dataset as follows:

```
def preprocess(data):
    return tokenizer(data['text'], padding=True, truncation=True)
```

Now, we preprocess the train and test sets using the `preprocess` function:

```
train_set = train_set.map(preprocess, batched=True,
                     batch_size=len(train_set))
test_set = test_set.map(preprocess, batched=True, batch_size=len(test_set))
```

Next, we use the `set_format` function and select the columns that we need in our dataset and the format we need them in as shown in the following code:

```
train_set.set_format('torch',
                columns=['input_ids', 'attention_mask', 'label'])
test_set.set_format('torch',
                columns=['input_ids', 'attention_mask', 'label'])
```

That's it. Now that we have the dataset ready, let's train the model.

Training the model

Define the batch size and epoch size:

```
batch_size = 8
epochs = 2
```

Define the warmup steps and weight decay:

```
warmup_steps = 500
weight_decay = 0.01
```

Define the training arguments:

```
training_args = TrainingArguments(
    output_dir='./results',
    num_train_epochs=epochs,
    per_device_train_batch_size=batch_size,
    per_device_eval_batch_size=batch_size,
    warmup_steps=warmup_steps,
    weight_decay=weight_decay,
    evaluate_during_training=True,
    logging_dir='./logs',
)
```

Now, define the trainer:

```
trainer = Trainer(
    model=model,
    args=training_args,
    train_dataset=train_set,
    eval_dataset=test_set
)
```

Start training the model:

```
trainer.train()
```

After training, we can evaluate the model using the `evaluate` function:

```
trainer.evaluate()
```

The preceding code will print the following:

```
{'epoch': 1.0, 'eval_loss': 0.68}
{'epoch': 2.0, 'eval_loss': 0.50}
```

In this way, we can fine-tune the pre-trained BERT model. Now that we have learned how to fine-tune BERT for a text classification task, in the next section, let's see how to fine-tune the BERT model for **Natural Language Inference** (**NLI**).

Natural language inference

In NLI, the goal of our model is to determine whether a hypothesis is an entailment (true), a contradiction (false), or undetermined (neutral) given a premise. Let's learn how to perform NLI by fine-tuning BERT.

Consider the sample dataset shown in the following figure; as we can see, we have a premise and a hypothesis with a label indicating whether they are entailment, contradiction, or undetermined:

Premise	Hypothesis	Label
He is playing	He is sleeping	Contradiction
A soccer game with multiple males playing	Some men are playing sport	Entailment
An older and a younger man smiling	Two men are smiling at the dogs playing on the floor	Neutral

Figure 3.7 – Sample NLI dataset

Now, the goal of our model is to determine whether a sentence pair (premise-hypothesis pair) is an entailment, a contradiction, or undetermined. Let's understand how to do this with an example. Consider the following premise-hypothesis pair:

Premise: He is playing

Hypothesis: He is sleeping

First, we tokenize the sentence pair, then add a [CLS] token at the beginning of the first sentence and an [SEP] token at the end of every sentence. The tokens are as follows:

```
tokens = [ [CLS], He, is, playing, [SEP], He, is, sleeping [SEP]]
```

Now, we feed the tokens to the pre-trained BERT model and get the embedding of each token. We learned that the representation of the [CLS] token holds the aggregate representation.

So, we take the representation of the [CLS] token, which is $R_{[CLS]}$, and feed it to a classifier (feeedforward + softmax), which returns the probability of the sentence being a contradiction, an entailment, or neutral. Our results will not be accurate in the initial iteration, but over a course of multiple iterations, we will get better results:

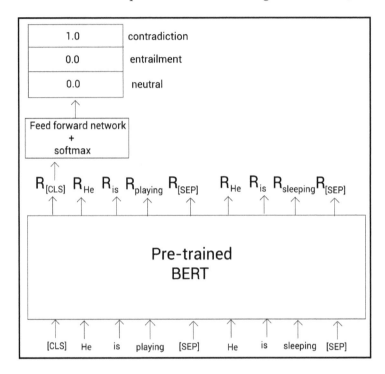

Figure 3.8 – Fine-tuning the pre-trained BERT model for NLI

Now that we have learned how to fine-tune BERT for NLI, in the next section, we will learn how to fine-tune BERT for question-answering.

Question-answering

In a question-answering task, we are given a question along with a paragraph containing an answer to the question. Our goal is to extract the answer from the paragraph for the given question. Now, let's learn how to fine-tune the pre-trained BERT model to perform a question-answering task.

The input to the BERT model will be a question-paragraph pair. That is, we feed a question and a paragraph containing the answer to the question to BERT and it has to extract the answer from the paragraph. So, essentially, BERT has to return the text span that contains the answer from the paragraph. Let's understand this with an example – consider the following question-paragraph pair:

Question = *"What is the immune system?"*

Paragraph = *"The immune system is a system of many biological structures and processes within an organism that protects against disease. To function properly, an immune system must detect a wide variety of agents, known as pathogens, from viruses to parasitic worms, and distinguish them from the organism's own healthy tissue."*

Now, our model has to extract an answer from the paragraph; it essentially has to return the text span containing the answer. So, it should return the following:

Answer = *"a system of many biological structures and processes within an organism that protects against disease"*

Okay, how can we fine-tune the BERT model to do this task? To do this, our model has to understand the starting and ending index of the text span containing the answer in the given paragraph. For example, take the question, *"What is the immune system?"* If our model understands that the answer to this question starts from index 4 ("*a*") and ends at index 21 ("*disease*"), then we can get the answer as shown here:

Paragraph = *"The immune system is **a system of many system of many biological structures and processes within an organism that protects against disease**" biological structures and processes within an organism that protects against disease. To function properly, an immune system must detect a wide variety of agents, known as pathogens, from viruses to parasitic worms, and distinguish them from the organism's own healthy tissue."*

Now, how do we find the starting and ending index of the text span containing the answer? If we get the probability of each token (word) in the paragraph of being the starting and ending token (word) of the answer, then we can easily extract the answer, right? Yes, but how we can achieve this? To do this, we use two vectors called the start vector S and the end vector E. The values of the start and end vectors will be learned during training.

First, we compute the probability of each token (word) in the paragraph being the starting token of the answer.

To compute this probability, for each token i, we compute the dot product between the representation of the token R_i and the start vector S. Next, we apply the softmax function to the dot product $S.R_i$ and obtain the probability:

$$P_i = \frac{e^{S.R_i}}{\sum_j e^{S.R_j}}$$

Next, we compute the starting index by selecting the index of the token that has a high probability of being the starting token.

In a very similar fashion, we compute the probability of each token (word) in the paragraph being the ending token of the answer. To compute this probability, for each token i, we compute the dot product between the representation of the token R_i and the end vector E. Next, we apply the softmax function to the dot product $E.R_i$ and obtain the probability:

$$P_i = \frac{e^{E.R_i}}{\sum_j e^{E.R_j}}$$

Next, we compute the ending index by selecting the index of the token that has a high probability of being the ending token. Now, we can select the text span that contains the answer using the starting and ending index.

As shown in the following figure, first, we tokenize the question-paragraph pair and feed the tokens to the pre-trained BERT model, which returns the embeddings of all the tokens. As shown in the figure, R_1 to R_N denotes the embeddings of the tokens in the question and R_1 R_M denotes the embedding of the tokens in the paragraph.

After computing the embedding, we compute the dot product with the start/end vectors, apply the softmax function, and obtain the probabilities of each token in the paragraph being the start/end word as shown here:

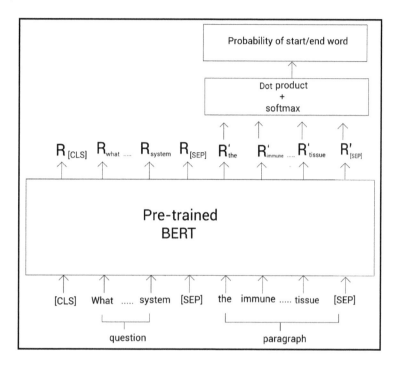

Figure 3.9 - Fine-tuning the pre-trained BERT for question-answering

From the preceding figure, we can see how we compute the probability of each token in the paragraph being the start/end word. Next, we select the text span containing the answer using the starting and ending indexes with the highest probability. To get a better understanding of how this works, let's see how to use the fine-tuned question-answering BERT model in the next section.

Performing question-answering with fine-tuned BERT

In this section, let's learn how to perform question answering with a fine-tuned question-answering BERT model. First, let's import the necessary modules:

```
from transformers import BertForQuestionAnswering, BertTokenizer
```

Now, we download and load the model. We use the `bert-large-uncased-whole-word-masking-fine-tuned-squad` model, which is fine-tuned on the **Stanford Question-Answering Dataset** (**SQUAD**):

```
model = BertForQuestionAnswering.from_pretrained('bert-large-uncased-whole-word-masking-fine-tuned-squad')
```

Next, we download and load the tokenizer:

```
tokenizer = BertTokenizer.from_pretrained('bert-large-uncased-whole-word-masking-fine-tuned-squad')
```

Now that we have downloaded the model and tokenizer, let's preprocess the input.

Preprocessing the input

First, we define the input to BERT, which is the question and paragraph text:

```
question = "What is the immune system?"
paragraph = "The immune system is a system of many biological structures
and processes within an organism that protects against disease. To function
properly, an immune system must detect a wide variety of agents, known as
pathogens, from viruses to parasitic worms, and distinguish them from the
organism's own healthy tissue."
```

Add a `[CLS]` token to the beginning of the question and an `[SEP]` token to the end of both the question and the paragraph:

```
question = '[CLS] ' + question + '[SEP]'
paragraph = paragraph + '[SEP]'
```

Now, tokenize the question and paragraph:

```
question_tokens = tokenizer.tokenize(question)
paragraph_tokens = tokenizer.tokenize(paragraph)
```

Combine the question and paragraph tokens and convert them to `input_ids`:

```
tokens = question_tokens + paragraph_tokens
input_ids = tokenizer.convert_tokens_to_ids(tokens)
```

Next, we define `segment_ids`. Now, `segment_ids` will be 0 for all the tokens of the question and 1 for all the tokens of the paragraph:

```
segment_ids = [0] * len(question_tokens)
segment_ids = [1] * len(paragraph_tokens)
```

Now we convert `input_ids` and `segment_ids` to tensors:

```
input_ids = torch.tensor([input_ids])
segment_ids = torch.tensor([segment_ids])
```

Now that we have processed the input, let's feed it to the model and get the result.

Getting the answer

We feed `input_ids` and `segment_ids` to the model, which returns the start score and end score for all of the tokens:

```
start_scores, end_scores = model(input_ids, token_type_ids = segment_ids)
```

Now, we select `start_index`, which is the index of the token that has the highest start score, and `end_index`, which is the index of the token that has the highest end score:

```
start_index = torch.argmax(start_scores)
end_index = torch.argmax(end_scores)
```

That's it! Now, we print the text span between the start and end indexes as our answer:

```
print(' '.join(tokens[start_index:end_index+1]))
```

The preceding code will print the following:

```
a system of many biological structures and processes within an organism
that protects against disease
```

Now that we have learned how to fine-tune BERT for question-answering, in the next section, we will learn how to fine-tune BERT for NER.

Named entity recognition

In NER, our goal is to classify named entities into predefined categories. For instance, consider the sentence *Jeremy lives in Paris*. In this sentence, "*Jeremy*" should be categorized as a *person*, and "*Paris*" should be categorized as a *location*.

Now, let's learn how to fine-tune the pre-trained BERT model to perform NER. First, we tokenize the sentence, then we add the [CLS] token at the beginning and the [SEP] token at the end. Then, we feed the tokens to the pre-trained BERT model and obtain the representation of every token. Next, we feed those token representations to a classifier (feedforward network + softmax function). Then, the classifier returns the category to which the named entity belongs. This is shown in the following figure:

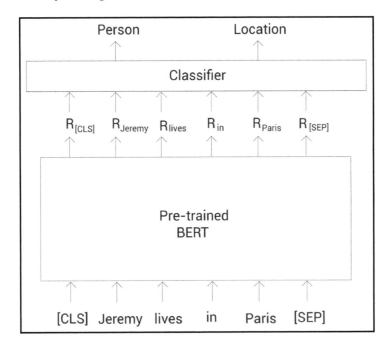

Figure 3.10 - Fine-tuning the pre-trained BERT model for NER

We can fine-tune the pre-trained BERT model for several downstream tasks. So far, we have learned how BERT works and also how to use the pre-trained BERT model. In the next chapter, we will learn about different variants of BERT.

Summary

We started the chapter by looking at different configurations of the pre-trained BERT model provided by Google. Then, we learned that we can use the pre-trained BERT model in two ways: as a feature extractor by extracting embeddings, and by fine-tuning the pre-trained BERT model for downstream tasks such as text classification, question-answering, and more.

Then, we learned how to extract embeddings from the pre-trained BERT model in detail. We also learned how to use Hugging Face's transformers library to generate embeddings. Then, we learned how to extract embeddings from all the encoder layers of BERT in detail.

Moving on, we learned how to fine-tune pre-trained BERT for downstream tasks. We learned how to fine-tune BERT for text classification, NLI, NER, and question-answering in detail. In the next chapter, we will explore several interesting variants of BERT.

Questions

Let's put our knowledge to the test. Try answering the following questions:

1. How do you use the pre-trained BERT model?
2. What is the use of the [PAD] token?
3. What is an attention mask?
4. What is fine-tuning?
5. How do you compute the starting index of an answer in question-answering?
6. How do you compute the ending index of an answer in question-answering?
7. How do you use BERT for NER?

Further reading

To learn more, refer to the following resources:

- Check out the Hugging Face transformers documentation, available at `https://huggingface.co/transformers/model_doc/bert.html`.
- *BERT: Pre-training of Deep Bidirectional Transformers for Language Understanding* by Jacob Devlin, Ming-Wei Chang, Kenton Lee, and Kristina Toutanova available at `https://arxiv.org/pdf/1810.04805.pdf`.

Section 2 - Exploring BERT Variants 2

In this section, we will explore several interesting variants of BERT. We will learn about popular variants of BERT such as ALBERT, RoBERTa, ELECTRA, and SpanBERT. We will also explore BERT variants based on knowledge distillation, such as DistilBERT and TinyBERT.

The following chapters are included in this section:

- Chapter 4, *BERT Variants I – ALBERT, RoBERTa, ELECTRA, and SpanBERT*
- Chapter 5, *BERT Variants II – Based on Knowledge Distillation*

4
BERT Variants I - ALBERT, RoBERTa, ELECTRA, and SpanBERT

In this chapter, we will understand different variants of BERT, such as ALBERT, RoBERTa, ELECTRA, and SpanBERT. We will start with understanding how ALBERT works. **ALBERT** is basically **A Lite version of BERT** model. The ALBERT model includes few architectural changes to the BERT to minimize the training time. We will cover how ALBERT works and how it differs from BERT in detail.

Moving on, we will learn about the **RoBERTa** model, which stands for a **Robustly Optimized BERT pre-training Approach**. RoBERTa is one of the most popular variants of the BERT and it is used in many state-of-the-art systems. RoBERTa works similar to BERT but with a few changes in the pre-training steps. We will explore how RoBERTa works and how it differs from the BERT model in detail.

Going ahead, we will learn about the **ELECTRA** model, which stands for **Efficiently Learning an Encoder that Classifies Token Replacements Accurately**. Unlike other BERT variants, ELECTRA uses a generator and a discriminator. It is pre-trained using a new task called a replaced token detection task. We will learn how exactly ELECTRA works in detail.

At the end of the chapter, we will learn about **SpanBERT**. It is popularly used in use cases such as question answering, relation extraction, and so on. We will understand how SpanBERT works by exploring its architecture.

In this chapter, we will learn the following topics:

- A Lite version of BERT
- Robustly Optimized BERT pre-training Approach
- Understanding ELECTRA
- Predicting span with SpanBERT

A Lite version of BERT

In this section, we will learn about **A Lite version of BERT**, also known as **ALBERT**. One of the challenges with BERT is that it consists of millions of parameters. BERT-base consists of 110 million parameters, which makes it harder to train, and it also has a high inference time. Increasing the model size gives us good results but it puts a limitation on the computational resources. To combat this, ALBERT was introduced. ALBERT is a lite version of BERT with fewer parameters compared to BERT. It uses the following two techniques to reduce the number of parameters:

- Cross-layer parameter sharing
- Factorized embedding layer parameterization

By using the preceding two techniques, we can reduce the training time and inference time of the BERT model. First, let's understand how these two techniques work in detail, and then we will see how ALBERT is pre-trained.

Cross-layer parameter sharing

Cross-layer parameter sharing is an interesting method for reducing the number of parameters of the BERT model. We know that BERT consists of N number of encoder layers. For instance, BERT-base consists of 12 encoder layers. During training, we learn the parameters of all the encoder layers. But with cross-layer parameter sharing, instead of learning the parameters of all the encoder layers, we only learn the parameters of the first encoder layer, and then we just share the parameters of the first encoder layer with all the other encoder layers. Let's explore this in detail.

The following figure shows the BERT model with N number of encoder layers; only the first encoder layer is expanded to reduce the clutter:

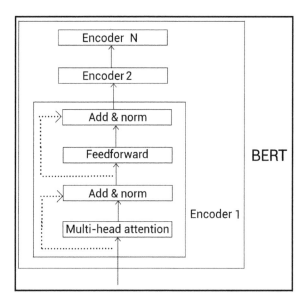

Figure 4.1 – BERT with N number of encoders

We know that each encoder layer is identical, that is, each encoder consists of sublayers called multi-head attention and feedforward layers. We can just learn the parameters of encoder 1 and share the parameters with all other encoders and this is known as cross-layer parameter sharing. We have several options for performing cross-layer parameter sharing, as listed here:

- **All-shared**: In all-shared, we share parameters of all the sublayers of the first encoder with all the sublayers of the other encoders.
- **Shared feedforward network**: Here, we only share the parameters of the feedforward network of the first encoder layer with the feedforward network of the other encoder layers.
- **Shared attention**: In this option, we only share the parameters of the multi-head attention of the first encoder layer with the multi-head attention of other encoder layers.

By default, ALBERT uses the all-shared option, that is, we share parameters of the first encoder layer with all the layers.

Now that we have learned how the cross-layer parameter sharing technique works, let's look into another interesting parameter reduction technique in the next section.

Factorized embedding parameterization

We learned that in BERT, we use the WordPiece tokenizer and create WordPiece tokens. The embedding size of the WordPiece tokens is set the same as the hidden layer embedding size (representation size). A WordPiece embedding is the non-contextual representation and it is learned from the one-hot-encoded vectors of vocabulary. Hidden layer embedding is the contextual representation and it is returned by the encoder.

Let's denote the vocabulary size as V. We learned that the vocabulary size of BERT is 30,000. Let's denote the hidden layer embedding size as H and the WordPiece embedding size as E.

To encode more information into hidden layer embedding, we usually set the size of hidden layer embeddings to a high value. For instance, in BERT-base, the hidden layer embedding size is set to 768. The dimension of our hidden layer embedding will be $V \times H$ = 30,000 x 768. Since the WordPiece embedding size is set the same as the hidden layer embedding size, if the hidden layer embedding H size is 768, then the size of the WordPiece embedding E size is also set to 768. Thus, the dimension of our WordPiece embedding will be $V \times E$ = 30,000 x 768. Thus, increasing the size of the hidden layer embedding, H, will also increase the size of the WordPiece embedding, E.

Both the WordPiece embedding and the hidden layer embedding are learned during training. Setting the WordPiece embedding size to the same as the hidden layer embedding size increases the number of parameters to learn. So, how do we avoid this? To avoid this, we use the factorized embedding parameterization method where we factorize the embedding matrix into smaller matrices.

We set the size of the WordPiece embedding to the same as the hidden layer embedding size because we directly project the one-hot-encoded vectors of the vocabulary to the hidden space. With factorization, instead of directly projecting the one-hot-encoded vectors of vocabulary to the hidden space ($V \times H$), first, we project one-hot-encoded vectors to low-dimensional embedding space ($V \times E$), and then we project this low-dimensional embedding to hidden space ($E \times H$). That is, instead of projecting $V \times H$ directly, we factorize this step into $V \times E$ and $E \times H$.

Let's understand this with an example. Say the size of our vocabulary, V, is 30,000. We don't have to set the WordPiece embedding size the same as the hidden layer embedding size. Say the WordPiece embedding, E, size is 128 and the hidden layer embedding, H, size is 768. Now, we project $V \times H$ with the following steps:

- First, we project the one-hot-encoded vectors of vocabulary V to the low-dimensional WordPiece embedding space E, that is, $V \times E$. The dimension of the WordPiece embedding becomes $V \times E = 30,000 \times 128$.
- Next, we project this WordPiece embedding space E into a hidden layer, H, that is, $E \times H$. The dimension becomes $E \times H = 128 \times 768$.

Thus, instead of directly projecting $V \times H$, we split it into $V \times E$ and $E \times H$.

In this way, by using cross-layer parameter sharing and factorized embedding parameterization, we can reduce our model parameters. We learned how ALBERT reduces the number of model parameters but how do we train the ALBERT model? Is it the same as BERT or does it use a different approach? Let's find out in the next section.

Training the ALBERT model

Similar to BERT, the ALBERT model is pre-trained using the English Wikipedia and Toronto BookCorpus datasets. We learned that BERT is pre-trained using the **masked language modeling** (**MLM**) and **next sentence prediction** (**NSP**) tasks. Similarly, the ALBERT model is pre-trained using the MLM task but instead of using the NSP task, ALBERT uses a new task called **sentence order prediction** (**SOP**). But why not use the NSP task?

The researchers of ALBERT pointed out that pre-training with the NSP task is not really useful and it is not a difficult task to perform compared to the MLM task. Also, the NSP task combines both topic prediction and coherence prediction into a single task. To alleviate this, researchers introduced the SOP task. SOP is based on inter-sentence coherence and not on topic prediction. Let's look at how the SOP task works in detail.

Sentence order prediction

Similar to the next sentence prediction task, SOP is a binary classification task. In the next sentence prediction task, we train the model to predict whether a sentence pair belongs to the `isNext` or `notNext` class, whereas in the SOP task, we train the model to predict whether a sentence order in a given sentence pair is swapped or not. Let's understand this with an example. Consider the following sentence pair:

Sentence 1: *She cooked pasta*

Sentence 2: *It was delicious*

In the given sentence pair, we can understand that sentence 2 is a consecutive sentence of sentence 1 and we label this sentence pair as a positive. Now, to create a negative class, we simply swap the sentence order, thus our sentence pair becomes the following:

Sentence 1: *It was delicious*

Sentence 2: *She cooked pasta*

From the preceding sentence pair, we can understand that the sentence order is swapped and we label this sentence pair as a negative.

Thus, SOP is basically a classification task where the goal of our model is to classify whether the sentence pair belongs to a positive class (sentence order not swapped) or a negative class (sentence order swapped). We can create a dataset for a SOP task using any monolingual corpus. Say we have a couple of documents. We simply take two consecutive sentences from a document and label them as positive. Next, we swap the sentences and label them as negative.

We learned that the ALBERT model is trained using the MLM and SOP tasks. But how efficient and powerful is our ALBERT model compared to BERT? Let's discuss this in the next section.

Comparing ALBERT with BERT

Similar to BERT, ALBERT is pre-trained with different configurations. In all configurations, ALBERT has few parameters compared to the BERT model. The following table shows a comparison of different configurations of the BERT and ALBERT models. We can notice how ALBERT has fewer parameters compared to BERT. For instance, BERT-large has 334 million parameters but ALBERT-large has only 18 million parameters:

Model	Parameters	Layer(L)	Hidden(H)	Embedding(E)
BERT-base	110M	12	768	768
BERT-large	334M	24	1024	1024
ALBERT-base	12M	12	768	128
ALBERT-large	18M	24	1024	128
ALBERT-xlarge	60M	24	2048	128
ALBERT-xxlarge	235M	12	4096	128

Figure 4.2 – Comparing BERT with ALBERT

Results as given in the ALBERT paper: `https://arxiv.org/pdf/1909.11942.pdf`

Just like BERT, after pre-training, we can fine-tune the pre-trained ALBERT model on any downstream task. The ALBERT-xxlarge model has significantly outperformed both BERT-base and BERT-large on several language benchmark datasets, including SQuAD1.1, SQuAD2.0, MNLI SST-2, and RACE.

Thus, the ALBERT model can be used as a good alternative to BERT. In the next section, let's explore how to extract embeddings from the pre-trained ALBERT model.

Extracting embeddings with ALBERT

With Hugging Face transformers, we can use the ALBERT model just like how we used BERT. Let's explore this with a small example. Suppose we need to get the contextual word embedding of every word in the sentence *Paris is a beautiful city*. Let's see how to do that with ALBERT.

Import the necessary modules:

```
from transformers import AlbertTokenizer, AlbertModel
```

Download and load the pre-trained ALBERT model and tokenizer. In this tutorial, we'll use the ALBERT-base model:

```
model = AlbertModel.from_pretrained('albert-base-v2')
tokenizer = AlbertTokenizer.from_pretrained('albert-base-v2')
```

Now, feed the sentence to the tokenizer and get the preprocessed input:

```
sentence = "Paris is a beautiful city"
inputs = tokenizer(sentence, return_tensors="pt")
```

Let's print the inputs:

```
print(inputs)
```

The preceding code prints the following. As we can observe, our inputs consist of `input_ids`, `token_type_ids` (segment ID), and `attention_mask`, all mapped to the given input sentence. The given sentence, *Paris is a beautiful city*, consists of five tokens (words), and with the `[CLS]` and `[SEP]` tokens, we will have seven tokens:

```
{
'input_ids': tensor([[   2, 1162,   25,   21, 1632,  136,    3]]),
'token_type_ids': tensor([[0, 0, 0, 0, 0, 0, 0]]),
'attention_mask': tensor([[1, 1, 1, 1, 1, 1, 1]])
}
```

Now, we just feed the inputs to the model and get the result. The model returns `hidden_rep`, which contains the hidden state representation of all the tokens from the final encoder layer, and `cls_head`, which contains the hidden state representation of the `[CLS]` token from the final encoder layer:

```
hidden_rep, cls_head = model(**inputs)
```

We can obtain the contextual word embedding of each word in the sentence just like BERT as follows:

- `hidden_rep[0][0]` contains the contextual embedding of the `[CLS]` token.
- `hidden_rep[0][1]` contains the contextual embedding of the `Paris` token.
- `hidden_rep[0][2]` contains the contextual embedding of the `is` token.

Similarly, in this manner, `hidden_rep[0][6]` contains the contextual embedding of the `[SEP]` token.

In this way, we can use the ALBERT model just like how we used the BERT model. We can also fine-tune the ALBERT model similar to how we fine-tuned the BERT model on any downstream task. Now that we have learned how ALBERT works, in the next section, let's explore RoBERTa, another interesting variant of BERT.

Robustly Optimized BERT pre-training Approach

RoBERTa is another interesting and popular variant of BERT. Researchers observed that BERT is severely undertrained and proposed several approaches to pre-train the BERT model. RoBERTa is essentially BERT with the following changes in pre-training:

- Use dynamic masking instead of static masking in the MLM task.
- Remove the NSP task and train using only the MLM task.
- Train with a large batch size.
- Use **byte-level BPE** (**BBPE**) as a tokenizer.

Now, let's look into the details and discuss each of the preceding points.

Using dynamic masking instead of static masking

We learned that we pre-train BERT using the MLM and NSP tasks. In the MLM task, we randomly mask 15% of the tokens and let the network predict the masked token.

For instance, say we have the sentence *We arrived at the airport in time.* Now, after tokenizing and adding [CLS] and [SEP] tokens, we have the following:

```
tokens = [ [CLS], we, arrived, at, the, airport, in, time, [SEP] ]
```

Next, we randomly mask 15% of the tokens:

```
tokens = [ [CLS], we, [MASK], at, the, airport, in, [MASK], [SEP] ]
```

Now, we feed the tokens to BERT and train it to predict the masked tokens. Note that the masking is done only once during the preprocessing step and we train the model over several epochs to predict the same masked token. This is known as static masking.

RoBERTa uses dynamic masking instead of static masking. Let's understand how dynamic masking works with an example.

First, we duplicate a sentence 10 times. Say we have 10 duplicates of the given sentence, *We arrived at the airport in time.* Next, we randomly mask 15% of the tokens in all of these 10 duplicates of the sentence. So, now we have 10 sentences with different tokens masked in each sentence, as shown:

Sentence	Tokens
Sentence 1	[CLS], we, [MASK], at, the, airport, in, [MASK], [SEP]
Sentence 2	[CLS], we, arrived, [MASK], the, [MASK], in, time, [SEP]
⋮	⋮
Sentence 10	[CLS], we, arrived, at, [MASK], airport, [MASK], time, [SEP]

Figure 4.3 – 10 duplicates of the given sentence

We train the model for 40 epochs. For each epoch, we feed the sentence with different tokens masked. For epoch 1, we feed sentence 1, for epoch 2, we feed sentence 2, and so on, as shown:

Epoch	Sentence
Epoch 1	Sentence 1
Epoch 2	Sentence 2
⋮	⋮
Epoch 10	Sentence 10
Epoch 11	Sentence 1
Epoch 12	Sentence 2
⋮	⋮
Epoch 40	Sentence 10

Figure 4.4 – Sentences used in each epoch

Our model will see a sentence with the same mask for only four epochs. For example, sentence 1 will be seen in epochs 1, 11, 21, and 31. Sentence 2 will be seen in epochs 2, 12, 22, and 32. In this way, we train the RoBERTa model using dynamic masking instead of static masking.

Removing the NSP task

Researchers observed that the NSP task is not really useful for pre-training the BERT model and so they pre-trained the RoBERTa only with the MLM task. To better understand the importance of the NSP task, the following experiments are conducted:

- **SEGMENT-PAIR + NSP**: In this setting, we train BERT with the NSP task. This is similar to how we train the vanilla BERT model and the input consists of a segment pair less than 512 tokens.
- **SENTENCE-PAIR + NSP**: Here as well, we train BERT with the NSP task and the input consists of a sentence pair, which is either sampled from a contiguous portion of one document or from different documents, and the input consists of less than 512 tokens.
- **FULL SENTENCES**: In this setting, we train BERT without the NSP task. Here, our input consists of a full sentence, which is sampled continuously from one or more documents. The input consists of at most 512 tokens. If we reach the end of one document, then we begin sampling from the next document.
- **DOC SENTENCES**: In this setting, we train BERT without the NSP task. It is similar to FULL-SENTENCES, but here, input consists of a full sentence that is sampled only from a single document. That is, if we reach the end of one document, then we will not sample from the next document.

The researchers pre-trained the BERT model in the preceding four settings and evaluated the model on several datasets, including SQuAD, MNLI-m, SST-2, and RACE. The following table shows the F1 score of our model on the SQuAD dataset and the accuracy scores for MNLI-m, SST-2, and RACE:

Model	SQuAD 1.1/2.0	MNLI-m	SST-2	RACE
SEGMENT-PAIR	90.4/78.7	84.0	92.9	64.2
SENTENCE-PAIR	88.7/76.2	82.9	92.1	63.0
FULL-SENTENCES	90.4/79.1	84.7	92.5	64.8
DOC-SENTENCES	90.6/79.7	84.7	92.7	65.6

Figure 4.5 – Performance of BERT in different settings

Results as given in the RoBERTa paper: https://arxiv.org/pdf/1907.11692.pdf

As we can observe from the preceding results, BERT performs better in the **FULL-SENTENCES** and **DOC-SENTENCES** settings where we trained it without the NSP task.

Comparing FULL-SENTENCES and DOC-SENTENCES, DOC-SENTENCES where we sample sentences only from a single document performs better than a FULL-SENTENCES setting where we sample sentences across documents. But in RoBERTa, we use the FULL-SENTENCES setting because the batch sizes vary in DOC-SENTENCES.

To conclude, in RoBERTa, we train the model only with the MLM task and not with the NSP task and the input consists of a full sentence, which is sampled continuously from one or more documents. The input consists of at most 512 tokens. If we reach the end of one document, then we begin sampling from the next document.

Training with more data points

We learned that we pre-train BERT with the Toronto BookCorpus and English Wikipedia datasets, which account for a total of 16 GB. Along with these two datasets, we pre-train RoBERTa using the **CC-News** (**Common Crawl-News**), Open WebText, and Stories (subset of Common Crawl) datasets.

Thus, the RoBERTa model is pre-trained using five datasets and the sum of the total size of these five datasets is 160 GB.

Training with a large batch size

We learned that BERT is pre-trained with a batch size of 256 sequences for 1 million steps. We pre-train RoBERTa with a larger mini-batch size. We pre-train RoBERTa with a batch size of 8,000 sequences for 300,000 steps. We can also pre-train longer with a batch size of 8,000 sequences for 500,000 steps.

But why do we have to increase the batch size? What is the advantage of training with a large batch size? Training with a larger batch size increases the speed and performance of the model.

Using BBPE as a tokenizer

We know that BERT uses the WordPiece tokenizer. We learned that the WordPiece tokenizer works similar to BPE and it merges the symbol pair based on likelihood instead of frequency. Unlike BERT, RoBERTa uses BBPE as a tokenizer.

We learned how BBPE works in Chapter 2, *Understanding the BERT Model*. We learned that BBPE works very similar to BPE but instead of using a character-level sequence, it uses a byte-level sequence. We know that BERT uses a vocabulary size of 30,000 tokens but RoBERTa uses a vocabulary size of 50,000 tokens. Let's explore the RoBERTa tokenizer further in the next section.

Exploring the RoBERTa tokenizer

First, let's import the necessary modules:

```
from transformers import RobertaConfig, RobertaModel, RobertaTokenizer
```

Download and load the pre-trained RoBERTa model:

```
model = RobertaModel.from_pretrained('roberta-base')
```

Let's check the configuration of our RoBERTa model:

```
model.config
```

The preceding code prints the following. We can observe that since we loaded the RoBERTa-base model, we have 12 encoder layers, 12 attention heads, and 768 hidden size:

```
RobertaConfig {
  "_name_or_path": "roberta-base",
  "architectures": [
    "RobertaForMaskedLM"
  ],

  "attention_probs_dropout_prob": 0.1,
  "bos_token_id": 0,
  "eos_token_id": 2,
  "gradient_checkpointing": false,
  "hidden_act": "gelu",
  "hidden_dropout_prob": 0.1,
  "hidden_size": 768,
  "initializer_range": 0.02,
  "intermediate_size": 3072,
  "layer_norm_eps": 1e-05,
  "max_position_embeddings": 514,
```

```
    "model_type": "roberta",
    "num_attention_heads": 12,
    "num_hidden_layers": 12,
    "pad_token_id": 1,
    "type_vocab_size": 1,
    "vocab_size": 50265
}
```

Now, let's download and load the RoBERTa tokenizer:

```
tokenizer = RobertaTokenizer.from_pretrained("roberta-base")
```

Let's tokenize the sentence *It was a great day* using RoBERTa:

```
tokenizer.tokenize('It was a great day')
```

The preceding code gives the following output:

```
['It', 'Ġwas', 'Ġa', 'Ġgreat', 'Ġday']
```

We can observe that the given sentence is tokenized, but what's that Ġ character? It is used to indicate a space. The RoBERTa tokenizer replaces all the white space with the Ġ character. We can notice that Ġ is present before all the tokens but not in front of the first token because in the given sentence, all other tokens have white space before them but the first token does not have white space before it. Let's tokenize the same sentence with additional white space at the front and see the results:

```
tokenizer.tokenize(' It was a great day')
```

The preceding code will print the following:

```
['ĠIt', 'Ġwas', 'Ġa', 'Ġgreat', 'Ġday']
```

As we can observe, since we have added a white space to the front of the first token, now all the tokens are preceded with the Ġ character.

Consider a different example. Let's tokenize the sentence *I had a sudden epiphany*:

```
tokenizer.tokenize('I had a sudden epiphany')
```

The preceding code prints the following:

```
['I', 'Ġhad', 'Ġa', 'Ġsudden', 'Ġep', 'iphany']
```

From the results, we can observe that the word `epiphany` is split into subwords `ep` and `iphany` since it is not present in the vocabulary. We can also observe how the white spaces are replaced with the Ġ character.

To summarize, RoBERTa is a variant of BERT and it uses only the MLM task for training. Unlike BERT, it uses dynamic masking instead of static masking and it is trained with a large batch size. It uses BBPE as a tokenizer and it has a vocabulary size of 50,000.

Now that we have learned how RoBERTa works, in the next section, let's look into another interesting variant of BERT, called ELECTRA.

Understanding ELECTRA

ELECTRA (Efficiently Learning an Encoder that Classifies Token Replacements Accurately) is yet another interesting variant of BERT. We learned that we pre-train BERT using the MLM and NSP tasks. We know that in the MLM task, we randomly mask 15% of the tokens and train BERT to predict the masked token. Instead of using the MLM task as a pre-training objective, ELECTRA is pre-trained using a task called replaced token detection.

The replaced token detection task is very similar to MLM but instead of masking a token with the [MASK] token, here we replace a token with a different token and train the model to classify whether the given tokens are actual or replaced tokens.

Okay, but why use the replaced token detection task instead of the MLM task? One of the problems with the MLM task is that it uses the [MASK] token during pre-training but the [MASK] token will not be present during fine-tuning on downstream tasks. This causes a mismatch between pre-training and fine-tuning. In the replaced token detection task, we don't use any [MASK] tokens for masking; instead, we just replace a token with a different token and train the model to classify whether the given tokens are actual or replaced tokens. This combats the issue of mismatch between the pre-training and fine-tuning.

Unlike BERT, which is pre-trained using the MLM and NSP tasks, ELECTRA is pre-trained using only the replaced token detection task. Okay, but how does the replaced token detection task work? Which token do we replace? How we train the model to perform this task? Let's find out the answers to all these questions in the next section.

Understanding the replaced token detection task

Let's learn how exactly the replaced token detection task works with an example. Let's use the same example used in the paper. Consider the sentence *The chef cooked the meal*. After tokenization, we have the following:

```
tokens = [ The, chef, cooked, the, meal]
```

Let's replace the first token, the, with a, and the third token, cooked, with ate. Then, we have the following:

```
tokens = [ a, chef, ate, the, meal]
```

As we can observe, we replaced two tokens. Now, we train the BERT model to classify whether the tokens are original or replaced tokens. We can call this BERT a discriminator model since it is just classifying whether the tokens are original or replaced tokens.

As shown in the following figure, we feed the tokens to the discriminator (BERT) and it returns whether the tokens are original or replaced:

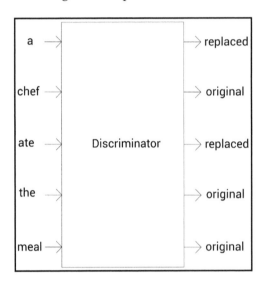

Figure 4.6 – Discriminator returning whether the tokens are original or replaced

We learned that we replace some tokens in the given sentence and feed it to the discriminator to classify whether the tokens are replaced or original. But the question is, before feeding the tokens to the discriminator, how exactly do we replace them? To replace tokens, we use MLM. Consider the original sentence, *The chef cooked the meal.* After tokenization, we have the following:

```
tokens = [ The, chef, cooked, the, meal]
```

Now, we randomly replace mask 15% of the tokens with the [MASK] token; then, we have the following:

```
tokens = [ [MASK] , chef, [MASK] ,the, meal]
```

Next, we feed the tokens to another BERT model and predict the masked tokens. We can call this BERT a generator since it returns the probability distribution over tokens. As we can notice from the following figure, we feed the masked tokens to the generator and it predicts the masked token as the one that has a high probability of being the masked token:

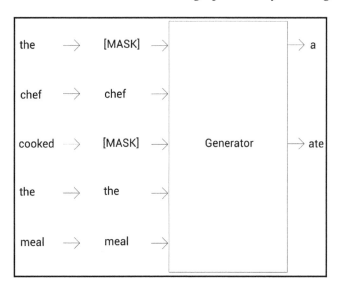

Figure 4.7 – Generator predicting the masked tokens

From the preceding figure, we can understand that our generator has predicted the masked token the as a and the masked token cooked as ate. Now, we take the tokens generated by the generator and use them for replacing. That is, we replace the tokens in the given sentence with the tokens generated by the generator. For instance, tokenizing the given sentence, *The chef cooked the meal,* we have the following:

```
tokens = [ The, chef, cooked, the, meal]
```

Now, we replace the tokens with the tokens generated by the generator. So, our tokens list becomes the following:

```
tokens = [ a, chef, ate, the, meal]
```

As we can notice, we replaced the The and cooked tokens with the a and ate tokens generated by the generator. Now, we feed the preceding tokens to the discriminator and train it to classify whether the given tokens are original or replaced.

As shown in the following figure, first we mask the tokens randomly and feed them to the generator. The generator predicts the masked tokens. Next, we replace the input tokens with tokens generated by the generator and feed it to the discriminator. The discriminator classifies whether the given tokens are original or replaced, as shown in the following figure:

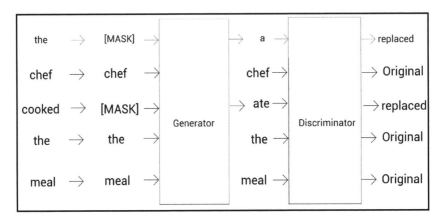

Figure 4.8 – Generator and discriminator of ELECTRA

The discriminator is basically our ELECTRA model. After training, we can remove the generator and use the discriminator as the ELECTRA model. Now that we have understood how the replaced token detection task works, let's take a closer look into the generator and discriminator in the next section.

Exploring the generator and discriminator of ELECTRA

First, let's have a look at the generator. We learned that the generator performs the MLM task. We randomly mask a few tokens with a 15% mask rate and train the generator to predict the masked token. Let's represent our input tokens as $X = [x_1, x_2, \ldots, x_n]$. We randomly mask some tokens and feed them as input to the generator, which returns the representation of each of the tokens. Let $h_G(X) = [h_1, h_2, \ldots, h_n]$ denote the representation of each token returned by the generator. That is, h_1 denotes the representation of the first token, x_1, h_2 denotes the representation of the second token, x_2, and so on.

Now, we feed the representation of the masked tokens to a classifier, which is basically the feedforward network with the softmax function, and it returns the probability distribution over the tokens, that is, the classifier returns the probability of each word in the vocabulary of being the masked word.

The generator is shown in the following figure; as you may notice, we take the sentence *'The chef cooked the meal'* and randomly mask a few tokens and feed them to the generator, which returns the probability of each word in the vocabulary being the masked word:

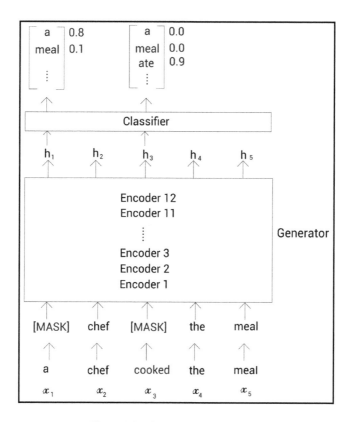

Figure 4.9 – Generator of ELECTRA

Let x_t be the masked word at position t; then, the generator returns the probability of each word in the vocabulary being the masked word, x_t, with the softmax function as follows:

$$P_G(x_t|X) = \frac{\exp(e(x_t)^T h_G(X)_t)}{\sum_{x'} \exp(e(x')^T h_G(X)_t)}$$

In the preceding equation, $e(\cdot)$ denotes the token embedding. With the probability distribution returned by the generator, we select the word that has a high probability as the masked token. Based on the probability distribution shown in the preceding figure, the masked token x_1 is predicted as *a*, and the masked token x_3 is predicted as *ate*. Next, we replace the input tokens with tokens generated by the generator and feed them to the discriminator. Now, let's have a look at the discriminator.

We learned that the goal of the discriminator is to classify whether the given tokens are replaced by the generator or the original tokens. First, we feed the tokens to the discriminator, which returns the representation of each token. Let $h_D(X) = [h_1, h_2, \ldots, h_n]$ denote the representation of each token returned by the discriminator. Next, we feed the representation of each token to a classifier, which is basically the feedforward network with a sigmoid function, and the classifier returns whether the given tokens are original or replaced.

The discriminator is shown in the following figure. As we can observe, we feed the tokens to the discriminator and it returns whether the given tokens are original or replaced:

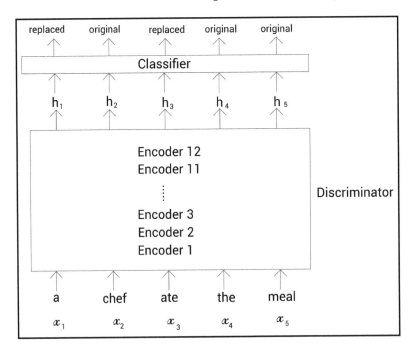

Figure 4.10 – Discriminator of ELECTRA

Let x_t be the token at position t; then, the discriminator returns whether the token is an original or replaced token with the sigmoid function as follows:

$$D(X, t) = \text{Sigmoid}(w^T h_D(X)_t)$$

To summarize, we feed the masked tokens to the generator and the generator predicts the masked tokens. Next, we replace the input tokens with tokens generated by the generator and feed them to the discriminator. The discriminator classifies whether the given tokens are original or replaced:

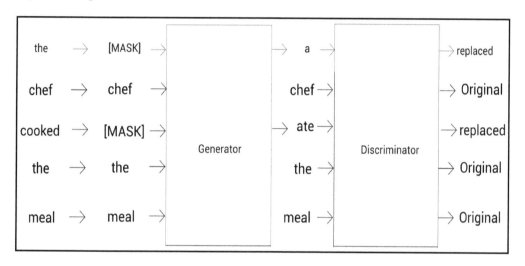

Figure 4.11 – Generator and discriminator of ELECTRA

The discriminator BERT is the ELECTRA model. Here, we are training the BERT (discriminator) to classify whether the given tokens are original or replaced tokens, hence the name ELECTRA, **Efficiently Learning an Encoder that Classifies Token Replacements Accurately**.

One of the advantages of ELECTRA compared to BERT is that in BERT, we use MLM as a training objective where we mask only 15% of the tokens, so the training signal to the model is only those 15% of the tokens since it predicts only those masked tokens. But in ELECTRA, the training signal is all the tokens since here, the model classifies whether all the given tokens are original or replaced.

Now that we have understood how the generator and discriminator work, in the next section, we will learn how to train ELECTRA.

Training the ELECTRA model

The generator is trained using the MLM task. So, for a given input, $X = [x_1, x_2, \ldots, x_n]$, we randomly select a few positions for masking. Let $M = [m_1, m_2, \ldots, m_n]$ denote the selected positions for masking. Then, we replace the tokens in the selected positions with the [MASK] token, which can be expressed as follows:

$$X^{\text{masked}} = \text{Replace}(X, M, [\text{MASK}])$$

After masking, we feed the X^{masked} tokens to the generator and the generator predicts the masked token.

Now, we corrupt (replace) a few tokens in the input, X, with tokens generated by the generator. We call it $X^{\text{corrupted}}$ since it consists of tokens corrupted (replaced) by the generator.

The loss function of the generator is expressed as follows:

$$L_G(X, \theta_G) = E\left(\sum_{i \in m} -\log P_G\left(x_i \mid X^{\text{masked}}\right) \right)$$

We feed the corrupted tokens, $X^{\text{corrupted}}$, to the discriminator and the discriminator classifies whether the given tokens are original or replaced. The loss function of the discriminator is expressed as follows:

$$L_D(X, \theta_D) = E\left(\sum_{t=1}^{n} -1(x_t^{\text{corrupt}} = x_t)\log D(X^{\text{corrupt}}, t) - 1(x_t^{\text{corrupt}} \neq x_t)\log(1 - D(X^{\text{corrupt}}, t)) \right)$$

We train the ELECTRA model by minimizing the combined loss of the generator and discriminator and it is expressed as follows:

$$min_{\theta_D, \theta_G} \sum_{X \in \mathbb{X}} L_G(X, \theta_G) + \lambda L_D(X, \theta_D)$$

In the preceding equation, θ_G and θ_D denote the parameters of the generator and discriminator, respectively, and $\mathbb{X}$ denotes a large text corpus. Next, let's look into some efficient methods for training ELECTRA.

Exploring efficient training methods

In order to train the ELECTRA model efficiently, we can share the weights between the generator and the discriminator. That is, if both the generator and the discriminator are the same size, then we can share the weights of the encoder.

But the problem is, if the generator and discriminator are the same size, then it will increase the training time, so to avoid that, we can use a smaller generator. When the generator is small, we can just share only the embedding layers (token and positional embeddings) between the generator and discriminator. This tied embedding between the generator and discriminator minimizes the training time.

The pre-trained ELECTRA model is open-sourced by Google and we can download it from here: `https://github.com/google-research/electra`. The pre-trained ELECTRA model is available in three different configurations:

- **ELECTRA-small**: With 12 encoder layers and 256 hidden size
- **ELECTRA-base**: With 12 encoders and 768 hidden size
- **ELECTRA-large**: With 24 encoders and 1,024 hidden size

We can use the ELECTRA model with the `transformers` library just like other BERT models. First, we import the necessary modules:

```
from transformers import ElectraTokenizer, ElectraModel
```

Suppose we use the ELECTRA-small discriminator; then, we can download and load the pre-trained ELECTRA-small discriminator as follows:

```
model = ElectraModel.from_pretrained('google/electra-small-discriminator')
```

Suppose we use the ELECTRA-small generator, then we can download and load the pre-trained ELECTRA-small generator as shown next:

```
model = ElectraModel.from_pretrained('google/electra-small-discriminator')
```

In this way, we can also load the other different configurations of ELECTRA. Now that we have learned how ELECTRA works, let's learn about a popular variant of BERT called SpanBERT in the next section.

Predicting span with SpanBERT

SpanBERT is another interesting variant of BERT. As the name suggests, SpanBERT is mostly used for tasks such as question answering where we predict the span of text. Let's understand how SpanBERT works by looking into its architecture.

Understanding the architecture of SpanBERT

Let's understand SpanBERT with an example. Consider the following sentence:

You are expected to know the laws of your country

After tokenizing the sentence, we will have the tokens as follows:

```
tokens = [ you, are, expected, to, know, the, laws, of, your, country]
```

Instead of masking the tokens randomly, in SpanBERT, we mask the random contiguous span of tokens as shown:

```
tokens = [ you, are, expected, to, know, [MASK], [MASK], [MASK], [MASK],
country]
```

We can observe that instead of masking the tokens at random positions, we have masked the random contiguous span of tokens. Now, we feed the tokens to SpanBERT and get the representation of the tokens. As shown in the following figure, we mask the random contiguous span of tokens and feed them to the SpanBERT model, which returns the representation, R_i, of each token, i:

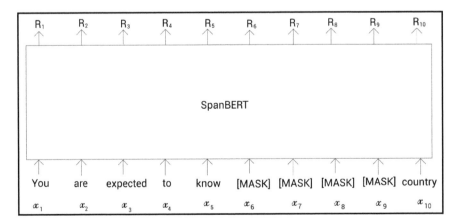

Figure 4.12 – SpanBERT

In order to predict the masked token, we train the SpanBERT model with the MLM objective along with a new objective called **span boundary objective** (**SBO**). Let's explore how this works in detail.

We know that in the MLM objective, to predict the masked token, our model uses the corresponding representation of the masked token. Suppose we need to predict the masked token x_7; so, with the representation R_7, we can predict the masked token. We just feed the representation R_7 to a classifier, which returns the probability of all the words in the vocabulary of being the masked word.

Now, let's look into the SBO. In the SBO, to predict any masked token, instead of using the representation of the corresponding masked token, we only use the representation of the tokens present in the span boundary. The span boundary includes immediate tokens that are before the start of the span and after the end of the span.

For instance, as shown in the following figure, we can observe that the tokens x_5 and x_{10} denote the tokens in the span boundary and R_5 and R_{10} are the representation of the tokens in the span boundary. Now, to predict any masked token, our model uses only these two representations. For instance, to predict the masked token x_7, our model uses only the span boundary token representations R_5 and R_{10}:

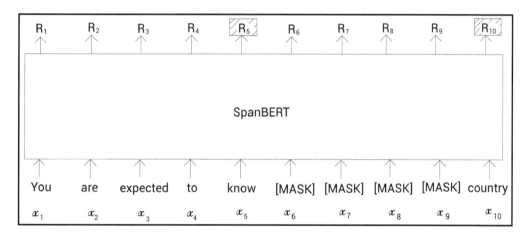

Figure 4.13 – SpanBERT

Wait. The question is if the model uses only the span boundary token representations to predict any masked token, then how will it distinguish between different masked tokens? For instance, to predict the masked token x_6, our model uses only the span boundary token representations R_5 and R_{10}, and to predict the masked token x_7, our model uses only the span boundary token representations R_5 and R_{10}. Similarly to predict any masked token, it uses only the span boundary representation. But if we do this, how does the model distinguish between the different masked tokens?

For this reason, apart from span boundary token representations, the model uses the position embedding of the masked token. Note that here, the position embeddings indicate the relative position of the masked token. That is, say we are predicting the masked token x_7. Now, out of all the masked tokens, we check the position of the masked token x_7. As shown in the following figure, the masked token x_7 is in the second position out of all the masked tokens. So now, to predict the masked token x_7, along with the span boundary token representations R_5 and R_{10}, we also use the position embedding of the masked token, which is P_2:

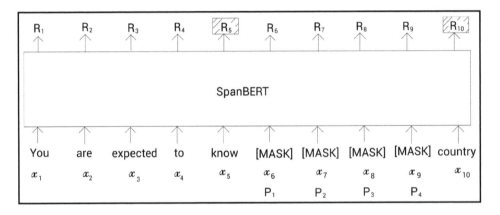

Figure 4.14 – SpanBERT

Thus, SpanBERT uses two objectives: one is MLM and the other is SBO. In the MLM objective, to predict the masked token, we just use the representation of the corresponding token, but in SBO, to predict the masked token, we use only the span boundary token representations and the position embedding of the masked token.

Now that we have a basic idea of how SpanBERT works, let's explore more details in the next section.

Exploring SpanBERT

We learned that in SpanBERT, we mask a contiguous span of tokens in the sentence. Let x_s and x_e be the start and end position of the masked tokens, respectively. We feed the tokens to SpanBERT and it returns the representation of all the tokens. The representation of token i is represented as R_i. The representation of the tokens in the span boundary is denoted as R_{e-1} and R_{e+1}.

Let's first look at the SBO. To predict the masked token, x_i, we use three values, which are the representation of the tokens in the span boundary (R_{e-1} and R_{e+1}), and the position embedding of the masked token (p_{i-s+1}). Okay, how exactly do we predict the masked token with these three values? First, we create a new representation called z_i using a function, $f(\cdot)$, with these three values as shown:

$$z_i = f(R_{s-1}, R_{e+1}, P_{i-s+1})$$

Okay, what about the $f(\cdot)$ function? It is basically a two-layer feedforward network with GeLU activations:

$$h_o = [R_{s-1}; R_{e+1}; p_{i-s+1}]$$

$$h_1 = \text{LayerNorm}(\text{GeLU}(W_1 h_0))$$

$$z_i = \text{LayerNorm}(\text{GeLU}(W_2 h_1))$$

Now, to predict the masked token, x_i, we just use the z_i representation. We feed the z_i representation to a classifier, which returns the probability of all the words in the vocabulary being the masked word. Thus, in SBO, we predict the masked token, x_i, using the representation z_i, which is created with span boundary tokens representations (R_{e-1} and R_{e+1}), and the position embedding of the masked token (p_{i-s+1}).

In the MLM objective, to predict masked token x_i, we just use the corresponding token representation, R_i. We feed the representation, R_i, to a classifier, which returns the probability of all the words in the vocabulary being the masked word.

The loss function of SpanBERT is the sum of the MLM loss and SBO loss. We train SpanBERT by minimizing the loss function. After pre-training, we can use the pre-trained SpanBERT model for any downstream task. Now that we have learned how SpanBERT works, in the next section, let's apply SpanBERT to the question answering task.

Performing Q and As with pre-trained SpanBERT

Let's learn how to perform question answering with a pre-trained SpanBERT model that is fine-tuned on the question answering task. In this section, we will use the pipeline API of the `transformers` library. The pipeline is the simple API provided by the `transformers` library for seamlessly performing complex tasks ranging from text classification to question answering. In this section, we will learn how to use the pipeline for the question answering task.

First, let's import the pipeline:

```
from transformers import pipeline
```

Now, we define our question answering pipeline. To the pipeline API, we pass the task that we want to perform, the pre-trained model, and the tokenizer as arguments. As shown in the following code, we are using the `spanbert-large-fine-tuned-squadv2` model, which is the pre-trained and fine-tuned SpanBERT for the question answering task:

```
qa_pipeline = pipeline(
    "question-answering",
    model="mrm8488/spanbert-large-finetuned-squadv2",
    tokenizer="SpanBERT/spanbert-large-cased"
)
```

Now, we just need to feed the question and the context to `qa_pipeline` and it will return the result containing the answer:

```
results = qa_pipeline({
    'question': "What is machine learning?",
    'context': "Machine learning is a subset of artificial intelligence. It
is widely for creating a variety of applications such as email filtering
and computer vision"
})
```

Let's print the result:

```
print(results['answer'])
```

The preceding code will print the following:

```
a subset of artificial intelligence
```

In this way, SpanBERT is popularly used for tasks where we need to predict the text span.

Thus, in this chapter, we learned about several variants of BERT. In the next chapter, we will learn another set of several variants of BERT that are based on knowledge distillation.

Summary

We started off the chapter by understanding how ALBERT works. We learned that ALBERT is a lite version of BERT and it uses two interesting parameter reduction techniques, called cross-layer parameter sharing and factorized embedding parameterization. We also learned about the SOP task used in ALBERT. We learned that SOP is a binary classification task where the goal of the model is to classify whether the given sentence pair is swapped or not.

After understanding the ALBERT model, we looked into the RoBERTa model. We learned that the RoBERTa is a variant of BERT and it uses only the MLM task for training. Unlike BERT, it uses dynamic masking instead of static masking and it is trained with a large batch size. It uses BBPE as a tokenizer and it has a vocabulary size of 50,000.

Following RoBERTa, we learned about the ELECTRA model. In ELECTRA, instead of using MLM task as a pre-training objective, we used a new pre-training strategy called replaced token detection. In the replaced token detection task, instead of masking a token with [MASK], we replaced a token with a different token and trained our model to predict whether the given tokens were actual tokens or replaced tokens. We also explored how the generator and discriminator of the ELECTRA model work in detail.

Then, at the end of the chapter, we learned about the SpanBERT model. We understood how SpanBERT uses the MLM objective and also a new objective called SBO in detail.

Questions

Let's evaluate our newly acquired knowledge by answering the following questions:

1. How does the SOP task differ from the NSP task?
2. What are the parameter reduction techniques used in ALBERT?
3. What is cross-layer parameter sharing?

4. What are the shared feedforward and shared attention options in cross-layer parameter sharing?

5. How does RoBERTa differ from the BERT model?

6. What is the replaced token detection task in ELECTRA?

7. How do we mask tokens in SpanBERT?

Further reading

For more information, refer to the following papers:

- *ALBERT: A Lite BERT for Self-supervised Learning of Language Representations* by *Zhenzhong Lan, Mingda Chen, Sebastian Goodman, Kevin Gimpel, Piyush Sharma, and Radu Soricut,* available at `https://arxiv.org/pdf/1909.11942.pdf`

- *RoBERTa: A Robustly Optimized BERT Pre-training Approach* by *Yinhan Liu, Myle Ott, et al.,* available at `https://arxiv.org/pdf/1907.11692.pdf`

- *ELECTRA: Pre-training Text Encoders as Discriminators Rather Than Generators* by *Kevin Clark, Minh-Thang Luong, Quoc V. Le,* and *Christopher D. Manning,* available at `https://arxiv.org/pdf/2003.10555.pdf`

- *SpanBERT: Improving Pre-training by Representing and Predicting Spans* by *Mandar Joshi, Danqi Chen, Yinhan Liu, Daniel S. Weld, Luke Zettlemoyer,* and *Omer Levy,* available at `https://arxiv.org/pdf/1907.10529v3.pdf`

5
BERT Variants II - Based on Knowledge Distillation

In the previous chapters, we learned how BERT works, and we also looked into different variants of BERT. We learned that we don't have to train BERT from scratch; instead, we can fine-tune the pre-trained BERT model on downstream tasks. However, one of the challenges with using the pre-trained BERT model is that it is computationally expensive and it is very difficult to run the model with limited resources. The pre-trained BERT model has a large number of parameters and also high inference time, which makes it harder to use it on edge devices such as mobile phones.

To alleviate this issue, we transfer knowledge from a large pre-trained BERT to a small BERT using knowledge distillation. In this chapter, we will learn about several variants of the BERT model that are based on knowledge distillation.

We will begin the chapter by understanding what knowledge distillation is and how it works in detail. Next, we will learn about DistilBERT. With DistilBERT, we will see how to transfer knowledge from a large pre-trained BERT to a small BERT by using knowledge distillation in detail.

Going forward, we will learn about TinyBERT. We will understand what TinyBERT is and how it acquires knowledge from a large pre-trained BERT using knowledge distillation. We will also look into the different data augmentation methods used in TinyBERT.

At the end of the chapter, we will learn how to transfer knowledge from a large pre-trained BERT to a simple neural network.

In this chapter, we will learn about the following topics:

- Introducing knowledge distillation
- DistilBERT – the distilled version of BERT
- Introducing TinyBERT
- Transferring knowledge from BERT to neural networks

Introducing knowledge distillation

Knowledge distillation is a model compression technique in which a small model is trained to reproduce the behavior of a large pre-trained model. It is also referred to as teacher-student learning, where the large pre-trained model is the teacher and the small model is the student. Let's understand how knowledge distillation works with an example.

Suppose we have pre-trained a large model to predict the next word in a sentence. We call this large pre-trained model a teacher network. If we feed in a sentence and let the network predict the next word in the sentence, then it will return the probability distribution of all the words in the vocabulary being the next word, as shown in the following figure. Note that for simplicity and better understanding, we'll assume we have only five words in our vocabulary:

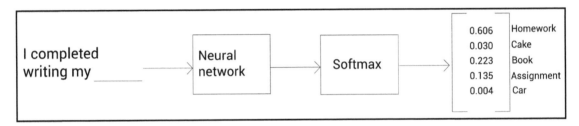

Figure 5.1 – Teacher network

From the preceding figure, we can observe the probability distribution returned by the network. This probability distribution is essentially obtained by applying the softmax function in the output layer and we select the word that has a high probability of being the next word in the sentence. Since the word **Homework** has a high probability, we select the next word in the sentence as **Homework**.

Apart from selecting the word that has a high probability, can we extract some other useful information from the probability distribution returned by our network? Yes! From the following figure, we can observe that apart from the word that has the highest probability, there are some words that have a high probability compared to other words. That is, as we can see, the words **Book** and **Assignment** have slightly higher probability compared to other words such as **Cake** and **Car**, as shown in the following figure:

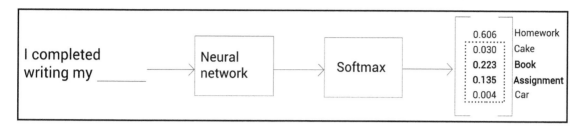

Figure 5.2 – Teacher network

This indicates that apart from the word **Homework**, the words **Book** and **Assignment** are more relevant to the given sentence compared to words like **Cake** and **Car**. This is known as **dark knowledge.** During knowledge distillation, we want our student network to learn this dark knowledge from the teacher.

Okay, but usually, any good model will return a high probability close to 1 for the correct class and probabilities very close to 0 for other classes, right? Yes! For instance, considering the same example we saw earlier, let's suppose our model has returned the following probability distribution:

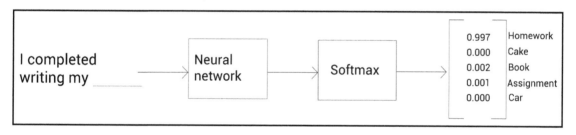

Figure 5.3 – Teacher network

From the preceding figure, we can notice that our model has returned a very high probability for the word **Homework** and probability close to 0 for all other words. We can observe that we don't have much information in the probability distribution apart from the ground truth (the correct word). So, how we can extract dark knowledge here?

In this case, we use the softmax function with a temperature. It is commonly referred to as softmax temperature. We use the softmax temperature in the output layer. It is used to smooth the probability distribution. The softmax function with temperature is expressed as follows:

$$P_i = \frac{\exp(z_i/T)}{\sum_j \exp(z_j/T)}$$

In the preceding equation, T is the temperature. When we set $T = 1$, then it is just our standard softmax function. Increasing the value of T makes the probability distribution softer and gives more information about other classes.

For example, as shown in the following figure, when $T = 1$, we have the same probability distribution returned by our network with the standard softmax function. When $T = 2$, the probability distribution is smoothed, and with $T = 5$, the probability distribution is further smoothed. So, by increasing the value of T, we get a smoothed probability distribution, which gives more information about other classes:

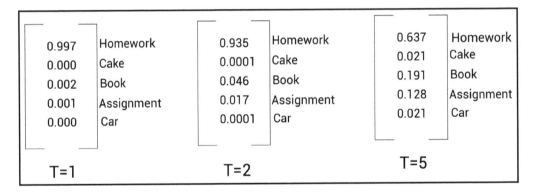

Figure 5.4 – Teacher network

Thus, with softmax temperature, we can obtain the dark knowledge. First, we pre-train the teacher network with softmax temperature to obtain dark knowledge. Then, during knowledge distillation (transferring knowledge from the teacher to the student), we transfer this dark knowledge from the teacher to the student.

Okay, but how do we transfer the dark knowledge from the teacher to the student? How is the student network trained and how does it acquires knowledge from the teacher? This is exactly what we discuss in the next section.

Training the student network

In the previous section, we looked into a pre-trained network that predicts the next word in a sentence. That pre-trained network is the teacher network. Now, let's learn how to transfer the knowledge from the teacher to the student network. Note that the student network is not pre-trained, only the teacher network is pre-trained and it is pre-trained with softmax temperature.

As shown in the following figure, we feed the input sentence to both teacher and student networks and get the probability distribution as output. We learned that the teacher network is a pre-trained network so the probability distribution returned by the teacher network will be our target. The output of the teacher network is called a **soft target**, and the prediction made by the student network is called a **soft prediction**.

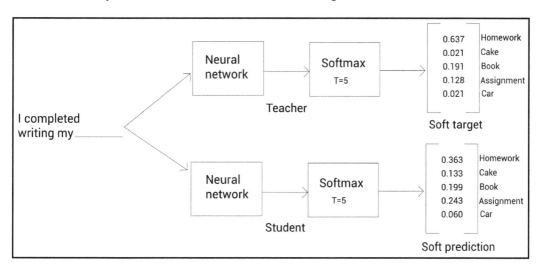

Figure 5.5 – Teacher-student architecture

Now, we compute the cross-entropy loss between the soft target and soft prediction and train the student network through backpropagation by minimizing the cross-entropy loss. The cross-entropy loss between the soft target and soft prediction is also known as the **distillation loss**. We can also observe from the following figure that we keep the softmax temperature T to the same value in both the teacher and student network and it is set greater than 1:

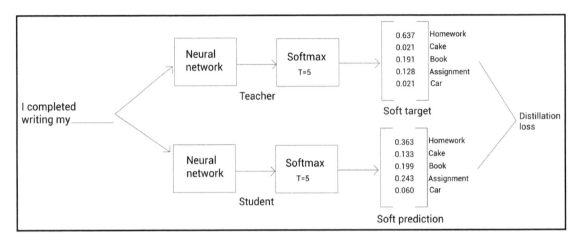

Figure 5.6 – Teacher-student architecture

Thus, we train the student network by minimizing the distillation loss through backpropagation. Apart from the distillation loss, we also use one more loss, called **student loss**.

To understand student loss, let's understand the difference between the soft target and the hard target. As shown in the following figure, directly taking the probability distribution returned by the teacher network is called the soft target, whereas, with the hard target, we simply set 1 where we have high probability and we set 0 for the rest of the values:

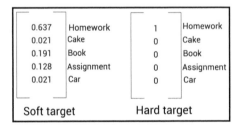

Figure 5.7 – Soft and hard target

Now, let's understand the difference between soft prediction and hard prediction. Soft prediction is the probability distribution predicted by the student network where temperature T is greater than 1, whereas hard prediction is the probability distribution predicted by the student network with temperature $T = 1$. That is, the hard prediction is standard softmax function prediction since T is set to 1.

The student loss is basically the cross-entropy loss between the hard target and hard prediction. The following figure helps us to understand how exactly we compute student loss and distillation loss. First, let's look into student loss. As we can observe from the following figure, to compute student loss, we use the softmax function with $T = 1$ in the student and get the hard prediction. We obtain the hard target by setting 1 where we have a high probability in the soft target and 0 in all other positions. Then we compute the student loss as the cross-entropy between the hard prediction and hard target.

To compute distillation loss, we use softmax function with T set greater than 1 and we compute the distillation loss as the cross-entropy loss between the soft prediction and soft target:

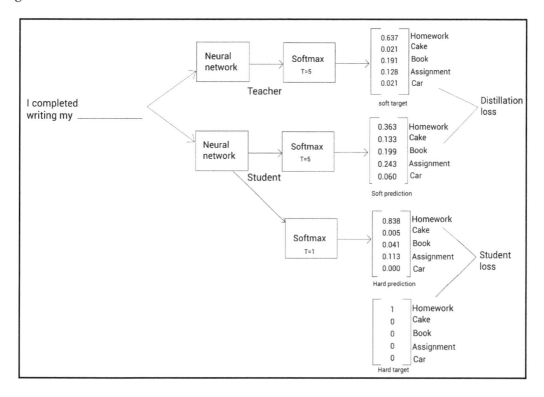

Figure 5.8 – Teacher-student architecture

Our final loss function is the weighted sum of student loss and distillation loss and it is expressed as follows:

$$L = \alpha \cdot \text{student loss} + \beta \cdot \text{distillation loss}$$

α and β are the hyperparameters used to compute the weighted average of student and distillation loss. We train our student network by minimizing the above loss function.

Thus, in knowledge distillation, we take the pre-trained network as the teacher network. We train the student network to obtain knowledge from the teacher network through distillation. We train the student network by minimizing the loss, which is the weighted sum of student and distillation loss.

Now that we have learned what knowledge distillation is and how it works, in the next section, we will learn how to apply knowledge distillation in BERT.

DistilBERT – the distilled version of BERT

The pre-trained BERT model has a large number of parameters and also high inference time, which makes it harder to use on edge devices such as mobile phones. To solve this issue, we use DistilBERT, which was introduced by researchers at Hugging Face. DistilBERT is a smaller, faster, cheaper, and lighter version of BERT.

As the name suggests, DistilBERT uses knowledge distillation. The ultimate idea of DistilBERT is that we take a large pre-trained BERT model and transfer its knowledge to a small BERT through knowledge distillation. The large pre-trained BERT is called a **teacher BERT** and the small BERT is called a **student BERT**.

Since the small BERT (student BERT) acquires its knowledge from the large pre-trained BERT (teacher BERT) through distillation, we can call our small BERT DistilBERT. DistilBERT is 60% faster and its size is 40% smaller compared to large BERT models. Now that we have a basic idea of DistilBERT, let's get into the details and learn how it works.

Teacher-student architecture

Let's begin by understanding the architecture of the teacher and student BERT in detail. First, we'll look at the teacher BERT, then we'll look at the student BERT.

The teacher BERT

The teacher BERT is a large pre-trained BERT model. We use the pre-trained BERT-Base model as the teacher. We have already learned how the BERT-Base model is pre-trained in the previous chapters. We know that the BERT model is pre-trained using masked language modeling and next sentence prediction tasks.

Since BERT is pre-trained using the masked language modeling task, we can use our pre-trained BERT model to predict the masked word. The pre-trained BERT-Base model is shown in the following figure:

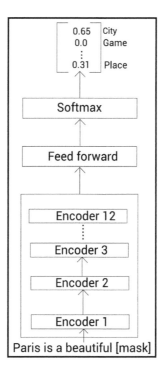

Figure 5.9 – Teacher BERT

From the preceding figure, we can notice that, given a masked input sentence, our pre-trained BERT gives the probability distribution of all the words in the vocabulary being the masked word. This probability distribution contains dark knowledge and we need to transfer this knowledge to the student BERT. Let's see how we do that in the upcoming sections.

The student BERT

Unlike the teacher BERT, the student BERT is not pre-trained. The student BERT has to learn from the teacher. The student BERT is a small BERT and it contains fewer layers compared to the teacher BERT. The teacher BERT consists of 110 million parameters, but the student BERT consists of only 66 million parameters.

Since we have fewer layers in the student BERT, it helps us train it faster compared to the teacher BERT (BERT-base).

The researchers of DistilBERT have kept the hidden state dimension of student BERT to 768, the same as what we have in the teacher BERT (BERT-base). They have observed that reducing the hidden state dimension does not significantly affect the computation efficiency. So, they have focused on only reducing the number of layers.

Okay. How can we train the student BERT? Now that we have understood the architecture of student BERT, let's learn how to train the student BERT by distilling knowledge from the teacher BERT in the next section.

Training the student BERT (DistilBERT)

We can train the student BERT with the same dataset we used for pre-training the teacher BERT (BERT-Base). We know that the BERT-Base model is pre-trained with English Wikipedia and the Toronto BookCorpus dataset, and we can use this same dataset to train the student BERT (small BERT).

We'll borrow a few training strategies from the RoBERTa model. Just as we learned with RoBERTa, in `Chapter 4`, *BERT variants I – ALBERT, RoBERTa, ELECTRA, and SpanBERT*, here, we train the student BERT with only the masked language modeling task, and during masked language modeling, we use dynamic masking. We also use a large batch size on every iteration.

As shown in the following figure, we take a masked sentence and feed it as input to the teacher BERT (pre-trained BERT-Base) and the student BERT and get the probability distribution over the vocabulary as an output. Next, we compute the distillation loss as cross-entropy loss between the soft target and soft prediction:

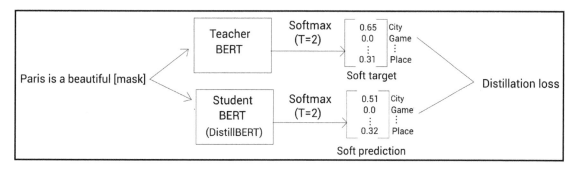

Figure 5.10 – DistilBERT

Along with distillation loss, we also compute the student loss, which is the masked language modeling loss, that is, cross-entropy loss over the hard target (ground truth) and hard prediction (standard softmax prediction with $T = 1$), as shown in the following figure:

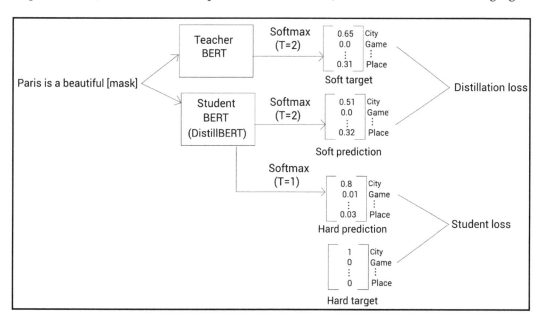

Figure 5.11 – DistilBERT

Apart from the distillation and student loss, we also compute cosine embedding loss. It is basically a distance measure between the representation learned by the teacher and student BERT. Minimizing the cosine embedding loss makes the representation of the student more accurate and similar to the teacher's embedding.

Thus, our loss function is the sum of the following three losses:

- Distillation loss
- Masked language modeling loss (student loss)
- Cosine embedding loss

We can train our student BERT (DistilBERT) by minimizing the sum of the above three losses. After training, the student BERT (DistilBERT) will acquire its knowledge from the teacher.

DistiBERT gives us almost 97% accurate results as the original BERT-Base model. Since DistilBERT is lighter, we can easily deploy it on any edge device and it is 60% faster at inference compared to the BERT model.

DistilBERT was trained on eight 16 GB V100 GPUs for approximately 90 hours. The pre-trained DistilBERT has been made publicly available by Hugging Face. We can download the pre-trained DistilBERT and fine-tune it for downstream tasks, just as we did with the original BERT model.

Researchers fine-tuned the pre-trained DistilBERT for the question-answering task and deployed it on iPhone 7 Plus and compared its inference time with the question-answering model based on BERT-Base. They observed that the DistilBERT inference time was 71% faster than BERT and the model weights were only 207 MB.

Now that we have learned how DistilBERT acquires its knowledge from the teacher using knowledge distillation, in the next section, we will learn about TinyBERT.

Introducing TinyBERT

TinyBERT is another interesting variant of BERT that also uses knowledge distillation. With DistilBERT, we learned how to transfer knowledge from the output layer of the teacher BERT to the student BERT. But apart from this, can we also transfer knowledge from the other layers of the teacher BERT? Yes! Apart from transferring knowledge from the output layer of the teacher to the student BERT, we can also transfer knowledge from other layers.

In TinyBERT, apart from transferring knowledge from the output layer (prediction layer) of the teacher to the student, we also transfer knowledge from embedding and encoder layers.

Let's understand this with an example. Suppose we have a teacher BERT with **N** encoder layers. For simplicity, we have shown only one encoder layer in the following figure. The following figure depicts the pre-trained teacher BERT model where we feed a masked sentence and it returns the logits of all the words in our vocabulary being the masked word.

In DistillBERT, **(1)** we took the logits produced by the output layer of the teacher BERT and trained the student BERT to produce the same logits. Apart from this, now, in TinyBERT, we also take the **(2)** hidden state and attention matrix produced by the teacher BERT and train the student BERT to produce the same hidden state and attention matrix. Next, we also take the **(3)** output of the embedding layer from the teacher BERT and train the student BERT to produce the same embedding as the teacher BERT:

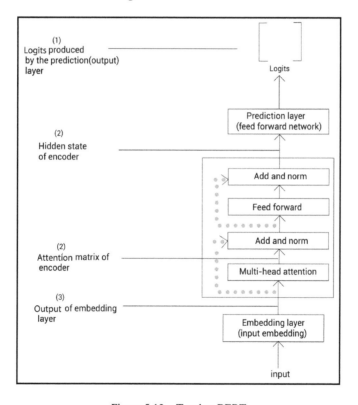

Figure 5.12 – Teacher BERT

Thus, in TinyBERT, apart from transferring knowledge from the output layer of the teacher BERT to the student BERT, we also transfer knowledge from the intermediate layers. Transferring knowledge of intermediate layers from the teacher to the student BERT helps the student BERT to learn more information from the teacher. For instance, the attention matrix encapsulates linguistic information, and thus transferring the knowledge from the attention matrix of the teacher to the student helps the student BERT to learn linguistic information from the teacher.

Apart from this, in TinyBERT, we use a two-stage learning framework where we apply distillation in both the pre-training and fine-tuning stage. We will learn how exactly this two-stage learning helps us as we go through the next sections. Now that we have got a basic idea and overview of TinyBERT, let's explore more about it in detail.

Teacher-student architecture

To understand how exactly TinyBERT works, first let's understand the premise and notation used. The following figure shows the teacher and student BERT:

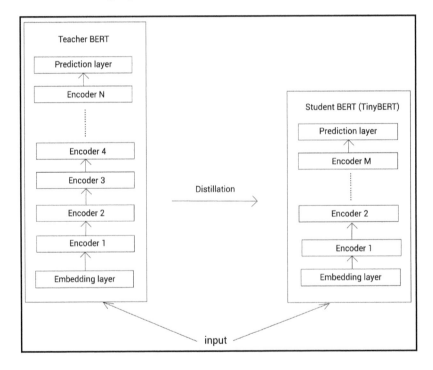

Figure 5.13 – Teacher-student architecture of TinyBERT

First, let's have a look at the teacher BERT, and then we will look at the student BERT.

Understanding the teacher BERT

From *Figure 5.13*, we can understand that the teacher BERT consists of N encoder layers. We take the input sentence and feed it to an embedding layer and get the input embeddings. Next, we pass the input embedding to the encoder layers. The encoder layers learn the contextual relation of the input sentence using the self-attention mechanism and return the representation. Next, we send the representation to the prediction layer.

The prediction layer is basically the feedforward network. If we are performing a masked language modeling task, then the prediction layer will return the logits of all the words in our vocabulary being the masked word.

We use the pre-trained BERT-Base model as the teacher BERT. We know that the BERT-Base model consists of 12 encoder layers and 12 attention heads, and the size of the representation (hidden state dimension d) produced by it is 768. The teacher BERT contains 110 million parameters. Now that we have understood the teacher BERT, let's have a look at the student BERT.

Understanding the student BERT

From the *Figure 5.13*, we can notice that the architecture of the student BERT is the same as the teacher BERT, but unlike the teacher BERT, the student BERT consists of M encoder layers. Note that N is greater than M, that is, the number of encoder layers in the teacher BERT is greater than the number of encoder layers in the student BERT.

We use the BERT model with 4 encoder layers as the student BERT and we set the representation size (hidden state dimension d') to 312. The student BERT contains only 14.5 million parameters.

We have understood the architecture of the teacher and student BERT, but how exactly does the distillation work? How can we transfer knowledge from the teacher BERT to the student BERT (TinyBERT)? Let's find that out in the next section.

Distillation in TinyBERT

As we learned at the beginning of the section, apart from transferring knowledge from the output layer (prediction layer) of the teacher to the student BERT, here, we transfer knowledge from other layers as well. Let's take a detailed look and understand how exactly the distillation happens in each of the following layers:

- Transformer layer (encoder layer)
- Embedding layer (input layer)
- Prediction layer (output layer)

The following figure shows the teacher BERT and the student BERT (TinyBERT):

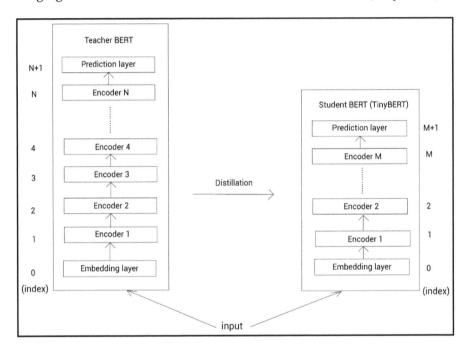

Figure 5.14 – Teacher-student architecture of TinyBERT

Note that in the teacher BERT, index 0 indicates the embedding layer, 1 indicates the first encoder layer, 2 indicates the second encoder layer, N indicates the Nth encoder layer, and $N + 1$ indicates the prediction layer. Similarly, in the student BERT, index 0 indicates the embedding layer, 1 indicates the first encoder layer, 2 indicates the second encoder layer, M indicates the Mth encoder layer, and $M + 1$ indicates the prediction layer.

We transfer knowledge from the teacher to the student BERT as follows:

$$n = g(m)$$

The preceding equation implies that we transfer the knowledge from the nth layer in the teacher to the mth layer in the student using a mapping function, g. That is, it implies that the mth layer in the student learns information from the nth layer in the teacher.

For instance:

- $0 = g(0)$ implies that we transfer knowledge from the 0th layer (embedding layer) in the teacher to the 0th layer (embedding layer) in the student.
- $N + 1 = g(M + 1)$ implies that we transfer knowledge from the $N + 1^{th}$ layer (prediction layer) in the teacher to the $M + 1^{th}$ layer (prediction layer) in the student.

Now that we have a basic idea of how distillation happens in TinyBERT, let's look at it in detail and learn how distillation happens in each layer.

Transformer layer distillation

The transformer layer is basically the encoder layer. We know that in the encoder layer, we compute the attention matrix using multi-head attention and the encoder layer returns the hidden state representation as output. In transformer distillation, we transfer the knowledge from the attention matrix of the teacher to the student and we also transfer knowledge from the hidden state of the teacher to the student. Thus, transformer layer distillation includes two distillations, as given here:

- Attention-based distillation
- Hidden state-based distillation

First, let's take a look at how attention-based distillation works, and then we will look at hidden state-based distillation.

Attention-based distillation

In **attention-based distillation**, we transfer the knowledge of the attention matrix from the teacher BERT to the student BERT. But what is the use of this? Why do we have to perform attention-based distillation? The attention matrix holds useful information such as language syntax, coreference information, and more, which are very useful in understanding more about the language in general. Hence, transferring the knowledge of the attention matrix from the teacher to the student would be very useful. Okay, how can we achieve this?

To perform attention-based distillation, we train the student network by minimizing the mean squared error between the attention matrix of the student and the teacher BERT. The attention-based distillation loss L_{attn} is expressed as follows:

$$L_{\text{attn}} = \frac{1}{h} \sum_{i=1}^{h} \text{MSE}(A_i^S, A_i^T)$$

We know that the transformer uses the multi-head attention mechanism. So, in the previous equation, the following applies:

- h denotes the number of attention heads.
- A_i^S denotes the attention matrix of the ith head of the student.
- A_i^T implies the attention matrix of the ith head of the teacher.
- **MSE** indicates the mean squared error.

Thus, we perform attention-based distillation by minimizing the mean squared error between the attention matrix of the student and teacher. It is also important to know that we use an *unnormalized attention matrix*, that is, the attention matrix without the softmax function. This is because the unnormalized attention matrix performs better and attains faster convergence in this setting. Attention-based distillation is shown in the following figure:

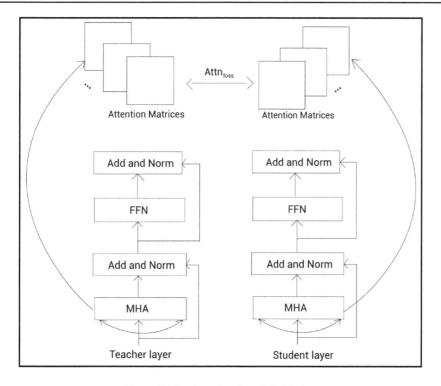

Figure 5.15 – Attention-based distillation

From the preceding figure, we can observe how we transfer knowledge of the attention matrix from the teacher to the student BERT.

Hidden state-based distillation

Now, let's see how to perform hidden state-based distillation. The hidden state is basically the output of the encoder, that is, the representation. So, in hidden-state distillation, we transfer knowledge from the hidden state of the teacher encoder to the hidden state of the student encoder. Let H^S be the hidden state of the student and H^T be the hidden state of the teacher. Then we perform distillation by minimizing the mean squared error between H^S and H^T as expressed here:

$$L_{\text{hidn}} = \text{MSE}(H^S, H^T)$$

But wait! The dimension of the hidden state of student H^S and teacher H^T varies, right? Yes! Let d be the dimension of the hidden state of the teacher H^T and d' be the dimension of the hidden state of the student H^S. We learned that the teacher BERT is basically BERT-Base and the student BERT is TinyBERT. Hence, the dimension of the hidden state of the teacher BERT d is always greater than the dimension of the hidden state of the student BERT d'.

So, to transform the hidden state of the student H^S to be in the same space as the hidden state of the teacher H^T, we perform linear transformation by multiplying H^S with a matrix W_h. Note that the values of W_h will be learned during training. Now, we can rewrite our loss function as:

$$L_{\text{hidn}} = \text{MSE}(H^S W_h, H^T)$$

As we can observe from the preceding equation, we multiply H^S with the matrix W_h to transform the H^S to be in the same space as H^T. From the following figure, we can observe how we transfer knowledge of hidden state from the teacher to the student BERT:

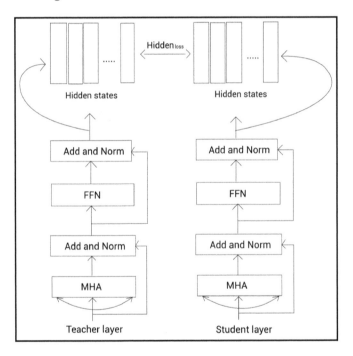

Figure 5.16 – Hidden state-based distillation

That's it. Now that we have learned how to perform transformer-layer distillation, in the next section, let's see how to perform embedding layer distillation.

Embedding layer distillation

In embedding layer distillation, we transfer knowledge from the embedding layer of the teacher to the embedding layer of the student. Let E^S denote the embedding of the student and E^T denote the embedding of the teacher, then we train the network to perform embedding layer distillation by minimizing the mean squared error between the embedding of student E^S and teacher E^T as shown in the following:

$$L_{\text{embd}} = \text{MSE}(E^S, E^T)$$

Similar to what we learned in the previous section, the dimension of embeddings of the student and teacher varies. So, we can just multiply the embedding of the student E^S by W_e to transform the embedding of the student to be in the same space as the embedding of the teacher. Thus, our loss function becomes the following:

$$L_{\text{embd}} = \text{MSE}(E^S W_e, E^T)$$

Now that we have learned how to perform embedding-layer distillation, in the next section, let's see how to perform prediction layer distillation.

Prediction layer distillation

In prediction layer distillation, we transfer knowledge from the final output layer, which is logits produced by the teacher BERT, to the student BERT. This is similar to the distillation loss we learned about with DistilBERT.

We perform prediction layer distillation by minimizing the cross-entropy loss between the soft target and soft prediction. Let Z^S be the logits of the student network and Z^T be the logits of the teacher network. Then we can represent our loss function as follows:

$$L_{\text{pred}} = -\text{softmax}(Z^t) \cdot \text{log\_softmax}(Z^s)$$

We learned how to perform distillation in different layers of TinyBERT, and we also saw the different loss functions. Now, let's look at the final loss function in the next section.

The final loss function

The loss function comprising the distillation loss in all the layers is expressed as follows:

$$L_{\text{layer}}\left(S_m, T_{g(m)}\right) = \begin{cases} L_{\text{embd}}\left(S_0, T_0\right), & m = 0 \\ L_{\text{hidn}}\left(S_m, T_{g(m)}\right) + L_{\text{attn}}\left(S_m, T_{g(m)}\right), & M \geq m > 0 \\ L_{\text{pred}}\left(S_{M+1}, T_{N+1}\right), & m = M + 1 \end{cases}$$

From the preceding equation, we can observe the following:

- When m is 0, it implies that our layer is an embedding layer so we use embedding layer loss.
- When m is between greater than 0 and less than or equal to M, then it implies that our layer is the transformer layer (encoder layer), so we use the sum of the hidden state loss and attention layer loss as the transformer layer loss.
- When m is $M + 1$ then it implies that our layer is the prediction layer, so we use the prediction layer loss.

The final loss function is expressed as follows:

$$L = \sum_{m=0}^{M+1} \lambda_m L_{\text{layer}}\left(S_m, T_{g(m)}\right)$$

In the preceding equation, L_{layer} denotes the loss function of the layer m and λ_m acts as a hyperparameter and it is used to control the importance of the mth layer. We train our student BERT (TinyBERT) by minimizing the preceding loss function. In the next section, we will learn how exactly we train the student BERT.

Training the student BERT (TinyBERT)

In TinyBERT, we will use a two-stage learning framework as follows:

- General distillation
- Task-specific distillation

This two-stage learning framework enables the distillation in both the pre-training and fine-tuning stages. Let's take a look at how each of the stages works in detail.

General distillation

General distillation is basically the pre-training step. Here, we use the large pre-trained BERT (BERT-Base) as the teacher and transfer its knowledge to the small student BERT (TinyBERT) by performing distillation. Note that we apply distillation at all the layers.

We know that the teacher BERT-Base model is pre-trained on the general dataset (Wikipedia and the Toronto BookCorpus dataset). So, while performing distillation, that is, while transferring knowledge from the teacher (BERT-Base) to the student (TinyBERT), we use the same general dataset.

After distillation, our student BERT will consist of knowledge from the teacher and we can call our pre-trained student BERT a **general TinyBERT**.

Thus, as a result of general distillation, we obtained a general TinyBERT, which is just the pre-trained student BERT. Now, we can fine-tune this general TinyBERT for downstream tasks. In the next section, we'll see how to fine-tune this general TinyBERT.

Task-specific distillation

Task-specific distillation is basically the fine-tuning step. Here, we fine-tune the general TinyBERT (pre-trained student BERT) for a specific task. Unlike DistilBERT, apart from applying distillation in the pre-training step, in TinyBERT, we apply distillation at the fine-tuning step as well.

First, we take a pre-trained BERT-Base model and fine-tune it for a specific task and we use this fine-tuned BERT-Base as the teacher. The general TinyBERT is the student BERT. We perform distillation and transfer the knowledge from the fine-tuned BERT-Base to the general TinyBERT. After distillation, our general TinyBERT will consist of task-specific knowledge from the teacher (fine-tuned BERT-Base) and thus now we can call our general TinyBERT a **fine-tuned TinyBERT** since it is fine-tuned for a specific task.

The following table helps us to clear up any confusion between general distillation and task-specific distillation:

	General distillation (pre-training step)	Task-specific distillation (fine-tuning step)
Teacher	Pre-trained BERT-base	Fine-tuned BERT-base
Student	TinyBERT(small BERT)	General TinyBERT (pre-trained TinyBERT)
Result	After distillation, the student BERT will consist of knowledge from the teacher and we can call the pre-trained student BERT a general TinyBERT	After distillation, the general TinyBERT will consist of task-specific knowledge from the teacher (fine-tuned BERT-base) and thus now we can call the general TinyBERT a fine-tuned TinyBERT since it is fine-tuned for a specific task

Figure 5.17 – The distinctions between general distillation and task-specific distillation

Note that to perform distillation at the fine-tuning step, we need more task-specific data points. That is, for task-specific distillation, we need more data points. So we use a data augmentation method to obtain the augmented dataset. We will fine-tune the general TinyBERT with this augmented dataset. The next section will show us how data augmentation is performed.

The data augmentation method

First, we will explore the algorithm of the data augmentation method step by step, and then we will understand it more clearly with an example.

Suppose we have a sentence: *Paris is a beautiful city*. First, we tokenize the sentence using the BERT tokenizer and store the tokens in the list called X as shown here: X = [Paris, is, a, beautiful, city].

We copy X to another list called X_masked. Thus, we will have X_masked = [Paris, is, a, beautiful, city].

Now, for every element (word), i, in the list, X, we do the following:

1. We check whether X[i] is a single-piece word. If it is a single-piece word, then we mask X_masked[i] with the [MASK] token. Next, we use the BERT-Base model to predict the masked word. We predict the first K most likely words and store them in a list called candidates. Say K = 5; then we predict the 5 most likely words and store them in the candidates list.

2. If X[i] is not a single-piece word, then we will not mask it. Instead, we check for the K words most similar to X[i] using the glove embeddings and store them in the candidates list.

   Next, we randomly sample a value, p, from a uniform distribution, $p \sim \text{Uniform}(0, 1)$. We introduce a new variable called a **threshold**, p_t. Let the threshold $p_t = 0.4$. Then, we do the following:

3. If p is less than or equal to p_t, then we replace X_masked[i] with any random word from the candidates list.

4. If p is not less than or equal to p_t, then we replace X_masked[i] with an actual word, X[i].

We perform the preceding steps for every word i in the sentence and append the updated X_masked list to a list called data_aug. We repeat this data augmentation method about N times for every sentence in our dataset. Say N=10; then for every sentence, we perform the data augmentation step and obtain 10 new sentences.

Now that we understood how the data augmentation method works, let's look at a small example. Say we have the following:

    X = [Paris, is, a, beautiful, city]

We copy X to a new list called X_masked and thus, we have this:

    X_masked = [Paris, is, a, beautiful, city]

Now, for every word i in the list, we perform the following.

Say i=0; then, we have X[0]=Paris. We check whether X[0] is a single-piece word. Since it is a single-piece word, we replace X_masked[0] with the [MASK] token as shown here:

    X_masked = [[MASK], is, a, beautiful, city]

Now, we use the BERT-Base model and predict the K most likely words for the masked token, and store them in the `candidates` list. Say we set K=3; then we store the 3 most likely words predicted by BERT-Base in the `candidates` list. Suppose the following are the 3 most likely words predicted by the BERT-Base model for the masked token:

```
candidates = [ Paris, it, that]
```

Next, we randomly sample a value, p, from a uniform distribution, $p \sim$ Uniform(0, 1). Say $p_t = 0.3$. Now, we check if p is less than or equal to the threshold value p_t. Let $p_t = 0.4$. Since p is less than the threshold p_t, we replace X_masked[0] with any random word from our `candidates` list. Say we randomly picked the word `it` from the `candidates` list, then our X_masked list becomes the following:

```
X_masked = [it, is, a, beautiful, city]
```

Now, we just append X_masked to a list, data_aug.

That's it. We repeat these steps for N times and obtain more data points. After obtaining this augmented dataset, we fine-tune the general TinyBERT (pre-trained TinyBERT) using the augmented dataset.

In a nutshell, in TinyBERT, we perform distillation at all the layers and we also apply distillation in both the pre-training and fine-tuning phase.

TinyBERT is 96% more effective, 7.5 times smaller, and 9.4 times faster during inference than the BERT-Base model. We can download the pre-trained TinyBERT here: `https://github.com/huawei-noah/pre-trained-Language-Model/tree/master/TinyBERT`.

So far, we have learned how to perform knowledge distillation from a large pre-trained BERT to a smaller BERT. Can we perform knowledge distillation and transfer knowledge from a pre-trained BERT to a simple neural network? Yes, and that's exactly what we discuss in the next section.

Transferring knowledge from BERT to neural networks

In this section, let's look at an interesting paper, *Distilling Task-Specific Knowledge from BERT into Simple Neural Networks* by the University of Waterloo. In this paper, the researchers have explained how to perform knowledge distillation and transfer task-specific knowledge from BERT to a simple neural network. Let's get into the details and understand how exactly this works.

Teacher-student architecture

To understand how exactly we transfer task-specific knowledge from BERT to a neural network, first let's take a look at the teacher BERT and student network in detail.

The teacher BERT

We use the pre-trained BERT as the teacher BERT. Here, we use the pre-trained BERT-large as the teacher BERT. Note that, here, we are transferring task-specific knowledge from the teacher to the student. So, first, we take the pre-trained BERT-large model, fine-tune it for a specific task, and then use it as the teacher.

Suppose we want to train our student network for the sentiment analysis task. In that case, we take the pre-trained BERT-large model, fine-tune it for a sentiment analysis task, and then use it as the teacher. Thus, our teacher is the pre-trained BERT, fine-tuned for a specific task of our interest.

The student network

The student network is a simple bidirectional LSTM and we can shortly represent this as BiLSTM. The architecture of the student network changes based on the task. Let's look at the architecture of the student network for a single-sentence classification task.

Suppose we are performing sentiment analysis. Say we have a sentence: *I love Paris*. First, we get the embeddings of the sentence, then we feed the input embeddings to the bidirectional LSTM. Bidirectional LSTM reads the sentence in both directions (that is, forward and backward). So, we obtain the forward and backward hidden states from bidirectional LSTM.

Next, we feed the forward and backward hidden states to the fully connected layer with ReLU activation, which then returns the logits as an output. We take the logits and feed them to the softmax function and obtain the probabilities of the sentence belonging to the positive and negative class as shown in the diagram:

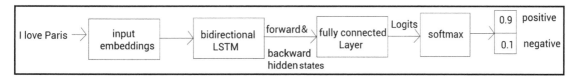

Figure 5.18 – Student network

Now, let's take a look at the architecture of the student network for sentence matching tasks. Suppose we want to understand whether the given two sentences are similar. In this case, our student network is the siamese BiLSTM.

First, we get the embeddings of sentence 1 and sentence 2 and feed them to the bidirectional LSTM 1 (BiLSTM 1) and bidirectional LSTM 2 (BiLSTM 2) respectively. We obtain the forward and backward hidden states from BiLSTM 1 and BiLSTM 2. Let h_{s1} be the forward and backward hidden state obtained from BiLSTM 1 and h_{s2} be the forward and backward hidden state obtained from BiLSTM 2 . We combine h_{s1} and h_{s2} using a concatenate–compare operation as given in the following equation:

$$f(h_{s1}, h_{s2}) = \left[h_{s1}, h_{s2}, h_{s1} \odot h_{s2}, |h_{s1} - h_{s2}|\right]$$

In the preceding equation, $\odot$ denotes the element-wise multiplication. Next, we feed the concatenated result to the fully connected layer with ReLU activations and get the logits. Then we feed the logits to the softmax function, which returns the probabilities of the given sentence pair being similar and dissimilar as shown in the following figure:

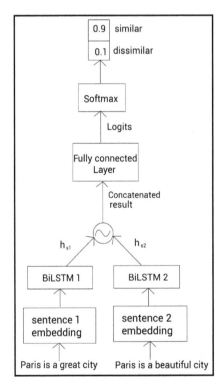

Figure 5.19 – Student network

Now that we have understood the architecture of the student network, let's see how to train the student network by acquiring knowledge from the teacher BERT in the next section.

Training the student network

Remember that, here, we are transferring task-specific knowledge from the teacher to the student. So, as we have learned, we take the pre-trained BERT model, fine-tune it for a specific task, and then use the fine-tuned BERT model as the teacher. Thus, our teacher is pre-trained, fine-tuned BERT and the student is the BiLSTM.

We train the student network by minimizing the loss, which is the weighted sum of student loss $L_{student}$ and distillation loss $L_{distill}$. This is similar to what we learned in the *Introducing knowledge distillation* section:

$$L = \alpha \cdot L_{student} + \beta \cdot L_{distill}$$

We set the value of β to (1 - α) and rewrite the preceding equation as follows:

$$L = \alpha \cdot L_{student} + (1 - \alpha) \cdot L_{distill}$$

We know that the distillation loss is basically the cross-entropy loss between the soft target and soft prediction. But here, we use the mean squared loss as the distillation loss since it performs better than the cross-entropy loss in this setting. It is expressed as follows:

$$L_{distill} = \text{MSE}(Z^T, Z^S)$$

In the preceding equation, Z^T denotes the logits of the teacher network and Z^S denotes the logits of the student network.

The student loss is just the standard cross-entropy loss between the hard target and hard prediction. Thus, our loss function is as follows:

$$L = \alpha \cdot L_{student} + (1 - \alpha) \cdot L_{distill}$$

We train the student network by minimizing the preceding loss function. Note that to distill knowledge from the teacher BERT to the student network, we need a large dataset. So, we use a task-agnostic data augmentation method to increase the number of data points. In the next section, we will learn how exactly the data augmentation method works in detail.

The data augmentation method

We use the following methods for performing task-agnostic data augmentation:

- Masking
- POS-guided word replacement
- n-gram sampling

Let's take a look at each one of them.

Understanding the masking method

In the masking method, with probability p_{mask}, we randomly mask a word in the sentence with the [MASK] token and create a new sentence with the masked token. For instance, suppose we are performing a sentiment analysis task and, say, in our dataset, we have the sentence *I was listening to music*. Now, with probability p_{mask}, we randomly mask a word. Say we have masked the word *music*, then we have a new sentence: *I was listening to [MASK]*.

But how is this useful? With the [MASK] token in the sentence, our model will not able to produce the confidence logits since [MASK] is an unknown token. Our model produces less confident logits for the sentence *I was listening to [MASK]* with a [MASK] token than for the sentence *I was listening to music* with the unmasked token. This helps our model understand the contribution of each word to the label.

Understanding the POS-guided word replacement method

In the POS-guided (parts of speech guided) word replacement method, with probability p_{pos}, we replace a word in a sentence with another word but with the same parts of speech.

For example, consider the sentence *Where did you go?* We know that in this sentence the word *did* is a verb. Now we can replace the word *did* with another verb. So now our sentence becomes *where do you go?* As you can see, we replaced the word *did* with *do* and obtained a new sentence.

Understanding the n-gram sampling method

In the n-gram sampling method, with probability p_{ng}, we just randomly sample an n-gram from a sentence, and the value of n is chosen randomly from 1 to 5.

We have learned three different methods for data augmentation. But how exactly do we apply them? Should we apply all of them together or one at a time? Let's discuss this in the next section.

The data augmentation procedure

Say we have a sentence – *Paris is a beautiful city*. Let $w_1, w_2, \ldots w_i, \ldots w_n$ be the words in the sentence. Now, for each word w_i in our sentence, we create a variable called X_i where the value of X_i is randomly sampled from the uniform distribution $X_i \sim \text{Uniform}(0, 1)$. Based on the value of X_i, we do the following:

- If $X_i < p_{mask}$, then we mask the word w_i.
- If $p_{mask} \leq X_i < p_{mask} + p_{pos}$, then we apply POS-guided word replacement.

Note that masking and POS-guided word replacement are mutually exclusive; if we apply one, then we can't apply the other.

After the preceding step, we will obtain a modified sentence (a synthetic sentence). Now, with probability p_{ng}, we apply n-gram sampling to our synthetic sentence and obtain a final synthetic sentence. Then we append the final synthetic sentence to a list, `data_aug`.

For every sentence, we perform the preceding steps **N** number of times and obtain **N** new synthetic sentences. Okay, if we have sentence pairs instead of sentences, then how we can obtain the synthetic sentence pairs? In that case, we can create synthetic sentence pairs with many combinations. Some of which are as follows:

- We can create a synthetic sentence only from the first sentence and hold the second sentence.
- We hold the first sentence and create a synthetic sentence only from the second sentence.
- We can create synthetic sentences from both the first and second sentences.

In this way, we can apply the data augmentation method and obtain more data points. Then, we train our student network with the augmented data points.

Thus, in this chapter, we have learned about different variants of BERT model using knowledge distillation and we have also learned how to transfer knowledge from the pre-trained BERT to a simple neural network.

Summary

We started off the chapter by understanding what knowledge distillation is and how it works. We learned that knowledge distillation is a model compression technique in which a small model is trained to reproduce the behavior of a large pre-trained model. It is also referred to as teacher-student learning, where the large pre-trained model is the teacher and the small model is the student.

Next, we learned about DistilBERT where we take a large pre-trained BERT as a teacher and transfer its knowledge to a small BERT through knowledge distillation.

Following DistilBERT, we learned how TinyBERT works. In TinyBERT, apart from transferring knowledge from the output layer of the teacher, we also transfer knowledge from other layers, such as the embedding layer, transformer layer, and prediction layer.

Moving on, at the end of the chapter, we learned how to transfer task-specific knowledge from BERT to a simple neural network. In the next chapter, we will learn how to fine-tune the pre-trained BERT for a text summarization task.

Questions

Let's put our knowledge to the test by answering the following questions:

1. What is knowledge distillation?
2. What are the soft target and soft prediction?
3. Define distillation loss.
4. What is the use of DistilBERT?
5. What is the loss function of DistilBERT?
6. How does transformer layer distillation work?
7. How does prediction layer distillation work?

Further reading

To learn more, check out the following papers:

- *Distilling the Knowledge in a Neural Network* by Geoffrey Hinton, Oriol Vinyals, Jeff Dean, available at `https://arxiv.org/pdf/1503.02531.pdf`
- *DistilBERT, a distilled version of BERT: smaller, faster, cheaper and lighter* by Victor Sanh, Lysandre Debut, Julien Chaumond, Thomas Wolf available at `https://arxiv.org/pdf/1910.01108.pdf`
- *TinyBERT: Distilling BERT for Natural Language Understanding* by Xiaoqi Jiao et al, available at `https://arxiv.org/pdf/1909.10351.pdf`
- *Distilling Task-Specific Knowledge from BERT into Simple Neural Networks* by Raphael Tang, Yao Lu, Linqing Liu, Lili Mou, Olga Vechtomova, and Jimmy Lin, available at `https://arxiv.org/pdf/1903.12136.pdf`

Section 3 - Applications of BERT

3

In this section, we will look into several interesting applications of BERT. We will learn how to fine-tune BERT for text summarization tasks using BERTSUM. Then, we will explore how to apply BERT for languages other than English. We will also learn about VideoBERT and other interesting models.

The following chapters are included in this section:

- Chapter 6, *Exploring BERTSUM for Text Summarization*
- Chapter 7, *Applying BERT to Other Languages*
- Chapter 8, *Exploring Sentence and Domain–Specific BERT*
- Chapter 9, *Working with VideoBERT, BART, and More*

6
Exploring BERTSUM for Text Summarization

Text summarization is one of the most popular applications of natural language processing. In this chapter, we will understand how to fine-tune the pre-trained BERT model for a text summarization task. The BERT model fine-tuned for the text summarization task is often called **BERTSUM** (**BERT for summarization**). In this chapter, we will understand what BERTSUM is and how it is used for text summarization in detail.

We will begin the chapter by understanding different types of text summarization called extractive and abstractive summarizations. First, we will learn how to perform extractive summarization using BERTSUM with a classifier, BERTSUM with a transformer, and BERTSUM with an LSTM. Next, we will look into how BERTSUM is used for performing the abstractive summarization task.

Going forward, we will learn about the text summarization evaluation metric called the ROUGE metric. We will understand ROUGE-N and ROUGE-L evaluation metrics in detail. Next, we will check the performance of the BERTSUM model. At the end of the chapter, we will also take a look at training the BERTSUM model.

In this chapter, we will learn about the following topics:

- Text summarization
- Fine-tuning BERT for text summarization
- Extractive summarization using BERT
- Abstractive summarization using BERT
- Understanding ROUGE evaluation metrics
- The performance of the BERTSUM model
- Training the BERTSUM model

Text summarization

Text summarization is the process of converting a long text into its summary. Suppose we have a Wikipedia article and say we don't want to read the whole article – we just need an overview of the article. In this case, summarizing the Wikipedia article will help us get an overview of the article. Text summarization is widely used for a variety of applications, from summarizing long documents, news articles, blog posts, ranging to many more. In the text summarization task, given a long text, our goal is to convert the given long text into its summary as shown in the figure:

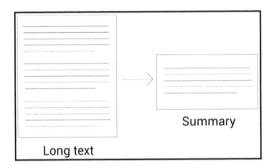

Figure 6.1 – Text summarization

Text summarization is of two types:

- Extractive summarization
- Abstractive summarization

Now let's explore extractive and abstractive summarization in detail.

Extractive summarization

In **extractive summarization**, we create a summary from a given text by extracting only the important sentences.

That is, say we are given a long document containing many sentences, with extractive summarization, we create a summary of the document by extracting only the important sentences that hold the essential meaning of the document.

Let's understand extractive summarization with a small example. Consider the following text from Wikipedia:

Machine learning is the study of computer algorithms that improve automatically through experience. It is seen as a subset of artificial intelligence. Machine learning algorithms build a mathematical model based on sample data, known as training data, in order to make predictions or decisions without being explicitly programmed to do so. Machine learning algorithms are used in a wide variety of applications, such as email filtering and computer vision, where it is difficult or infeasible to develop conventional algorithms.

Now, with extractive summarization, we only extract the important sentences from the given text. So, as a result of extractive summarization, our summary will look like the following:

Machine learning is the study of computer algorithms that improve automatically through experience. It is seen as a subset of artificial intelligence. Machine learning algorithms are used in a wide variety of applications, such as email filtering and computer vision, where it is difficult or infeasible to develop conventional algorithms.

From the preceding result, we can observe that our summary consists of only the important sentences that hold the essential meaning of the given text.

Abstractive summarization

Unlike extractive summarization, in **abstractive summarization**, we will not create a summary by just extracting important sentences from the given text. Instead, in this type, we create a summary by paraphrasing the given text. Okay, what is paraphrasing? Paraphrasing implies that we re-express the given text using different words to provide more clarity.

So, in abstractive summarization, given a text, we will create a summary by re-expressing the given text using different words holding only the essential meaning of the given text.

Let's understand abstractive summarization with a small example. Let's consider the same text we saw in the previous section:

Machine learning is the study of computer algorithms that improve automatically through experience. It is seen as a subset of artificial intelligence. Machine learning algorithms build a mathematical model based on sample data, known as training data, in order to make predictions or decisions without being explicitly programmed to do so. Machine learning algorithms are used in a wide variety of applications, such as email filtering and computer vision, where it is difficult or infeasible to develop conventional algorithms.

Now, with abstractive summarization, we create a summary by paraphrasing the given text. So, as a result of abstractive summarization, our summary will look as shown here:

Machine learning is a subset of artificial intelligence and it is widely used for creating a variety of applications such as email filtering and computer vision.

From the preceding result, we can observe that our summary is basically paraphrased from the given text, holding only the essential meaning of the text.

Now that we have understood what extractive and abstractive summarizations are, in the next section, we will learn how to fine-tune the BERT model to perform extractive and abstractive summarizations.

Fine-tuning BERT for text summarization

In this section, let's understand how to fine-tune the BERT model to perform text summarization. First, we will understand how to fine-tune BERT for extractive summarization, and then we will see how to fine-tune BERT for abstractive summarization.

Extractive summarization using BERT

To fine-tune the pre-trained BERT for the extractive summarization task, we slightly modify the input data format of the BERT model. Before looking into the modified input data format, first, let's recall how we feed the input data to the BERT model.

Say we have two sentences: *Paris is a beautiful city. I love Paris.* First, we tokenize the sentences and we add a [CLS] token only at the beginning of the first sentence and we add a [SEP] token at the end of every sentence. Before feeding the tokens to the BERT, we convert them into embedding using three embedding layers known as **token embedding, segment embedding**, and **position embedding**. We sum up all the embeddings together element-wise and then we feed them as input to the BERT. The input data format of BERT is shown in the following figure:

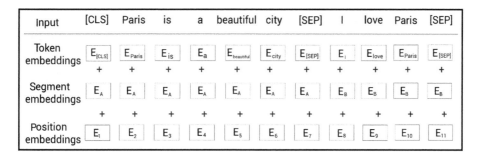

Figure 6.2 – Input data format of BERT

The BERT model takes this input and returns the representation of every token as output as shown in the following figure:

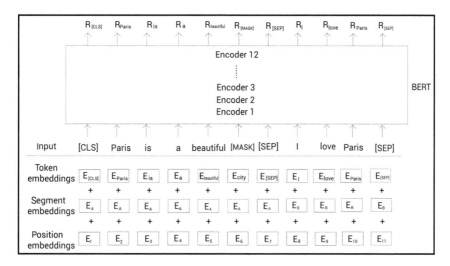

Figure 6.3 – BERT

Now the question is how can we use the BERT for the text summarization task? We know that the BERT model gives a representation of every token. But we don't need a representation of every token. Instead, we need a representation of every sentence. But why?

We learned that in extractive summarization, we create a summary by just selecting only the important sentences. We know that a representation of a sentence will hold the meaning of the sentence. If we get a representation of every sentence, then based on the representation, we can decide whether the sentence is important or not. If it is important, then we will add it to the summary, else we will discard it. Thus, if we obtain the representation of every sentence using BERT, then we can feed the representation to the classifier and the classifier will tell us whether the sentence is important or not.

Okay, how can we get the representation of a sentence? Can we use the representation of the [CLS] token as the representation of the sentence? Yes! But there is a small catch here. We learned that we add the [CLS] token only at the beginning of the first sentence, but in the text summarization task, we feed multiple sentences to the BERT model and we need the representation of all the sentences.

So, in this case, we modify our input data format to the BERT model. We add the [CLS] token at the beginning of every sentence so that we can use the representation of the [CLS] token added at the beginning of every sentence as the representation.

Say we have three sentences: *sent one, sent two,* and *sent three*. First, we tokenize the sentences and we add the [CLS] token at the beginning of every sentence and we also separate each sentence with the [SEP] token. The input tokens are shown in the following. As we can observe, we have added the [CLS] token at the beginning of every sentence and we added the [SEP] token at the end of every sentence:

```
Input tokens = [ [CLS], sent, one, [SEP], [CLS], sent, two, [SEP], [CLS],
sent, three, [SEP] ]
```

Next, we feed the input tokens to the token, segment, and position embedding layers and convert the input tokens into embeddings. The token embedding layer is shown in the following figure:

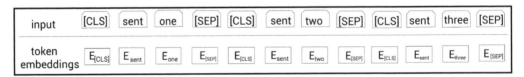

Figure 6.4 – Token embeddings

The next layer is the segment embedding layer. We know that segment embedding is used to distinguish between the two given sentences. The segment embedding layer returns either of two embeddings, E_A or E_B. That is, if the input token belongs to sentence A, then the token will be mapped to the embedding E_A and if the input token belongs to sentence B, then the token will be mapped to embedding E_B. But in the text summarization setting, we feed more than two sentences to the BERT model. Now how can we map the tokens from more than two sentences to embedding E_A and E_B?

In this case, we use an interval segment embedding. The interval segment embedding is used to distinguish between the multiple given sentences. With internal segment embedding, we map the tokens of the sentence occurring in the odd index to E_A and we map the tokens of the sentence occurring in the even index to E_B. Say we have four sentences, then:

- All tokens from sentence 1 will be mapped to E_A.
- All tokens from sentence 2 will be mapped to E_B.
- All tokens from sentence 3 will be mapped to E_A.
- All tokens from sentence 4 will be mapped to E_B.

The interval segment embedding layer is shown in the following figure. As we can observe, tokens from sentence one are mapped to E_A, tokens from sentence two are mapped to E_B, and tokens from sentence three are mapped to E_A:

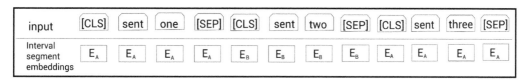

Figure 6.5 – Interval segment embeddings

The next layer is the position embedding layer. The position embedding layer works in the same way as we learned before. The position embedding layer encodes the positional information of every token in the input. The positional embedding layer is shown in the following figure:

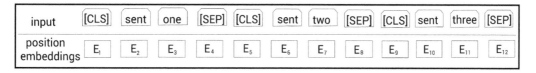

Figure 6.6 – Position embeddings

The final modified input data format with the token, interval segment, and position embedding layers for the extractive summarization task is shown in the following figure:

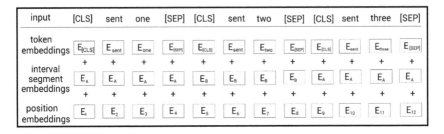

Figure 6.7 – Input data format

Now, we feed the input to the BERT model with this modified input data format. As shown in the following figure, the BERT model takes this input and returns the representation of every token as an output. Since we added the [CLS] token at the beginning of every sentence, we can use the representation of the [CLS] token as the sentence representation. As shown in the following figure, R_1 denotes the representation of sent one, R_2 denotes the representation of sent two, and R_3 denotes the representation of sent three. We can call the following BERT model with the modified input data format BERTSUM:

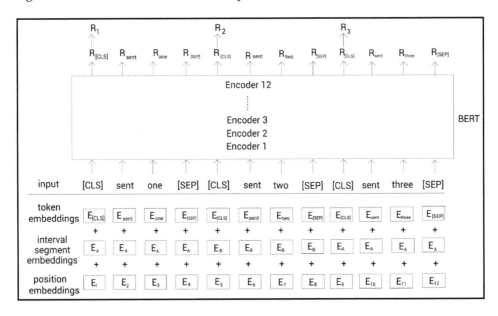

Figure 6.8 – BERTSUM

Note that to obtain the sentence representation, we don't have to train BERT from scratch. Instead, we can use any pre-trained BERT model but we just need to modify the input data format in the way we discussed earlier so that we can use the representation of every [CLS] token as the corresponding sentence representation.

We learned how to obtain the representation of every sentence in the given text using a pre-trained BERT model, but how can we make use of those representations for the extractive summarization task? Let's find that out in the next section.

BERTSUM with a classifier

We learned that in extractive summarization, we create a summary by just selecting only the important sentences from the given text. In the previous section, we learned how to obtain the representation of every sentence in the given text using a pre-trained BERT model. Now, we feed the representation of a sentence to a simple binary classifier and the classifier tells us whether the sentence is important or not. That is, the classifier returns the probability of the sentence being included in the summary. The classification layer is often called the **summarization layer**. This is shown in the following figure:

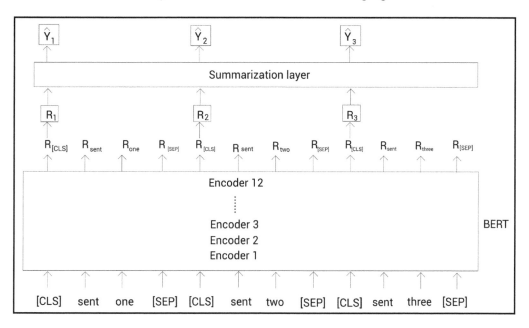

Figure 6.9 – BERTSUM with a classifer

From the preceding figure, we can observe that we feed all the sentences from a given text to the pre-trained BERT model. The pre-trained BERT model will return the representation of each sentence, $R_1, R_2, \ldots, R_i, \ldots, R_n$. Then we feed the representation to a classifier (summarization layer). The classifier then returns the probability of the sentence being included in the summary.

For each sentence i in the document, we will get the sentence representation R_i, and we feed the representation to the summarization layer, which returns the probability $\hat{Y}_i$ of including the sentence in the summary:

$$\hat{Y}_i = \sigma(W_o R_i + b_o)$$

From the preceding equation, we can observe that we are using a simple sigmoid classifier to obtain the probability $\hat{Y}_i$. Our results will not be accurate in the initial iterations. So, we will fine-tune the model by minimizing the binary classification loss between the predicted probability $\hat{Y}_i$ and the actual probability Y_i. We will fine-tune the pre-trained BERT model jointly with the summarization layer.

We learned that we use a simple sigmoid classifier in the summarization layer. But instead of a simple classifier, can we try something else? Yes, and that's exactly what we will discuss in the next section.

BERTSUM with a transformer and LSTM

We learned how to use BERTSUM. Instead of using only the simple sigmoid classifier in the summarization layer, researchers have proposed two different approaches:

- An inter-sentence transformer
- **Long short-term memory (LSTM)**

That is, instead of feeding the sentence representation R obtained from the BERT directly to the sigmoid classifier, we can feed it to a transformer and LSTM and learn even better representation. Let's understand this in detail in the next sections.

BERTSUM with an inter-sentence transformer

With an inter-sentence transformer, we feed the result of the BERT to the transformer layers. That is, we feed the sentence representation R obtained from BERT to the transformer's encoder layers. But why exactly do we have to do this? What is the advantage of this? The transformer's encoder takes the representation R obtained from BERT and returns its hidden state representation. This hidden state representation will help in learning the document-level features focusing on the summarization task. Confused? Let's understand this in detail.

Before going ahead, let's quickly recap the transformer's encoder. We know that the transformer consists of an **L** number of encoders. Each encoder in the transformer consists of two sublayers – multi-head attention and a feedforward network with layer normalization. The following figure shows two encoders (only encoder 1 is expanded). We can observe that the encoder consists of two sublayers. We can also notice that before feeding the input to the encoder, we add the positional embedding to the input. The final encoder (topmost encoder) returns the hidden state representation as an output:

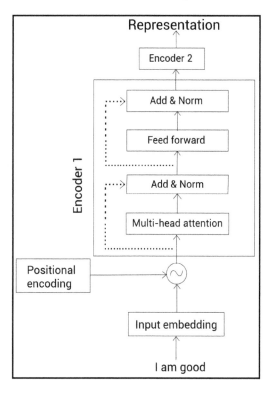

Figure 6.10 – Encoder

Now let's understand how the transformer's encoder is going to help us. We know that the transformer consists of many encoders $(1, 2, \ldots, l, \ldots, L)$.

Let's represent the encoder by l and the hidden state representation obtained from the encoder by h. So, h^l denotes the hidden state representation obtained from an encoder l.

We feed the sentence representation R obtained from BERT as an input to the encoder. Before feeding the input R directly to the encoder, we add the positional embeddings. The input representation R along with the position embedding is represented as h^0:

$$h^0 = \text{PosEmb}(R)$$

In the preceding equation, **PosEmb** denotes the positional embedding. Now, we feed the input h^0 to the encoder. We learned that each encoder consists of two sublayers – a multi-head attention layer and a feedforward network. For an encoder, l, the equations of sublayers are given as follows:

$$\tilde{h}^l = \text{LN}(h^{l-1} + \text{MHAtt}(h^{l-1}))$$

$$h^l = \text{LN}(\tilde{h}^l + \text{FNN}(\tilde{h}^l))$$

For example, say encoder $l = 1$, then we have the following:

$$\tilde{h}^1 = \text{LN}(h^0 + \text{MHAtt}(h^0))$$

$$h^1 = \text{LN}(\tilde{h}^1 + \text{FNN}(\tilde{h}^1))$$

In the preceding equation, **LN** denotes the layer normalization, **MHAtt** denotes the multi-head attention, and **FNN** denotes the feedforward network.

The topmost encoder is represented by L and the hidden state representation obtained from the topmost encoder is represented by h^L. We take the hidden state representation obtained from the topmost encoder h^L and feed it to the sigmoid classifier, which returns the probability of including the sentence in the summary:

$$\hat{Y}_i = \sigma(W_o h_i^L + b_o)$$

In a nutshell, we take the representation R_i of a sentence i obtained from BERT and feed it to the transformer's encoder. The encoder takes this representation R_i as an input and returns the hidden state representation obtained from the topmost encoder h_i^L as an output.

Next, we feed the hidden state representation h_i^L to the sigmoid classifier, which returns the probability of including the sentence in the summary. Thus, instead of using the representation R_i directly from the BERT, we feed it to the encoder and use the representation h_i^L. The following figure provides us with clarity:

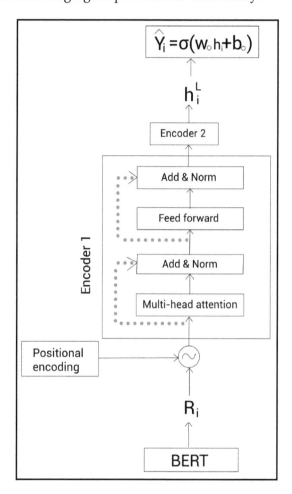

Figure 6.11 – BERTSUM with an inter-sentence transformer

Now that we have learned how to use BERTSUM with an inter-sentence transformer, in the next section, let's see how to use BERTSUM with LSTM.

BERTSUM with LSTM

We take the representation R_i of a sentence i obtained from BERT and feed it to the LSTM cell. The LSTM cell takes this representation R_i as an input and returns hidden state representation h_i as an output. Next, we feed the hidden state representation h_i to the sigmoid classifier, which returns the probability of including the sentence in the summary:

$$\hat{Y}_i = \sigma(W_o h_i + b_o)$$

Thus, instead of using the representation R_i directly from the BERT model, we feed it to the LSTM and use the representation h_i. The following figure provides us with clarity:

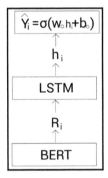

Figure 6.12 – BERTSUM with LSTM

Thus, we have learned how to use BERTSUM. We learned that we can use BERTSUM in the following three ways:

- BERTSUM with a simple classifier
- BERTSUM with an inter-sentence transformer
- BERTSUM with LSTM

We learned how to fine-tune the pre-trained BERT model for a summarization task. We fine-tune the pre-trained BERT jointly with the summarization layer. For instance, we can fine-tune the pre-trained *bert-base-uncased* model jointly with the summarization layer to perform an extractive summarization task. We use the Adam optimizer with the following learning rate:

$$lr = 2e^{-3} . \min(\text{step}^{-0.5}, \text{step. warmup}^{-1.5})$$

In the preceding equation, **warmup$_e$ = 10,000**.

We learned how to fine-tune the pre-trained BERT for an extractive summarization task. Can we also use BERT to perform abstractive summarization? Yes! We will learn about this in the next section.

Abstractive summarization using BERT

In this section, we will learn how to perform abstractive summarization using BERT. We know that in abstractive summarization our goal is to create a summary by paraphrasing the given text. That is, in abstractive summarization, given a text, we will create a summary by re-expressing the given text using different words holding only the essential meaning of the given text. But how can we do this with BERT? Because BERT will return only the representation of tokens. How can we generate a new text with BERT? Let's explore this in detail.

To perform abstractive summarization, we use the transformer model with encoder-decoder architecture. We feed the input text to the encoder and the encoder will return the representation of the given input text. We take the representation returned by the encoder and feed it as an input to the decoder. The decoder uses this representation and generates the summary.

We already learned how to fine-tune BERTSUM in the previous section. We learned how to use BERTSUM to generate sentence representation. Now, in our transformer model with encoder-decoder architecture, we can use pre-trained BERTSUM as an encoder. So, the pre-trained BERTSUM model will generate meaningful representation and the decoder uses this representation and learns how to generate the summary.

There is a small catch here: in our transformer model, the encoder is a pre-trained BERTSUM model but the decoder is randomly initialized. This will cause a discrepancy during fine-tuning. Since the encoder is already pre-trained, it might overfit and since the decoder is not pre-trained, it might underfit.

So, to combat this, we use two Adam optimizers, one for the encoder and the other for the decoder. We use different learning rates for the encoder and decoder. Since the encoder is already pre-trained, we set the small learning rate and smooth decay for the encoder. The learning rate of the encoder is given as $lr_e = \tilde{lr}_e . \min(\text{step}^{-0.5}, \text{step. warmup}_e^{-1.5})$ where $\tilde{lr}_e = 2e^{-3}$ and **warmup$_e$ = 20,000**.

The learning rate of the decoder is given as follows:

$$lr_d = \tilde{lr}_d . \min(\text{step}^{-0.5}, \text{step. warmup}_d^{-1.5})$$

Where, $\bar{l}r_d = 0.1$ and **warmup$_e$ = 10,000**.

The abstractive summarization process is shown in the following figure:

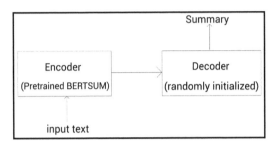

Figure 6.13 – BERT for abstractive summarization

From the preceding figure, we can observe how abstractive summarization happens with pre-trained BERTSUM as an encoder and a randomly initialized decoder. We can call our model **BERTSUMABS** (**BERT for abstractive summarization**).

We learned how to fine-tune BERT for extractive and abstractive summarization. But how do we measure the performance of BERTSUM? How accurately does our BERTSUM model perform summarization? We will discuss this in the next section.

Understanding ROUGE evaluation metrics

In order to evaluate a text summarization task, we use a popular set of metrics called **ROUGE**, which stands for **Recall-Oriented Understudy for Gisting Evaluation**. First, we will understand how the ROUGE metric works, and then we will check the ROUGE score for text summarization with the BERTSUM model.

The ROUGE metric was first introduced in the paper *ROUGE: A Package for Automatic Evaluation of Summaries* by Chin-Yew Lin. The five different ROUGE evaluation metrics include the following:

- ROUGE-N
- ROUGE-L
- ROUGE-W
- ROUGE-S
- ROUGE-SU

We will focus only on ROUGE-N and ROUGE-L. First, let's understand how ROUGE-N is computed, and then we will look at ROUGE-L.

Understanding the ROUGE-N metric

ROUGE-N is an n-gram recall between a candidate summary (predicted summary) and a reference summary (actual summary).

The recall is defined as a ratio of the total number of overlapping n-grams between the candidate and reference summary to the total number of n-grams in the reference summary:

$$\text{Recall} = \frac{\text{Total number of overlapping n-grams}}{\text{Total number of n-grams in the reference summary}}$$

Let's understand how ROUGE-N works with ROUGE-1 and ROUGE-2.

ROUGE-1

ROUGE-1 is a unigram recall between a candidate summary (predicted summary) and a reference summary (actual summary). Consider the following candidate and reference summary:

- **Candidate summary** – Machine learning is seen as a subset of artificial intelligence.
- **Reference summary** – Machine Learning is a subset of artificial intelligence.

Now, we can compute ROUGE-1 as follows:

$$\text{Recall} = \frac{\text{Total number of overlapping unigrams}}{\text{Total number of unigrams in the reference summary}}$$

The unigrams in the candidate and reference summary are given as follows:

- **Candidate summary unigrams** – Machine, learning, is, *seen, as,* a, subset, of, artificial, intelligence.
- **Reference summary unigrams** – Machine, Learning, is, a, subset, of, artificial, intelligence.

We can observe that the total number of overlapping unigrams between the candidate and reference summary is 8 and the total number of unigrams in the reference summary is also 8. So, we can compute recall as follows:

$$\text{Recall} = 8/8 = 1$$

Thus, our ROUGE-1 score is 1. Next, we will see how to compute ROUGE-2.

ROUGE-2

ROUGE-2 is a bigram recall between a candidate summary (predicted summary) and a reference summary (actual summary). Let's consider the same candidate and reference summary:

- **Candidate summary** – Machine learning is seen as a subset of artificial intelligence.
- **Reference summary** – Machine Learning is a subset of artificial intelligence.

Now, we can compute ROUGE-2 as follows:

$$\text{Recall} = \frac{\text{Total number of overlapping bigrams}}{\text{Total number of bigrams in the reference summary}}$$

The bigrams in the candidate and reference summary are given as follows:

- **Candidate summary bigrams** – (machine learning), (learning is), **(is seen), (seen as), (as a),** (a subset), (subset of), (of artificial) (artificial intelligence)
- **Reference summary bigrams** – (machine learning), (learning is), (is a), (a subset), (subset of), (of artificial) (artificial intelligence)

We can observe that the total number of overlapping bigrams between the candidate and reference summary is 6 and the total number of bigrams in the reference summary is 7. So, we can compute recall as follows:

$$\text{Recall} = 6/7 = 0.85$$

Thus, our ROUGE-2 score is 0.85. In this manner, we can compute the ROUGE-N score for n-grams. Now that we have understood how ROUGE-N is computed, let's understand how the ROUGE-L metric works in the next section.

Understanding ROUGE-L

ROUGE-L is based on the **longest common subsequence** (**LCS**). The LCS between two sequences is the common subsequence with a maximum length. So, if the candidate and reference summary have an LCS, then we can say that our candidate summary matches the reference summary.

ROUGE-L is calculated using the F-measure. Before looking at the F-measure, let's see how recall and precision are computed for ROUGE-L.

Recall R_{lcs} is computed as the ratio of LCS between the candidate and reference summary to the total number of words in the reference summary:

$$R_{lcs} = \frac{\text{LCS(candidate, reference)}}{\text{Total Number of words in the reference summary}}$$

Precsion P_{lcs} is computed as the ratio of LCS between the candidate and reference summary to the total number of words in the candidate summary:

$$P_{lcs} = \frac{\text{LCS(candidate, reference)}}{\text{Total Number of words in the candidate summary}}$$

Now the F-measure is computed as follows:

$$F_{lcs} = \frac{(1 + b^2)R_{lcs}P_{lcs}}{R_{lcs} + b^2 P_{lcs}}$$

In the preceding equation, b is used for controlling the importance of precision and recall. The preceding F-measure is basically the ROUGE-L score.

We learned how to compute the ROUGE-N and ROUGE-L score. But what is the ROUGE score of our BERTSUM model? Let's find that out in the next section.

The performance of the BERTSUM model

The researchers of BERTSUM have used the CNN/DailyMail news dataset. The CNN/DailyMail dataset consists of news articles along with their highlights. We split the CNN/DailyMail news dataset into train and test sets. We train the model using the train set and evaluate it on the test set.

The following shows the ROUGE score of an extractive summarization task using BERTSUM with a classifier, a transformer, and LSTM. We can observe that BERTSUM with the transformer performs slightly better than the others:

Model	ROUGE-1	ROUGE-2	ROUGE-L
BERT+classifier	43.23	20.22	39.60
BERT+transformer	43.25	20.24	39.63
BERT+LSTM	43.22	20.17	39.59

Figure 6.14 – ROUGE score of an extractive summarization task using BERTSUM

The following shows the ROUGE score of the abstractive summarization task using BERTSUMABS:

Model	ROUGE-1	ROUGE-2	ROUGE-L
BERTSUMABS	41.72	19.39	38.76

Figure 6.15 – ROUGE score of the abstractive summarization task using BERTSUMABS

Thus, we have learned how to fine-tune the BERT model for abstractive and extractive summarization tasks. In the next section, we will see how to train the BERTSUM model.

Training the BERTSUM model

The code for training the BERTSUM model is open-sourced by the researchers of BERTSUM and it is available at `https://github.com/nlpyang/BertSum`. In this section, let's explore this and learn how to train the BERTSUM model. We will train the BERTSUM model on the CNN/DailyMail news dataset. We can also access the complete code from the GitHub repository of the book. In order to run the code smoothly, clone the GitHub repository of the book and run the code using Google Colab.

First, let's install the necessary libraries:

```
!pip install pytorch-pre-trained-bert
!pip install torch==1.1.0 pytorch_transformers tensorboardX multiprocess
pyrouge
!pip install googleDriveFileDownloader
```

If you are working with Google Colab, switch to the content directory with the following code:

```
cd /content/
```

Clone the BERTSUM repository:

```
!git clone https://github.com/nlpyang/BertSum.git
```

Now switch to the bert_data directory:

```
cd /content/BertSum/bert_data/
```

The researchers have also made the preprocessed CNN/DailyMail news dataset available. So, first, let's download it:

```
from googleDriveFileDownloader import googleDriveFileDownloader
gdrive = googleDriveFileDownloader()
gdrive.downloadFile("https://drive.google.com/uc?id=1x0d61LP9UAN389YN00z0Pv
-7jQgirVg6&export=download")
```

Unzip the downloaded dataset:

```
!unzip /content/BertSum/bert_data/bertsum_data.zip
```

Switch to the src directory:

```
cd /content/BertSum/src
```

Now train the BERTSUM model. In the following code, the -encoder classifier argument implies that we are training the BERTSUM model with a classifier:

```
!python train.py -mode train -encoder classifier -dropout 0.1 -
bert_data_path ../bert_data/cnndm -model_path ../models/bert_clas
sifier -lr 2e-3 -visible_gpus 0 -gpu_ranks 0 -world_size 1 -report_every 50
-save_checkpoint_steps 1000 -batch_size 3000 -decay_method noam -
train_steps 50 -accum_count 2 -log_file ../logs/bert_classifier -
use_interval true -warmup_steps 10000
```

That's it. During training, you can see how the ROUGE score changes over a series of epochs. In the next chapter, we will learn how to apply BERT for other languages using multilingual-BERT.

Summary

We started off the chapter by understanding what text summarization is. We learned that there are two types of text summarization tasks – one is extractive summarization and the other is abstractive summarization. In extractive summarization, we create a summary from a given text by just extracting only the important sentences. Unlike extractive summarization, in abstractive summarization, we will not create a summary by just extracting important sentences from the given text. Instead, in this type, we create a summary by paraphrasing the given text.

Next, we learned how to fine-tune BERT to perform the summarization task. We learned how BERTSUM works and how it used for summarization tasks. After understanding BERTSUM, we learned how to use BERTSUM with a classifier, with a transformer, and with LSTM for an extractive summarization task.

Later, we learned how to perform abstractive summarization using BERTSUM. For abstractive summarization, we used a transformer architecture with pre-trained BERTSUM as an encoder, but the decoder was randomly initialized. We also understood how we use different learning rates for the encoder and decoder.

Moving on, we learned how to evaluate a summarization task with the ROUGE measure. We learned about two popular ROUGE metrics called ROUGE-N and ROUGE-L. ROUGE-N is an n-gram recall between a candidate summary (predicted summary) and a reference summary (actual summary), whereas ROUGE-L is based on the longest common subsequence. The longest common subsequence between two sequences is the common subsequence with a maximum length.

At the end of the chapter, we learned how to train the BERTSUM model. In the next chapter, we will learn how to apply BERT to other languages using multilingual-BERT.

Questions

Let's evaluate our understanding of BERTSUM. Try answering the following questions:

1. What is the difference between extractive and abstractive summarization tasks?
2. What is interval segment embedding?
3. How is abstractive summarization performed with BERT?
4. What is ROUGE?
5. What is ROUGE-N?
6. Define recall in ROUGE-N.
7. Define the ROUGE-L metric.

Further reading

For more information, refer to the following papers:

- *Fine-tune BERT for Extractive Summarization* by Yang Liu, available at https://arxiv.org/pdf/1903.10318.pdf
- *Text Summarization with pre-trained Encoders* by Yang Liu and Mirella Lapata, available at https://arxiv.org/pdf/1908.08345.pdf
- *ROUGE: A Package for Automatic Evaluation of Summaries* by Chin-Yew Lin, available at https://www.aclweb.org/anthology/W04-1013.pdf

Applying BERT to Other Languages

7

In previous chapters, we learned how BERT works and we also explored its different variants. Hitherto, however, we have only applied BERT to the English language. Can we also apply BERT to other languages? The answer to this question is yes, and that's precisely what we will learn in this chapter. We will use **multilingual BERT (M-BERT)** to compute the representation of different languages other than English. We will begin the chapter by understanding how M-BERT works and how to use it.

Next, we will understand how multilingual the M-BERT model is by investigating it in detail. Following this, we will learn about the XLM model. XLM stands for the cross-lingual language model, which is used to obtain cross-lingual representations. We will understand how XLM works and how it differs from M-BERT in detail.

Following on from this, we will learn about XLM-R, which is the XLM-RoBERTa model. XLM-R is the state-of-the-art, cross-lingual model. We will explore how XLM-R works and how it differs from XLM. At the end of the chapter, we will look at some of the pre-trained monolingual BERT models for languages including French, Spanish, Dutch, German, Chinese, Japanese, Finnish, Italian, Portuguese, and Russian.

In this chapter, we will cover the following topics:

- Understanding multilingual BERT
- How multilingual is multilingual BERT?
- The cross-lingual language model
- Understanding XLM-R
- Language-specific BERT

Understanding multilingual BERT

BERT provides representation for only English text. Let's suppose we have an input text in a different language, say, French. Now, how we can use BERT to obtain a representation of the French text? Here is where we use M-BERT.

Multilingual BERT, referred to hereinafter as M-BERT, is used to obtain representations of text in different languages and not just English. We learned that the BERT model is trained with **masked language modeling** (**MLM**) and **next sentence prediction** (**NSP**) tasks using the English Wikipedia text and the Toronto BookCorpus. Similar to BERT, M-BERT is also trained with MLM and NSP tasks, but instead of using the Wikipedia text of only English language, M-BERT is trained using the Wikipedia text of 104 different languages.

But the question is, the size of the Wikipedia text for some languages would be higher than others right? Yes! The size of Wikipedia text would be large for high-resource languages, such as English, compared to low-resource languages, such as Swahili. If we train our model with this dataset, then this will lead to the problem of overfitting. To avoid overfitting, we use sampling methods. We apply undersampling for high-resource languages, and oversampling for low-resource languages.

Since M-BERT is trained using Wikipedia text of 104 different languages, it learns the general syntactic structure of different languages. M-BERT consists of a 110K shared WordPiece vocabulary across all 104 languages.

M-BERT understands the context from different languages without any paired or language-aligned training data. It is important to note that we have not trained M-BERT with any cross-lingual objective; it has been trained just like how we trained the BERT model. M-BERT produces a representation that generalizes across multiple languages for downstream tasks.

The pre-trained M-BERT model is open sourced by Google and can be downloaded from the following link: `https://github.com/google-research/bert/blob/master/multilingual.md`. The various configurations of pre-trained M-BERT models provided by Google are provided here:

- BERT-base, multilingual cased
- BERT-base, multilingual uncased

Both of the preceding models consist of 12 encoder layers, 12 attention heads, and a hidden size of 768. It consists of a total of 110 million parameters.

The pre-trained M-BERT is also compatible with the Hugging Face's transformers library. So, we can use it with the transformers library in precisely the same way as we use BERT. Let's now see how to use the pre-trained M-BERT model and obtain sentence representation:

First, let's import the necessary modules:

```
from transformers import BertTokenizer, BertModel
```

Download and load the pre-trained M-BERT model:

```
model = BertModel.from_pretrained('bert-base-multilingual-cased')
```

Now, download and load the pre-trained M-BERT model's tokenizer:

```
tokenizer = BertTokenizer.from_pretrained('bert-base-multilingual-cased')
```

Define the input sentence. Let's provide a French sentence as input:

```
sentence = "C'est une si belle journée"
```

Tokenize the sentence and get the tokens:

```
inputs = tokenizer(sentence, return_tensors="pt")
```

Feed the tokens to the model and get the representation:

```
hidden_rep, cls_head = model(**inputs)
```

`hidden_rep` contains the representation of all the tokens in our sentence, and `cls_head` contains the representation of the [CLS] token, which holds the aggregate representation of the sentence. In this way, we can use the pre-trained M-BERT model in the same way as other BERT models. Now that we understand how M-BERT works, in the next section, we will evaluate them.

Evaluating M-BERT on the NLI task

Let's evaluate M-BERT by fine-tuning it on the **natural language inference** (**NLI**) task. We know that in the NLI task, the goal of our model is to determine whether a hypothesis is an entailment (true), a contradiction (false), or undetermined (neutral) given a premise. Thus, we feed a sentence pair (premise-hypothesis pair) to the model and it has to classify whether the sentence pair (premise-hypothesis pair) belongs to entailment, contradiction, or is an undetermined class.

Okay, what dataset can we use for this task? For the NLI task, we generally use the **Stanford Natural Language Inference** (**SNLI**) dataset. But since we are evaluating M-BERT in this instance, we use a different dataset, called **cross-lingual NLI** (**XNLI**). The XNLI dataset is based on a MultiNLI dataset. So, first, let's take a look at the MultiNLI dataset.

MultiNLI stands for **Multi-Genre Natural Language Inference** and is a corpus similar to SNLI. It consists of premise-hypothesis pairs across various genres. A sample of the MultiNLI dataset is shown in the following diagram. As we can observe, we have a genre, along with the premise-hypothesis pair and the corresponding label:

Genre	Premise	Hypothesis	Label
Letters	Will you add your dreams to ours?	Will you help us build the best school in the nation?	Neutral
911	For the rescue efforts, see FDNY report,Report from the Chief of Department, Anthony L. Fusco, in Manning,ed	Anthony L. Fusco, the Chief of Department, wrote a report on the rescue efforts.	Entailment
Fiction	That was in Bridgetown on the night of the Spanish raid.	There was never a raid on Bridgetown.	Contradiction
Travel	Just a few blocks in back of the malecen are a growing collection of unique clubs with a more urban edge.	The collection is growing, but not as fast as it did last year.	Neutral
Verbatim	Serious crime down, but murders increase.	There has been a rise in murders.	Entailment

Figure 7.1 – MLNI dataset

Now let's see how the XNLI dataset is based on the MultiNLI dataset. The XNLI dataset is an extension of the MultiNLI dataset. The XNLI training set consists of 433K English sentence pairs (premise-hypothesis pairs) from the MultiNLI corpus.

To create an evaluation set, we use 7,500 sentence pairs. We take 7,500 sentence pairs (premise-hypothesis pairs) and translate them into 15 different languages. Thus, our evaluation set consists of 7,500 x 15 = 112,500 sentence pairs in 15 different languages. Hence, to summarize, in the XNLI dataset, the training set consists of 433K sentence pairs in just the English language, while the evaluation set consists of 112.5K sentence pairs in 15 different languages:

Training set: 433K English sentence pairs

Evaluation set: 112.5k sentence pairs in 15 languages

The following table shows a few data points from the XNLI dataset:

Language	Genre	Premise	Hypothesis	Label
English	Travel	Kuala Perlis, south of the state capital, Kangar, is the departure point for the less than an hour's ferry journey to Langkawi.	Kuala Perlis was 17 miles south.	Neutral
Swedish	Face to face conversation	Sikujua nini nilichoendea au kitu chochote, hivyo ilikuwa na ni ripoti mahali paliopangwa huko Washington.	Sikuwa na hakika kabisa nilichokuwa nikienda kufanya hivyo nilikwenda Washington ambako nilipewa kazi ya kuripoti.	Entailment
Russian	911	Не было намеков на внутреннюю угрозу.	У нас были веские основания подозревать, что сигналы о терроре будут подняты в ближайшее время.	Contradiction
French	Fiction	Il fit appel à Lord Julian.	Il voulut demander à Lord Julian d'épargner sa femme.	Neutral
Vietnamaese	Letters	Đầu tư của bạn tiếp tục đạt chất lượng cao về tất cả khía cạnh của Museum và tạo ra những thành tựu mới có thể.	Đầu tư không ảnh hưởng đến Bảo tàng theo bất kỳ cách nào.	Contradiction

Figure 7.2 – XNLI dataset

Now that we understand the XNLI dataset, let's see how to evaluate M-BERT using the XNLI dataset. To evaluate M-BERT, we fine-tune M-BERT on the NLI task using the XNLI dataset in various settings. Let's explore each of these in turn.

Zero-shot

In this type, we fine-tune M-BERT for the NLI task on the English training set and then we evaluate the model on each language in the test set. It is called zero-shot because our model is only fine-tuned on the English language, but tested on other languages present in the test set. This helps us to understand the cross-lingual ability of M-BERT. In this type, we perform the following actions:

Fine-tuning: On the English training set

Evaluation: On all languages in the test set

If the zero-shot knowledge transfer is due to vocabulary overlap, then we can say that M-BERT accuracy for zero-shot transfer is highly dependent on languages that have a high vocabulary overlap. Let's conduct a small experiment to see whether the zero-shot transfer is due to the vocabulary overlap.

Let's suppose we are performing an NER task. Let's say we are fine-tuning M-BERT in one language and evaluating it in a different language. Let E_{train} denote the WordPiece tokens in the fine-tuning language, and E_{eval} denote the WordPiece tokens in the evaluation language. Then we can compute the WordPiece tokens that overlap between the fine-tuning and evaluation language as follows:

$$\text{overlap} = \frac{|E_{train} \cap E_{eval}|}{|E_{train} \cup E_{eval}|}$$

Suppose we have an NER dataset with 16 languages. First, we take the M-BERT model, fine-tune it for the NER task in one language, and then we evaluate this fine-tuned model in a different language and get the F1 score. Let's call this score a zero-shot F1 score. We compute the zero-shot F1 score between every language pair in our 16 languages.

The following plot shows the zero-shot F1 score between every language pair against the average vocabulary overlap. We can observe that the zero-shot F1 score is independent of the vocabulary overlap. That is, we can observe that we have a high zero-shot F1 score even when there is low vocabulary overlap:

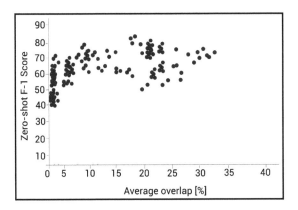

Figure 7.4 – Zero-shot F-1 score versus average overlap

We can conclude that zero-shot knowledge transfer in M-BERT is not dependent on the vocabulary overlap. That is, the vocabulary overlap has no effect on the zero-shot knowledge transfer in M-BERT. Thus, we can say that M-BERT is able to generalize well in relation to other languages, indicating that it learns multilingual representation deeper than simply memorizing vocabulary.

Generalization across scripts

In this section, let's investigate whether the M-BERT model can generalize across languages that are written in different scripts. Let's conduct a small experiment to understand this. Say we are performing a POS tagging task. First, we fine-tune M-BERT for the POS tagging task in the Urdu language. Then, we evaluate the fine-tuned M-BERT model in a different language, say Hindi. Note that Urdu follows Arabic script, while Hindi follows Devanagari script. A simple example of Urdu and Hindi text is given here:

Urdu: آپ کا نام کیا ہے

Hindi: आपका नाम क्या है

From the preceding example, we can observe that Urdu and Hindi follow different scripts. Surprisingly, the M-BERT model fine-tuned for the POS-tagging task on the Urdu text achieves 91.1% evaluation accuracy on the Hindi text. This indicates that M-BERT has mapped the Urdu annotations to the Hindi words. This helps us to understand that the M-BERT model can generalize across different scripts.

However, our M-BERT model does not generalize well across scripts for language pairs such as English-Japanese. This is mainly due to the effect of typological similarity. We will explore the effect of typological similarity in detail in the next section. We can conclude that M-BERT generalizes well across scripts for some language pairs, but not all.

Generalization across typological features

In this section, let's investigate how well the M-BERT model generalizes across the typological features. We fine-tune M-BERT to perform POS tagging in the English language and we evaluate the fine-tuned model in Japanese. In this case, our accuracy will be less because English and Japanese have different orders of subject, verb, and object. But if we evaluate our fine-tuned M-BERT model on the Bulgarian language, then the level of accuracy will be high. This is because English and Bulgarian have the same order of subject, verb, and object. Thus, the word orders are important for multilingual knowledge transfer.

The following table shows the accuracy of the POS tagging task using the M-BERT model. The row represents the fine-tuning language, and the column represents the evaluation language. For instance, we can observe that the accuracy of the model fine-tuned on English and evaluated on Bulgarian is 87.1 %, while the accuracy of the model fine-tuned on English and evaluated on Japanese is only 49.4%:

		Evaluation language		
		EN	BG	JA
Fine-tuning language	EN	96.8	87.1	49.4
	BG	82.2	98.9	51.6
	JA	57.4	67.2	96.5

Figure 7.5 – Accuracy of the POS tagging task

We can observe that zero-shot transfer in M-BERT works better across languages that have the same word order compared with languages that have a different word order. Thus, we can conclude that the generalizability of our M-BERT model depends on the typological similarity between the languages. This indicates that M-BERT does not learn systematic transformations.

Effect of language similarity

In this section, let's explore how language similarity affects the zero-shot transfer in M-BERT. It is observed that zero-shot transfer in M-BERT performs well when the linguistic structures are similar between the fine-tuning and evaluation languages. Let's understand this with the help of an example. The **World Atlas of Language Structures**, referred to hereinafter as **WALS**, is a large database comprising the structural properties of languages, such as grammatical, lexical, and phonological properties.

Let's make a plot of zero-shot transfer accuracy against the number of common WALS features between fine-tuning and evaluation languages. From the following graph, we can observe that zero-shot accuracy is high when the number of common WALS features is high between fine-tuning and evaluation languages, but it is low when the number of common WALS features is high:

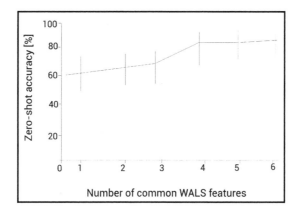

Figure 7.6 – Zero-shot accuracy versus the number of common WALS features

Thus, we can conclude that M-BERT can generalize well across languages that share similar linguistic structures.

Effect of code switching and transliteration

In this section, let's investigate how M-BERT handles code switching and transliteration. Before moving on, let's understand what code switching and transliteration are.

Code switching

Mixing, or alternating different languages in a conversation, is called code switching. For instance, let's consider the following English sentence:

"Nowadays, I'm a little busy with work."

Instead of uttering the sentence just in English, let's incorporate some Hindi words in between. Hence, the sentence becomes the following:

"आजकल I'm थोड़ा busy with work."

As we can observe in the preceding sentence, the words *nowadays* and *little* are uttered in Hindi. This is an example of code switched text.

Transliteration

In transliteration, instead of writing a text in the source language script, we use the target language script. Let's understand transliteration with the help of an example. Consider the following code switched text we saw in the previous section:

"आजकल I'm थोड़ा busy with work."

Now, instead of writing the preceding sentence in both Hindi and English, we also write the Hindi words in English. That is, we write how the Hindi words are pronounced in the English script. So, now our sentence becomes the following:

"Aajkal I'm thoda busy with work."

The preceding text is an example of transliterated and code switched text. Now that we understand what code switching and transliteration are, in the next section, let's see how M-BERT handles them.

M-BERT on code switching and transliteration

Let's understand how M-BERT performs in the code switched and transliterated text with the help of an example. In this section, we use the code switched Hindi/English UD corpus (https://universaldependencies.org/).

The dataset consists of text in two formats:

- Transliterated: Here, the Hindi text is written in Latin script. Here is an example: "Aajkal I'm thoda busy with work."
- Code switched: Here, the Hindi text from Latin is converted and rewritten in Devanagari script. Here is an example: "आजकल I'm थोड़ा busy with work."

First, let's see how M-BERT handles the transliterated text. Let's fine-tune M-BERT for the POS tagging task on the transliterated HI/EN corpus and also on the monolingual HI +EN corpus. First, we fine-tune directly on the transliterated corpus and see how the accuracy changes when we fine-tune M-BERT on the monolingual HI +EN corpus. The accuracy is shown in the following table. We can observe that when we fine-tune M-BERT directly on the transliterated corpus, we achieve 85.64% accuracy, but when fine-tuned on the monolingual HI +EN corpus, the accuracy is greatly reduced to 50.41%. Since the level of accuracy was reduced significantly, we can deduce that M-BERT is unable to handle the transliterated text:

Corpus	Accuracy
Transliterated	85.64
Monolingual	50.41

Figure 7.7 – Accuracy in terms of the POS task

Now, let's see how M-BERT handles code switching. Let's fine-tune M-BERT for the POS tagging task on the code switched HI/EN corpus and also on the monolingual HI +EN corpus. First, we fine-tune directly on the code switched corpus and see how the accuracy changes when we fine-tune M-BERT on the monolingual HI +EN corpus. The accuracy is shown in the following table. We can observe that when we fine-tune M-BERT directly on the code switched corpus, we achieve 90.56% accuracy, and when fine-tuned on the monolingual corpus, the accuracy is 86.59%. Since the accuracy is not reduced much, we can deduce that M-BERT can handle the code switched text:

Corpus	Accuracy
Code-switched	90.56
Monolingual	86.59

Figure 7.8 – Accuracy in terms of the POS task

We can conclude that M-BERT performs well on code switched text compared with transliterated text.

Thus, in this section, we investigated the multilingual ability of the M-BERT model. We learned the following:

- M-BERT's generalizability does not depend on the vocabulary overlap.
- M-BERT's generalizability depends on typological and language similarity.
- M-BERT can handle code switched text but not transliterated text.

Now that we have learned how M-BERT works and about its multilingual ability, in the next section, we will learn about another interesting model, known as a cross-lingual language model.

The cross-lingual language model

In the previous sections, we learned how M-BERT works and we also investigated how multilingual M-BERT is. We understood that the M-BERT model is pre-trained just like the regular BERT model, without any specific cross-lingual objective. In this section, let's learn how to pre-train BERT with a cross-lingual objective. We refer to BERT trained with a cross-lingual objective as a **cross-lingual language model** (**XLM**). The XLM model performs better than M-BERT and it learns cross-lingual representations.

The XLM model is pre-trained using the monolingual and parallel datasets. The parallel dataset consists of text in a language pair, that is, it consists of the same text in two different languages. Say we have an English sentence, and then we will have a corresponding sentence in another language, French, for example. We can call this parallel dataset a cross-lingual dataset.

The monolingual dataset is obtained from Wikipedia, and the parallel dataset is obtained from several sources, including MultiUN (a multilingual corpus from United Nations documents), OPUS (the open parallel corpus), and the IIT Bombay corpus. XLM uses **byte pair encoding** (**BPE**) and creates shared vocabulary across all languages.

Pre-training strategies

The XLM model is pre-trained using the following tasks:

- Causal language modeling
- Masked language modeling
- Translation language modeling

Let's take a look at how each of the preceding tasks works.

Causal language modeling

Causal language modeling (**CLM**) is the simplest pre-training method. In CLM, the goal of our model is to predict the probability of a word given the previous set of words. It is represented as $P(w_t|w_1, w_2, \ldots, w_{t-1}; \theta)$.

Masked language modeling

We know that in the **masked language modeling** (**MLM**) task, we randomly mask 15% of the tokens and train the model to predict the masked tokens. We mask 15% of tokens with the 80-10-10% rule:

- For 80% of the time, we replace a token (word) with a [MASK] token.
- For 10% of the time, we replace a token with a random token (random word).
- For 10% of the time, we leave the tokens unchanged.

We train the XLM model using the MLM task, just like how we trained the BERT model, but with the following two variations:

1. We learned that in BERT, we take a sentence pair and randomly mask a few tokens in the sentence pair, and then feed the sentence pair as an input. But in XLM, we don't have to feed just the sentence pair. Instead, we can feed an arbitrary number of sentences to the model. We keep the total token length to 256.
2. To balance the frequent and rare words, we sample tokens according to a multinomial distribution whose weights are proportional to the square root of their inverse frequencies.

The following diagram shows the XLM model with the MLM objective. We can observe that, unlike BERT, where we feed only a sentence pair, here we are feeding an arbitrary number of sentences separated by a special token, [/s]. We can also observe that along with token and positional embeddings, here we have language embeddings. Language embeddings are used to represent a language:

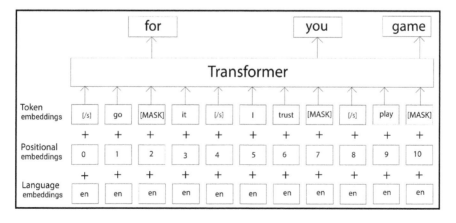

Figure 7.9 – Masked language modeling

As shown in the preceding diagram, we mask 15% of tokens and train the model to predict the masked token. Next, let's look at another task, known as translation language modeling.

Translation language modeling

Translation language modeling (**TLM**) is another interesting pre-training strategy. In CLM and MLM, we train our model on monolingual data, but in TLM, we train the model on cross-lingual data, that is, the parallel data that consists of the same text in two different languages.

The TLM method works just like MLM we saw in the previous section. Similar to MLM, here, we train the model to predict the masked word. However, instead of feeding an arbitrary number of sentences, we feed the parallel sentence for learning the cross-lingual representation.

The following diagram shows the XLM model with the TLM objective. As shown in the following diagram, we feed a parallel sentence as an input, that is, the same text in two different languages. In this example, we are feeding the English sentence "I am a student" along with its French equivalent, "Je suis étudiant". We randomly mask a few words in both English and French sentences and feed it to the model, as shown in the following diagram:

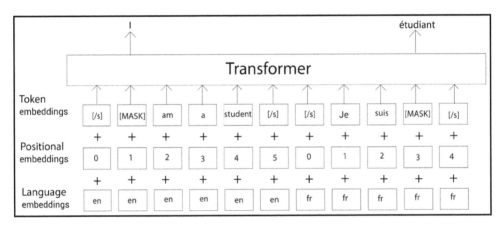

Figure 7.10 – Translation language modeling

We train the model to predict the masked token. The model learns to predict the masked token by understanding the context from nearby tokens. Say the model is learning to predict the masked token (word) in an English sentence, then it can not only use the context of the tokens (words) in the English sentence, but it can also use the context of the tokens (words) in the French sentence. This enables the model to align the cross-lingual representation.

We can also observe from the preceding diagram that language embedding is used to represent different languages and we can observe that we use separate positional embedding for both the sentences.

We learned that in XLM, we use three pre-training strategies – CLM, MLM, and TLM. But how exactly do we pre-train the XLM model? Should we use all of these strategies or should we train the model with just one? Let's find out the answer to this question in the next section.

Pre-training the XLM model

We pre-train the XLM model in the following ways:

- Using the CLM task
- Using the MLM task
- Using the MLM task combined with the TLM task

If we train the XLM using CLM or MLM, then we use the monolingual dataset for training. We use an arbitrary number of sentences with a total of 256 tokens. For the TLM task, we use a parallel dataset. If we use MLM and TLM tasks for training the model, we alternate the MLM and TLM objectives.

After pre-training, we can use the pre-trained XLM model directly or fine-tune it on downstream tasks, just like the BERT model. In the next section, let's look at the performance of the XLM model.

Evaluation of XLM

The researchers of XLM have evaluated the XLM model on the cross-lingual classification task. They fine-tuned the XLM model on the English NLI dataset and evaluated it on the 15 different XNLI languages. The results (test accuracy) of the cross-lingual classification task are shown in the following table. The XLM (MLM) indicates the XLM model trained using only the MLM task on the monolingual data, whereas XLM (MLM + TLM) indicates that the XLM model is trained using both MLM and TLM tasks. Δ denotes the average. We can observe that on average, our XLM (MLM+TLM) model achieves 75.1% accuracy:

Model	en	fr	es	de	el	bg	ru	tr	ar	vi	th	zh	hi	sw	ur	Δ
XLM(MLM)	83.2	76.5	76.3	74.2	73.1	74.0	73.1	67.8	68.5	71.2	69.2	71.9	65.7	64.6	63.4	71.5
XLM (MLM+TLM)	85.0	78.7	78.9	77.8	76.6	77.4	75.3	72.5	73.1	76.1	73.2	76.5	69.6	68.4	67.3	75.1

Figure 7.11 – Evaluation of XLM

The researchers also tested the XLM model in the TRANSLATE-TRAIN and TRANSLATE-TEST settings, as shown in the following table. We can observe that the XLM model performs better than the M-BERT model:

Model	en	fr	es	de	el	bg	ru	tr	ar	vi	th	zh	hi	sw	ur	Δ
TRANSLATE-TRAIN																
M-BERT	81.9	-	77.8	75.9	-	-	-	-	70.7	-	-	76.6	-	-	61.6	-
XLM(MLM+TLM)	85.0	80.2	80.8	80.3	78.1	79.3	78.1	74.7	76.5	76.6	75.5	78.6	72.3	70.9	63.2	76.7
TRANSLATE-TEST																
M-BERT	81.4	-	74.9	74.4	-	-	-	-	70.4	-	-	70.1	-	-	62.1	-
XLM(MLM+TLM)	85.0	79.0	79.5	78.1	77.8	77.6	75.5	73.7	73.7	70.8	70.4	73.6	69.0	64.7	65.1	74.2

Figure 7.12 – Evaluation of XLM

We can use the pre-trained XLM model with the transformers library, just like how we used the BERT model. We can view all the available pre-trained XLM models from here: `https:/ /huggingface.co/transformers/multilingual.html`.

Now that we have learned how the XLM model works, in the next section, let's look at another interesting cross-lingual model, called XLM-R.

Understanding XLM-R

The XLM-R model is basically an extension of XLM with a few modifications to improve performance. **XLM-R** is the **XLM-RoBERTa** model and represents the state of the art for learning cross-lingual representation. In the previous section, we learned how XLM works. We learned that XLM is trained with MLM and TLM tasks. The MLM task uses the monolingual dataset, and the TLM task uses the parallel dataset. However, obtaining this parallel dataset is difficult for low-resource languages. So, in the XLM-R model, we train the model only with the MLM objective and we don't use the TLM objective. Thus, the XLM-R model requires only a monolingual dataset.

XLM-R is trained on a huge dataset whose size is 2.5 TB. The dataset is obtained by filtering the unlabeled text of 100 languages from the CommonCrawl dataset. We also increase the proportion of small languages in our dataset through sampling. The following diagram provides a comparison of the corpus size of the CommonCrawl and Wikipedia datasets. We can observe that CommonCrawl has a large data size compared to Wikipedia, especially for low-resource languages:

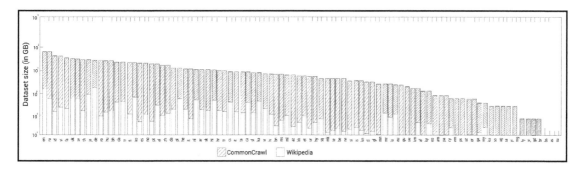

Figure 7.13 – Comparing the CommonCrawl and Wikipedia dataset sizes across languages

We use the CommonCrawl dataset for training the XLM-R model and it is trained with the MLM task. The XLM uses a SentencePiece tokenizer (https://github.com/google/sentencepiece) and it consists of a vocabulary of 250, 000 tokens.

The XLM-R model is trained with the following two different configurations:

- **XLM-R$_{base}$** with 12 encoder layers, 12 attention heads, and a hidden size of 768
- **XLM-R** with 24 encoder layers, 16 attention heads, and a hidden size of 1,024

After pre-training, we can fine-tune the XLM-R model for the downstream tasks, just like XLM. XLM-R performs better than both the M-BERT and XLM models. The researchers of XLM-R evaluated the XLM-R model on the cross-lingual classification task. They fine-tuned the XLM-R model on the English NLI dataset and evaluated it on the 15 different XNLI languages. The results (test accuracy) of the cross-lingual classification task are shown in the following table:

Model	D	#M	#lg	en	fr	es	de	el	bg	ru	tr	ar	vi	th	zh	hi	sw	ur	Avg
M-BERT	Wiki	N	102	82.1	73.8	74.3	71.1	66.4	68.9	69.0	61.6	64.9	69.5	55.8	69.3	60.0	50.4	58.0	66.3
XLM(MLM+TLM)	Wiki+MT	N	15	85.0	78.7	78.9	77.8	76.6	77.4	75.3	72.5	73.1	76.1	73.2	76.5	69.6	68.4	67.4	75.1
XLM-R	CC	1	100	89.1	84.1	85.1	83.9	82.9	84.0	81.2	79.6	79.8	80.8	78.1	80.2	76.9	73.9	73.8	80.9

Figure 7.14 – Evaluation of XLM-R

In the preceding table, **D** denotes the dataset used, and **#lg** denotes the number of languages that the model was pre-trained on. We can observe that our XLM-R performs better than both the M-BERT and XLM models.

For instance, we can observe that the accuracy of M-BERT on the Swedish (sw) language is only 50.4%, but XLM-R has attained 73.9. We can also observe that the average accuracy of our model is 80.9%, which is comparatively higher than other models.

Researchers have also evaluated the performance of XLM-R in the TRANSLATE-TEST, TRANSLATE-TRAIN, and TRANSLATE-TRAIN-ALL settings, as shown in the following table. We can observe that XLM-R performs better than both the XLM (MLM) and XLM (MLM+TLM) models:

Model	D	#M	#lg	en	fr	es	de	el	bg	ru	tr	ar	vi	th	zh	hi	sw	ur	avg
TRANSLATE-TEST																			
BERT-en	Wiki	1	1	88.8	81.4	82.3	80.1	80.3	80.9	76.2	76.0	75.4	72.0	71.9	75.6	70.0	65.8	65.8	76.2
RoBERTa	Wiki+CC	1	1	91.3	82.9	84.3	81.2	81.7	83.1	78.3	76.8	76.6	74.2	74.1	77.5	70.9	66.7	66.8	77.8
TRANSLATE-TRAIN																			
XLM(MLM)	Wiki	N	100	82.9	77.6	77.9	77.9	77.1	75.7	75.5	72.6	71.2	75.8	73.1	76.2	70.4	66.5	62.4	74.2
TRANSLATE-TRAIN-ALL																			
XLM(MLM+TLM)	Wiki+MT	1	15	85.0	80.8	81.3	80.3	79.1	80.9	78.3	75.6	77.6	78.5	76.0	79.5	72.9	72.8	68.5	77.8
XLM(MLM)	Wiki	1	100	84.5	80.1	81.3	79.3	78.6	79.4	77.5	75.2	75.6	78.3	75.7	78.3	72.1	69.2	67.7	76.9
XLM-R$_{Base}$	CC	1	100	85.4	81.4	82.2	80.3	80.4	81.3	79.7	78.6	77.3	79.7	77.9	80.2	76.1	73.1	73.0	79.1
XLM-R	CC	1	100	89.1	85.1	86.6	85.7	85.3	85.9	83.5	83.2	83.1	83.7	81.5	83.7	81.6	78.0	78.1	83.6

Figure 7.15 – Evaluation of XLM-R

We have learned about several interesting models, including M-BERT, XLM, and XLM-R, which are used for multilingual and cross-lingual knowledge transfer. In the next section, we will learn about several interesting language-specific BERT models.

Language-specific BERT

In the previous sections, we learned how M-BERT works. We learned how M-BERT is used in many different languages. However, instead of having a single M-BERT model for many languages, can we train a monolingual BERT for a specific target language? We can, and that is precisely what we will learn in this section. We will look into several interesting and popular monolingual BERT models for various languages, as indicated here:

- FlauBERT for French
- BETO for Spanish
- BERTje for Dutch
- German BERT
- Chinese BERT
- Japanese BERT
- FinBERT for Finnish
- UmBERTo for Italian
- BERTimbay for Portuguese
- RuBERT for Russian

FlauBERT for French

FlauBERT, which stands for **French Language Understanding via BERT**, is a pre-trained BERT model for the French language. The FlauBERT model performs better than the multilingual and cross-lingual models on many downstream French NLP tasks.

FlauBERT is trained on a huge heterogeneous French corpus. The French corpus consists of 24 sub-corpora containing data from various sources, including Wikipedia, books, internal crawling, WMT19 data, French text from OPUS (an open source parallel corpus), and Wikimedia.

First, we preprocess and tokenize the data using a tokenizer called a **Moses tokenizer**. The Moses tokenizer preserves special tokens, including URLs, dates, and more. After preprocessing and tokenizing, we use BPE and create a vocabulary. FlauBERT consists of a vocabulary of 50,000 tokens.

FlauBERT is trained only on the MLM task and, while masking tokens, we use dynamic masking instead of static masking. Similar to BERT, FlauBERT is available in various configurations. FlauBERT-base and FlauBERT-large are the commonly used ones. The pre-trained FlauBERT model is open sourced and can be downloaded from here: `https://github.com/getalp/Flaubert`. The different configurations of the FlauBERT model are shown in the following table:

Model name	Number of layers	Attention heads	Embedding Dimensions	Total parameters
flaubert-small-cased	6	8	512	54 M
flaubert-base-uncased	12	12	768	137 M
flaubert-base-cased	12	12	768	138 M
flaubert-large-cased	24	16	1024	373 M

Figure 7.16 – Different configurations of FlauBERT

We can download the pre-trained FlauBERT model and fine-tune it on the downstream tasks, just like BERT. FlauBERT is also available in the Hugging Face's transformers library, so we can use FlauBERT directly from the transformers library. Now, let's see how to use FlauBERT and obtain a representation of a French sentence.

Getting a representation of a French sentence with FlauBERT

Let's explore how to use the pre-trained FlauBERT to obtain a French sentence representation. First, let's import `FlaubertTokenizer, FlaubertModel` from Transformers, and also the Torch library:

```
from transformers import FlaubertTokenizer, FlaubertModel
import torch
```

Let's download and load the pre-trained `flaubert_base_cased` model:

```
model = FlaubertModel.from_pretrained('flaubert/flaubert_base_cased')
```

Next, we download and load the tokenizer that was used for pre-training the `flaubert_base_cased` model:

```
tokenizer = \
FlaubertTokenizer.from_pretrained('flaubert/flaubert_base_cased')
```

Now, let's define the input sentence for which we want to compute the embedding:

```
sentence = "Paris est ma ville préférée"
```

Next, we tokenize the sentence and get the token IDs:

```
token_ids = tokenizer.encode(sentence)
```

Then, we convert the token IDs to torch tensors:

```
token_ids = torch.tensor(token_ids).unsqueeze(0)
```

We then obtain the representation of each token in our sentence using the pre-trained `flaubert_base_cased` model:

```
representation = model(token_ids)[0]
```

Let's now check the shape of the representation:

```
representation.shape
```

The preceding code prints the following:

```
torch.Size([1, 7, 768])
```

As we can observe, our representation size is [1, 7, 768], including the [CLS] and [SEP] tokens. We learned that the [CLS] token holds the aggregate representation of a sentence, so we get the representation of the [CLS] token and use it as the sentence representation:

```
cls_rep = representation[:, 0, :]
```

That's it. In this way, we use the pre-trained FlauBERT and obtain the representation for the French text. We can also use the pre-trained FlauBERT model and fine-tune it for any downstream tasks.

French Language Understanding Evaluation

The researchers of FlauBERT have also introduced a new unified evaluation benchmark for downstream tasks, called **FLUE**, which stands for French Language Understanding Evaluation. FLUE is similar to the GLUE benchmark for the French language.

The dataset in FLUE includes the following:

- CLS-FR
- PAWS-X-FR
- XNLI-FR
- French Treebank
- FrenchSemEval

Now that we have learned how to use the FlauBERT to obtain representation for the French language, in the next section, let's look into BETO.

BETO for Spanish

BETO is the pre-trained BERT model for the Spanish language from the Universidad de Chile. It is trained using the MLM task with WWM. The configuration of BETO is the same as the standard BERT-base model. The researchers of BETO provided two variants of the BETO model, called BETO-cased and BETO-uncased, for cased and uncased text, respectively.

The pre-trained BETO is open sourced, so we can download it directly and use it for downstream tasks. Researchers have also shown that the performance of BETO is better than M-BERT for many downstream tasks, as indicated here:

Task	BETO-cased	BETO-uncased
POS	98.97	98.44
NER-C	88.43	82.67
MLDoc	95.60	96.12
PAWS-X	89.05	89.55
XNLI	82.01	80.15

Figure 7.17 – Performance of BETO

In the preceding table, the **POS** task means **part-of-speech** tagging, NER-C is the **named entity recognition** (**NER**) task, MLDoc is the document classification task, PAWS-X is the paraphrasing task, and XNLI is the cross-lingual natural language inference task.

The pre-trained BETO models can be downloaded from here: `https://github.com/dccuchile/beto`. We can also use the pre-trained BETO models directly from the Hugging Face's transformers library, as shown here:

```
tokenizer = \
BertTokenizer.from_pretrained('dccuchile/bert-base-spanish-wwm-uncased')
model = \
BertModel.from_pretrained('dccuchile/bert-base-spanish-wwm-uncased')
```

Next, let's learn to predict masked words using BETO.

Predicting masked words using BETO

In this section, we will learn how to use the pre-trained BETO model and predict masked words in a Spanish text.

Let's use the `transformers pipeline` API:

```
from transformers import pipeline
```

First, we define our masked word prediction pipeline. To the pipeline API, we pass the task that we want to perform, the pre-trained model, and the tokenizer as arguments. As shown in the following code, we are using the `dccuchile/bert-base-spanish-wwm-uncased` model, which is the pre-trained BETO model:

```
predict_mask = pipeline(
    "fill-mask",
    model= "dccuchile/bert-base-spanish-wwm-uncased",
    tokenizer="dccuchile/bert-base-spanish-wwm-uncased"
)
```

Let's take a sentence *"todos los caminos llevan a roma"* and mask the first word in the sentence with a [MASK] token and feed the sentence with the masked token to our `predict_mask` pipeline and get the result:

```
result = predict_mask('[MASK] los caminos llevan a Roma')
```

Print the result:

```
print(result)
```

The preceding code prints the following:

```
[{'score': 0.9719983339309692,
 'sequence': '[CLS] todos los caminos llevan a roma [SEP]',
 'token': 1399,
```

```
'token_str': 'todos'},
{'score': 0.007171058561652899,
'sequence': '[CLS] todas los caminos llevan a roma [SEP]',
'token': 1825,
'token_str': 'todas'},
{'score': 0.0053519923239946365,
'sequence': '[CLS] - los caminos llevan a roma [SEP]',
'token': 1139,
'token_str': '-'},
{'score': 0.004154071677476168,
'sequence': '[CLS] todo los caminos llevan a roma [SEP]',
'token': 1300,
'token_str': 'todo'},
{'score': 0.003964308183640242,
'sequence': '[CLS] y los caminos llevan a roma [SEP]',
'token': 1040,
'token_str': 'y'}]
```

From the preceding results, we can observe that we have scores, filled sequences, and also the predicted masked token (word). We can observe that our model has correctly predicted the masked word as 'todos' with a score of 0.97.

Now that we have learned how to use the BETO model for Spanish, in the next section, we will look at BERTje.

BERTje for Dutch

BERTje is the pre-trained monolingual BERT model for the Dutch language from the University of Groningen. The BERTje model is pre-trained using MLM and **sentence order prediction** (**SOP**) tasks with **whole word masking** (**WWM**).

The BERTje model is trained using several Dutch corpora, including TwNC (a Dutch news corpus), SoNAR-500 (a multi-genre reference corpus), Dutch Wikipedia text, web news, and books. The model has been pre-trained for about 1 million iterations. The pre-trained BERTje model can be downloaded from here: `https://github.com/wietsedv/bertje`. It is also compatible with the Hugging Face's transformers library, so we can use the pre-trained BERTje model directly with the transformers library.

Next sentence prediction with BERTje

Let's now see how to use the pre-trained BERTje model for the NSP task. That is, we feed two sentences, A and B, to the model, and predict whether sentence B follows on from sentence A. First, let's import the necessary modules:

```
from transformers import BertForNextSentencePrediction, BertTokenizer
from torch.nn.functional import softmax
```

Download and load the pre-trained BERTje model:

```
model = BertForNextSentencePrediction.from_pretrained("wietsedv/bert-base-dutch-cased")
```

Download and load the pre-trained BERTje tokenizer:

```
tokenizer = BertTokenizer.from_pretrained("wietsedv/bert-base-dutch-cased")
```

Define the input sentence pairs:

```
sentence_A = 'Ik woon in Amsterdam'
sentence_B = 'Een geweldige plek'
```

Get the embeddings of the sentence pairs:

```
embeddings = tokenizer(sentence_A, sentence_B, return_tensors='pt')
```

Compute the logits:

```
logits = model(**embeddings)[0]
```

Compute the probability using the softmax function:

```
probs = softmax(logits, dim=1)
```

Print the probability:

```
print(probs)
```

The preceding code prints the following:

```
tensor([[0.8463, 0.1537]])
```

In the preceding result, index 0 indicates the probability of the isNext class, and index 1 indicates the probability of the notNext class. Since we got a high probability of 0.8463, we can deduce that sentence_B follows on from sentence_A. Now that we have learned how to use the BERTje model for Dutch, in the next section, we will look at German BERT.

German BERT

German BERT was developed by an organization called *deepset.ai*. They trained the BERT model from scratch using German text. The pre-trained German BERT model is open sourced and free to use. German BERT is trained using recent German Wikipedia text, news articles, and data from OpenLegalData on a single Cloud TPU v2 for a period of 9 days.

German BERT is evaluated on many downstream tasks, including classification, NER, document classification, and more. German BERT outperforms M-BERT on all these tasks. We can use the pre-trained German BERT model directly with the Hugging Face's transformers library, as shown here.

In this section, let's use the auto classes from the transformers library. The auto classes will automatically identify the correct architecture of the model and create the relevant class just with the model name we are passing. Let's explore this in more detail.

First, we import the `AutoTokenizer` and `AutoModel` modules:

```
from transformers import AutoTokenizer, AutoModel
```

Now, let's download and load the pre-trained German BERT model. We use the `AutoModel` class to create the model. `AutoModel` is a generic class and, according to the model name we are passing to the `from_pretrained()` method, it will automatically create the relevant model class. Since we are passing `bert-base-german-cased`, `AutoModel` will create a model that is an instance of the `BertModel` class:

```
model = AutoModel.from_pretrained("bert-base-german-cased")
```

Now, we download and load the tokenizer with which the German BERT model was pre-trained. We use the `AutoTokenizer` class for the tokenizer. `AutoTokenizer` is a generic class and, according to the model name we are passing to the `from_pretrained()` method, it will automatically create the relevant tokenizer class. Since we are passing `bert-base-german-cased`, `AutoTokenizer` will create a tokenizer that is an instance of the `BertTokenizer` class:

```
tokenizer = AutoTokenizer.from_pretrained("bert-base-german-cased")
```

That's it. Now we can use it just like BERT for the German text. We can also download the pre-trained German BERT model from here: `https://int-deepset-models-bert.s3.eu-central-1.amazonaws.com/tensorflow/bert-base-german-cased.zip`.

Now that we have learned how to use the German BERT model, in the next section, let's look into Chinese BERT.

Chinese BERT

Along with M-BERT (M-BERT), Google Research has also open sourced the Chinese BERT model. The configuration of the Chinese BERT model is the same as the vanilla BERT-base model. It consists of 12 encoder layers, 12 attention heads, and 768 hidden units with 110 million parameters. The pre-trained Chinese BERT model can be downloaded from here: `https://github.com/google-research/bert/blob/master/multilingual.md`.

We can use the pre-trained Chinese BERT model with the transformers library, as shown here:

```
from transformers import AutoTokenizer, AutoModel
tokenizer = AutoTokenizer.from_pretrained("bert-base-chinese")
model = AutoModel.from_pretrained("bert-base-chinese")
```

Now, let's look into another Chinese BERT model described in the paper entitled *Pre-Training with Whole Word Masking for Chinese BERT*, available at `https://arxiv.org/pdf/1906.08101.pdf`.

The Chinese BERT model is pre-trained using the WWM scheme. To recap, in WWM, if a subword is masked, then we mask all the words corresponding to that subword. For instance, consider the following sentence:

sentence = "The statement was contradicting."

After tokenizing the sentence using the WordPiece tokenizer and adding `[CLS]` and `[SEP]` tokens, we have the following:

```
tokens = [ [CLS], the, statement, was, contra, ##dict, ##ing, [SEP] ]
```

Now, say we randomly mask some tokens and obtain the following:

```
tokens = [ [CLS], [MASK], statement, was, contra, ##dict, [MASK], [SEP] ]
```

As we can observe, we have masked the tokens `the` and *##ing*. The token `##ing` is a subword and is part of the word *contradicting*, so, in WWM, we mask all the tokens corresponding to the masked subword. As we can observe, we have masked the tokens `contra` and `##dict` since they correspond to the masked subword `##ing`:

```
tokens = [ [CLS], [MASK], statement, was, [MASK], [MASK], [MASK], [SEP] ]
```

Chinese BERT is pre-trained using the MLM task with WWM. The dataset used for training includes Wikipedia text containing both simplified and traditional Chinese.

The researchers have used LTP for Chinese word segmentation. **LTP** stands for the **Language Technology Platform**, from the Harbin Institute of Technology. It is used to process the Chinese language. It is mainly used to perform word segmentation, POS tagging, and syntactic analysis. The LTP helps in identifying the boundaries of Chinese words. The following screenshot shows the use of the LTP for Chinese word segmentation:

[Original Sentence]
使用语言模型来预测下一个词的probability。
[Original Sentence with CWS]
使用 语言 **模型** 来 **预测** 下 一 个 词 的 **probability** 。

Figure 7.18 – Chinese word segmentation

The preceding image is from the following paper: `https://arxiv.org/pdf/1906.08101.pdf`.

The following screenshot shows how we apply WWM:

[Original BERT Input]
使 用 语 言 [MASK] 型 来 [MASK] 测 下 一 个 词 的 **pro** [MASK] **##lity** 。
[Whold Word Masking Input]
使 用 语 言 [MASK] [MASK] 来 [MASK] [MASK] 下 一 个 词 的 [MASK] [MASK] [MASK] 。

Figure 7.19 – Whole word masking

The preceding image is from the following paper: `https://arxiv.org/pdf/1906.08101.pdf`.

The Chinese BERT model is pre-trained with different configurations and they can be downloaded from here: `https://github.com/ymcui/Chinese-BERT-wwm`. We can also use the pre-trained Chinese BERT model with the transformers library, as shown here:

```
tokenizer = BertTokenizer.from_pretrained("hfl/chinese-bert-wwm")
model = BertModel.from_pretrained("hfl/chinese-bert-wwm")
```

Now that we have learned how to use Chinese BERT, in the next section, let's look into Japanese BERT.

Japanese BERT

The Japanese BERT model is pre-trained using the Japanese Wikipedia text with WWM. We tokenize the Japanese texts using MeCab. MeCab is a morphological analyzer for Japanese text. After tokenizing with MeCab, we use the WordPiece tokenizer and obtain the subwords. Instead of using the WordPiece tokenizer and splitting the text into subwords, we can also split the text into characters. So, Japanese BERT comes in two variants:

- `mecab-ipadic-bpe-32k`: First, tokenize the text with the MeCab tokenizer and then split it into subwords. The vocabulary size is 32K.
- `mecab-ipadic-char-4k`: First, tokenize the text with the MeCab tokenizer and then split it into characters. The vocabulary size is 4K.

The pre-trained Japanese BERT models can be downloaded from here: `https://github.com/cl-tohoku/bert-japanese`. We can also use the pre-trained Japanese BERT model with the transformers library, as shown here:

```
from transformers import AutoTokenizer, AutoModel
model = AutoModel.from_pretrained("cl-tohoku/bert-base-japanese-whole-word-masking")
tokenizer = AutoTokenizer.from_pretrained("cl-tohoku/bert-base-japanese-whole-word-masking")
```

Now that we have learned how to use the Japanese BERT model, in the next section, let's look into FinBERT.

FinBERT for Finnish

FinBERT is the pre-trained BERT model for the Finnish language. FinBERT outperforms M-BERT on many downstream Finnish NLP tasks. We learned that M-BERT is trained using the Wikipedia text of 104 languages, but it comprises only 3% Finnish text. FinBERT is trained using the Finnish text from news articles, online discussions, and internet crawling. It consists of about 50K WordPiece vocabulary items, covering many Finnish words compared to M-BERT. This makes FinBERT better than M-BERT.

The architecture of FinBERT is similar to the BERT-base model and has two configurations, FinBERT-cased and FinBERT-uncased, for cased and uncased text, respectively. It is pre-trained on MLM and NSP tasks with a WWM scheme.

We can download the pre-trained FinBERT model from here: `https://github.com/ TurkuNLP/FinBERT`. We can also use the pre-trained FinBERT model with the transformers library, as shown here:

```
tokenizer = BertTokenizer.from_pretrained("TurkuNLP/bert-base-finnish-
uncased-v1")
model = BertModel.from_pretrained("TurkuNLP/bert-base-finnish-uncased-v1")
```

The following table shows the performance of FinBERT compared to M-BERT for the named entity recognition and POS tagging tasks:

Model	Task	Accuracy
M-BERT	NER	90.29
FinBERT	NER	92.40
M-BERT	POS	96.97
FinBERT	POS	98.23

Figure 7.20 – The performance of FinBERT

As we can observe, FinBERT performs better than M-BERT. Now that we have learned how to use the FinBERT model, in the next section, we will look at UmBERTo.

UmBERTo for Italian

UmBERTo is the pre-trained BERT model for the Italian language by Musixmatch research. The UmBERTo model inherits the RoBERTa model architecture. We learned that RoBERTa is essentially BERT with the following changes in pre-training:

- Dynamic masking is used instead of static masking in the MLM task.
- The NSP task is removed and trained using only the MLM task.
- Training is undertaken with a large batch size.
- Byte-level BPE is used as a tokenizer.

UmBERTo extends the RoBERTa architecture by using the SentencePiece tokenizer and WWM. Researchers have released two pre-trained UmBERTo models:

- `umberto-wikipedia-uncased-v1`: Trained on the Italian Wikipedia corpus
- `umberto-commoncrawl-cased-v1`: Trained on the CommonCrawl dataset

The pre-trained UmBERTo models can be downloaded from here: `https://github.com/musixmatchresearch/umberto`. We can also use the pre-trained UmBERTo model with the transformers library, as shown here:

```
tokenizer = \
AutoTokenizer.from_pretrained("Musixmatch/umberto-commoncrawl-cased-v1")
model = \
AutoModel.from_pretrained("Musixmatch/umberto-commoncrawl-cased-v1")
```

In this way, we can use the UmBERTo model for the Italian language. Next, let's look into BERTimbau.

BERTimbau for Portuguese

BERTimbau is a pre-trained BERT model for the Portuguese language. The model is pre-trained on the **brWaC (Brazilian Web as Corpus)**, which is a large, open source Brazilian Portuguese language corpus. The researchers used MLM with WWM for training and the model is trained for 1 million steps. The pre-trained BERTimbau model can be downloaded from here: `https://github.com/neuralmind-ai/portuguese-bert`.

It can be used with the transformers library, as shown here:

```
from transformers import AutoModel, AutoTokenizer
tokenizer = \
AutoTokenizer.from_pretrained('neuralmind/bert-base-portuguese-cased')
model = AutoModel.from_pretrained('neuralmind/bert-base-portuguese-cased')
```

Next, let's look into RuBERT for the Russian language.

RuBERT for Russian

RuBERT is the pre-trained BERT for the Russian language. RuBERT is trained differently from what we have learned so far. RuBERT is trained by transferring knowledge from M-BERT. We know that M-BERT is trained on Wikipedia text of 104 languages and has good knowledge of each language. So, instead of training the monolingual RuBERT from scratch, we train it by obtaining knowledge from M-BERT. Before training, we initialize all the parameters of RuBERT with the parameters of the M-BERT model, except the word embeddings.

RuBERT is trained using Russian Wikipedia text and news articles. **Subword Neural Machine Translation** (**Subword NMT**) is used to segment text into subword units. That is, we create a subword vocabulary using the Subword NMT. RuBERT's subword vocabulary will consist of longer and more Russian words compared to the vocabulary of the M-BERT model.

There will be some words that occur in both the M-BERT vocabulary and the monolingual RuBERT vocabulary. So, we can take the embeddings of them directly. For example, as shown here, the word Здравствуйте occurs in both the M-BERT and RuBERT vocabularies. For the common words that appear in both the M-BERT and monolingual RuBERT vocabularies, we can just use the embeddings of the M-BERT model directly:

Figure 7.21 – M-BERT and RuBERT vocabulary

There will be some words that are basically subwords and are part of longer words. Considering the same example used in the paper, from the following diagram, we can observe that in the M-BERT vocabulary, we have the tokens '*bi*' and '*##rd*'. We know that two ## signs basically imply that the token ##rd is a subword. We can observe that in the RuBERT vocabulary, we have a token called 'bird', but there is no token called 'bird' in the M-BERT vocabulary. In this case, we can just initialize the embedding of 'bird' in the RuBERT vocabulary by taking the mean embeddings of the tokens *bi* and *##rd* from the M-BERT vocabulary:

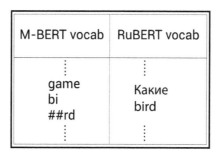

Figure 7.22 – M-BERT and RuBERT vocabulary

We can download the pre-trained RuBERT models from here: `http://docs.deeppavlov.ai/en/master/features/models/bert.html`. We can also use the pre-trained RuBERT model with the transformers library, as shown here:

```
from transformers import AutoTokenizer, AutoModel
tokenizer = AutoTokenizer.from_pretrained("DeepPavlov/rubert-base-cased")
model = AutoModel.from_pretrained("DeepPavlov/rubert-base-cased")
```

In this way, we can train the monolingual BERT for any language. In this chapter, we learned how to apply BERT to languages other than English. In the next chapter, we will learn how to compute sentence representation using sentence BERT.

Summary

We started off the chapter by understanding how the M-BERT model works. We understood that M-BERT is trained without any cross-lingual objective, just like how we trained the BERT model, and it produces a representation that generalizes across multiple languages for downstream tasks.

Moving on, we investigated how multilingual our M-BERT is. We learned that M-BERT's generalizability does not depend on the vocabulary overlap, relying instead on typological and language similarity. We also saw that M-BERT can handle code switched text, but not transliterated text.

Later, we learned about the XLM model, where we train BERT with a cross-lingual objective. We train XLM with MLM and TLM tasks. The TLM task works just like MLM, but in TLM, we train the model on cross-lingual data, that is, parallel data consisting of the same text in two different languages.

Next, we explored the XLM-R model, which uses the RoBERTa architecture. We train the XLM-R model only on the MLM task and we use the CommonCrawl dataset containing about 2.5 TB of text.

In the final section, we explored several different pre-trained monolingual BERT models for different languages, including French, Spanish, Dutch, German, Chinese, Japanese, Finnish, Italian, Portuguese, and Russian. In the next chapter, we will learn how to compute the representation of a sentence using sentence BERT. We will also look into some interesting domain-specific BERT models.

Questions

To assess our knowledge acquired in this chapter, try answering the following questions:

1. What is M-BERT?
2. How is M-BERT pre-trained?
3. What is the effect of word order in M-BERT?
4. Define code switching and transliteration.
5. How is an XLM model pre-trained?
6. How does TLM differ from other pre-training strategies?
7. Define FLUE.

Further reading

To learn more, refer to the following papers:

- **Cross-lingual Language Model Pretraining**, by *Guillaume Lample* and *Alexis Conneau*, available at `https://arxiv.org/pdf/1901.07291.pdf`.

- **Unsupervised Cross-lingual Representation Learning at Scale**, by *Alexis Conneau, Kartikay Khandelwal, et al.*, available at `https://arxiv.org/pdf/1911.02116.pdf`.

- **FlauBERT: Unsupervised Language Model Pre-training for French**, by *Hang Le, Loic Vial, et al.*, available at `https://arxiv.org/pdf/1912.05372.pdf`.

- **Spanish Pre-Trained BERT Model and Evaluation Data**, by *Jou-Hui Ho, Hojin Kang, et al.*, available at `https://users.dcc.uchile.cl/~jperez/papers/pml4dc2020.pdf`.

- **BERTje: A Dutch BERT Model**, by *Wietse de Vries, Andreas van Cranenburgh, Arianna Bisazza, Tommaso Caselli, Gertjan van Noord*, and *Malvina Nissim*, available at `https://arxiv.org/pdf/1912.09582.pdf`.

- **Pre-Training with Whole Word Masking for Chinese BERT**, by *Yiming Cui, Wanxiang Che, Ting Liu, Bing Qin, Ziqing Yang, Shijin Wang*, and *Guoping Hu*, available at `https://arxiv.org/pdf/1906.08101.pdf`.

- **Multilingual is not enough: BERT for Finnish**, by *Antti Virtanen, Jenna Kanerva, Rami Ilo, Jouni Luoma, Juhani Luotolahti, Tapio Salakoski, Filip Ginter*, and *Sampo Pyysalo*, available at `https://arxiv.org/pdf/1912.07076.pdf`.

- **Adaptation of Deep Bidirectional Multilingual Transformers for the Russian Language**, by *Yuri Kuratov* and *Mikhail Arkhipov*, available at `https://arxiv.org/pdf/1905.07213.pdf`.

8
Exploring Sentence and Domain-Specific BERT

Sentence-BERT is one of the most interesting variants of BERT and is popularly used for computing sentence representation. We will begin the chapter by understanding how Sentence-BERT works in detail. We will explore how Sentence-BERT computes sentence representation using the Siamese and triplet network architectures. Next, we will learn about the `sentence-transformers` library. We will understand how to use the pre-trained Sentence-BERT model to compute sentence representation with the `sentence-transformers` library.

Moving on, we will understand how to make the monolingual model multilingual with knowledge distillation in detail. Next, we will learn about several interesting domain-specific BERT models, such as ClinicalBERT and BioBERT. We will learn how ClinicalBERT is trained and how it is used for predicting the probability of re-admission.

Next, we will understand how BioBERT is trained and we will see how to fine-tune the pre-trained BioBERT for **named-entity recognition** (**NER**) and question answering tasks.

In this chapter, we will learn about the following topics:

- Learning about sentence representation with Sentence-BERT
- Exploring the `sentence-transformers` library
- Learning multilingual embeddings through knowledge distillation
- Domain-specific BERT models such as ClinicalBERT and BioBERT

Learning about sentence representation with Sentence-BERT

Sentence-BERT was introduced by the **Ubiquitous Knowledge Processing Lab (UKP-TUDA)**. As the name suggests, Sentence-BERT is used for obtaining fixed-length sentence representations. Sentence-BERT extends the pre-trained BERT model (or its variants) to obtain the sentence representation. Wait! Why do we need Sentence-BERT for obtaining sentence representations? We can directly use the vanilla BERT or its variants to obtain the sentence representation, right? Yes!

But one of the challenges with the vanilla BERT model is its high inference time. Say we have a dataset with n number of sentences; then, to find a sentence pair with high similarity, it takes about $n(n-1)/2$ computations.

To combat this high inference time, we use Sentence-BERT. Sentence-BERT drastically reduces the inference time of BERT. Sentence-BERT is popularly used in tasks such as sentence pair classification, computing similarity between two sentences, and so on. Before understanding how Sentence-BERT works in detail, first, let's take a look at computing sentence representation using the pre-trained BERT model in the next section.

Computing sentence representation

Consider the sentence *Paris is a beautiful city*. Suppose we need to compute the representation of the given sentence. First, we will tokenize the sentence and add a [CLS] token at the beginning and a [SEP] token at the end, so our tokens become the following:

```
tokens = [ [CLS], Paris, is, a, beautiful, city, [SEP] ]
```

Now, we feed the tokens to the pre-trained BERT and it will return the representation, R_i, for each of the tokens, i, as shown in the following figure:

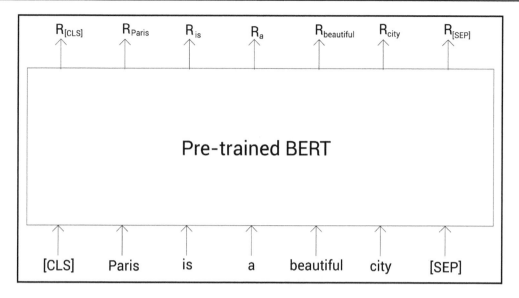

Figure 8.1 – Pre-trained BERT

Okay, we have obtained the representation, Ri, for each of the tokens. How can we obtain the representation of the complete sentence? We learned that the representation of the [CLS] token, $R_{[CLS]}$, holds the aggregate representation of the sentence. So, we can use the representation of the [CLS] token, $R_{[CLS]}$, as the sentence representation:

$$\text{Sentence representation} = R_{[CLS]}$$

But the problem with using the representation of the [CLS] token as a sentence representation is that the sentence representation will not be accurate, especially if we are using the pre-trained BERT model directly without fine-tuning it. So, instead of using the representation of the [CLS] token as a sentence representation, we can use pooling. That is, we compute sentence representation by pooling the representation of all the tokens. Mean pooling and max pooling are the two most popularly used pooling strategies. Okay, how would mean and max pooling be useful here?

- If we obtain the sentence representation by applying mean pooling to the representation of all the tokens, then essentially, the sentence representation holds the meaning of all the words (tokens).
- If we obtain the sentence representation by applying max pooling to the representation of all the tokens, then essentially, the sentence representation holds the meaning of important words (tokens).

Thus, we can compute the representation of a sentence by pooling the representation of all the tokens as shown in the following figure:

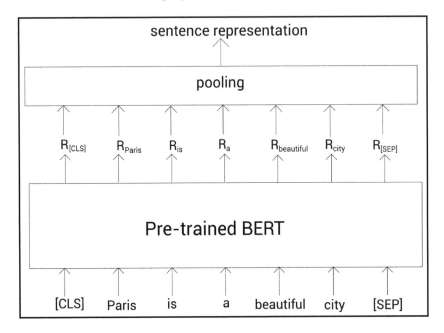

Figure 8.2 – Pre-trained BERT

Now that we have learned how to compute sentence representation using a pre-trained BERT model, let's see how Sentence-BERT works in detail in the next section.

Understanding Sentence-BERT

Note that we don't train Sentence-BERT from scratch. In Sentence-BERT, we take the pre-trained BERT model (or its variants) and fine-tune it for obtaining the sentence representation. In other words, Sentence-BERT is basically a pre-trained BERT model that is fine-tuned for computing sentence representation. Okay, then what is special about Sentence-BERT? For fine-tuning the pre-trained BERT, Sentence-BERT uses Siamese and triplet network architectures, which makes the fine-tuning faster and helps in obtaining accurate sentence representation.

Sentence-BERT uses a Siamese network architecture for tasks that involve a sentence pair as input. It uses triplet network architecture for the triplet loss objective function. Let's take a closer look at each of them.

Sentence-BERT with a Siamese network

Sentence-BERT uses the Siamese network architecture for fine-tuning the pre-trained BERT model for sentence pair tasks. In this section, let's understand how the Siamese network architecture is useful and how we fine-tune the pre-trained BERT for sentence pair tasks. First, we will see how Sentence-BERT works for a sentence pair classification task, then we will learn how Sentence-BERT works for a sentence pair regression task.

Sentence-BERT for a sentence pair classification task

Suppose we have a dataset containing sentence pairs and a binary label indicating whether the sentence pairs are similar (1) or dissimilar (0), as shown in the following figure:

Sentence 1	Sentence 2	Label
I completed my assignment	I completed my homework	1
The game was boring	This is a great place	0
The food is delicious	The food is tasty	1
⋮	⋮	⋮

Figure 8.3 – Sample dataset

Now, let's see how to fine-tune the pre-trained BERT model with the preceding dataset using the Siamese architecture for the sentence pair classification task. Let's take the first sentence pair from our dataset:

Sentence 1: *I completed my assignment*

Sentence 2: *I completed my homework*

We need to classify whether the given sentence pair is similar (1) or dissimilar (0). First, we tokenize the sentence and add [CLS] and [SEP] tokens at the beginning and end of the sentence, respectively, as shown:

```
Tokens 1 = [ [CLS], I completed, my, assignment, [SEP]]

Tokens 2 = [ [CLS], I, completed, my, homework, [SEP]]
```

Now, we feed the tokens to the pre-trained BERT model and obtain the representation of each of the tokens. We learned that Sentence-BERT uses a Siamese network. We know that the Siamese network consists of two identical networks that share the same weights. So, here we use two identical pre-trained BERT models. We feed the tokens from sentence 1 to one BERT and the tokens from sentence 2 to another BERT and compute the representation of the given two sentences.

To compute the representation of a sentence, we apply mean or max pooling. By default, in Sentence-BERT, we use mean pooling. After applying the pooling operation, we will have a sentence representation for the given sentence pair, as shown in the following figure:

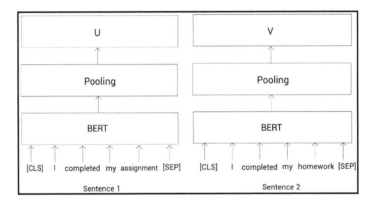

Figure 8.4 – Sentence-BERT

In the preceding figure, u denotes the representation of **Sentence 1** and v denotes the representation of **Sentence 2**. Now, we concatenate the sentence representations u and v with an element-wise difference and multiply by the weight, W, as given here:

$$(W_t(u, v, |u - v|))$$

Note that the dimension of weight W is n x k, where n is the dimension of the sentence embedding and k is the number of classes. Next, we feed the result to a softmax function, which returns the probability of similarity between the given sentence pair:

$$\text{Softmax}(W_t(u, v, |u - v|))$$

This is shown in the following figure. As we observe, first we feed the sentence pair to the pre-trained BERT models and obtain the sentence representation through pooling, then we concatenate the representation of the sentence pair and multiply it by the weights, W, and feed the result to the softmax function:

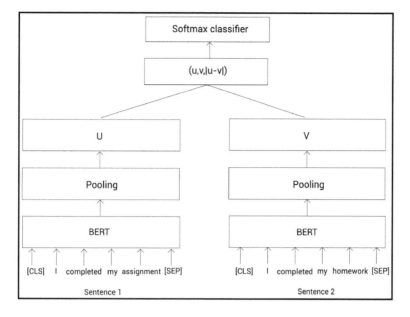

Figure 8.5 – Sentence-BERT

We train the preceding network by minimizing the cross-entropy loss and updating the weight, *W*. In this way, we can use Sentence-BERT for a sentence pair classification task.

Sentence-BERT for a sentence pair regression task

In the previous section, we learned how Sentence-BERT uses the Siamese architecture for a sentence pair classification task. In this section, let's see how Sentence-BERT works for a sentence pair regression task. Suppose we have a dataset containing sentence pairs and their similarity scores as shown in the following figure:

Sentence 1	Sentence 2	Score
How old are you	What is your age	0.99
The food is tasty	The food is delicious	0.98
I played the chess	He was sleeping	0.00
⋮	⋮	⋮

Figure 8.6 – Sample dataset

Now, let's see how to fine-tune the pre-trained BERT model with the preceding dataset using the Siamese architecture for the sentence pair regression task. In the sentence pair regression task, our goal is to predict the semantic similarity between two given sentences. Let's take the first sentence pair from our dataset:

Sentence 1: *How old are you*

Sentence 2: *What is your age*

Now, we need to compute the similarity score between the given two sentences.

Just like we saw in the previous section, first, we tokenize the given two sentences and add [CLS] and [SEP] tokens at the beginning and end of the sentences, respectively, as shown:

```
Tokens 1 = [ [CLS], How, old, are, you, [SEP]]

Tokens 2 = [ [CLS], What, is, your, age, [SEP]]
```

Now, we feed the tokens to the pre-trained BERT model and obtain the representation of each of the tokens. We learned that Sentence-BERT uses a Siamese network. So, here we use two identical pre-trained BERT models. We feed the tokens from sentence 1 to one BERT model and the tokens from sentence 2 to another BERT model and compute the representation of the given two sentences by applying pooling.

Let u be the representation of sentence 1 and v be the representation of sentence 2. Then, we compute the similarity between the two sentences using a similarity measure such as cosine similarity, as follows:

$$Similarity = cosine\ (u,v)$$

As shown in the following figure, we feed two sentences to two pre-trained BERT models and obtain their sentence representation through pooling. Then, we compute the similarity between the sentence representations using the cosine similarity function:

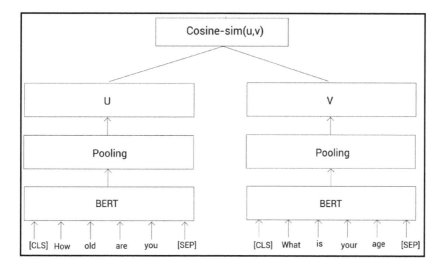

Figure 8.7 – Sentence-BERT

We train the preceding network by minimizing the mean squared loss and updating the weight of the model. In this way, we can use Sentence-BERT for the sentence pair regression task.

Sentence-BERT with a triplet network

In the previous section, we looked into the architecture of Sentence-BERT for sentence pair regression and classification tasks. We learned that Sentence-BERT uses the Siamese network architecture for fine-tuning the pre-trained BERT with the sentence pair inputs. In this section, let's see how Sentence-BERT uses the triplet network architecture.

Suppose we have three sentences – an anchor sentence, a positive sentence (entailment), and a negative sentence (contradiction), as follows:

- **Anchor sentence**: *Play the game*
- **Positive sentence**: *He is playing the game*
- **Negative sentence**: *Don't play the game*

Our task is to compute a representation such that the similarity between the anchor and positive sentences should be high and the similarity between the anchor and negative sentences should be low. Let's see how to fine-tune the pre-trained BERT model for this task. Since we have three sentences, in this case, Sentence-BERT uses the triplet network architecture.

First, we tokenize and feed the anchor, positive, and negative sentences to the three pre-trained BERT models, and then obtain the representation of each of the sentences through pooling, as shown in the following figure:

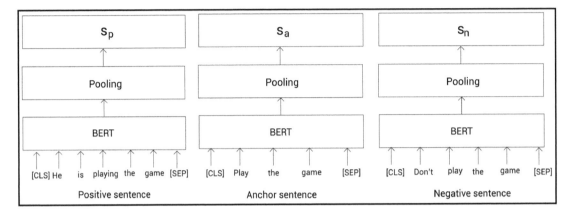

Figure 8.8 – Sentence-BERT

As we can observe, in the preceding figure, s_a, s_p, and s_n denote the representation of the anchor, positive, and negative sentences, respectively. Next, we train our network to minimize the following triplet objective function:

$$\max(||s_a - s_p|| - ||s_a - s_n|| + \epsilon, 0)$$

In the preceding equation, $||\cdot||$ denotes the distance metric. We use the Euclidean distance as the distance metric. ε denotes the margin; it is used to ensure that the positive sentence representation, s_p, is at least ε closer to the anchor sentence, s_a, than the negative sentence representation, s_n.

As shown in the following figure, we feed the anchor, positive, and negative sentences to the BERT model and get their representation through pooling. Then, we train the network to minimize the triplet loss function. Minimizing the triplet loss function ensures that the similarity between the positive and anchor sentences is greater than the similarity between the negative and anchor sentences:

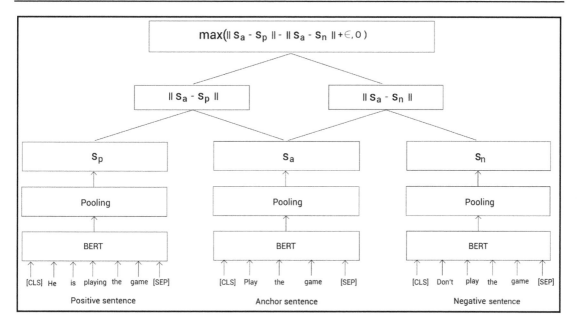

Figure 8.9 – Sentence-BERT

Thus, in this way, we can use Sentence-BERT with a triplet loss objective function. The researchers of Sentence-BERT also open-sourced their `sentence-transformers` library, which is used for computing sentence representation through Sentence-BERT. In the next section, we will learn how to use the `sentence-transformers` library.

Exploring the sentence-transformers library

The `sentence-transformers` library can be installed using `pip` as shown in the following code:

```
pip install -U sentence-transformers
```

The researchers of Sentence-BERT have also made their pre-trained Sentence-BERT models available online. All available pre-trained models can be found here: `https://public.ukp.informatik.tu-darmstadt.de/reimers/sentence-transformers/v0.2/`.

We can find pre-trained models named `bert-base-nli-cls-token`, `bert-base-nli-mean-token`, `roberta-base-nli-max-tokens`, `distilbert-base-nli-mean-tokens`, and so on. Let's understand what this means:

- `bert-base-nli-cls-token` is a pre-trained Sentence-BERT model where we have taken a pre-trained BERT-base model and fine-tuned it with the NLI dataset, and the model uses a `[CLS]` token as the sentence representation.
- `bert-base-nli-mean-token` is a pre-trained Sentence-BERT model where we have taken a pre-trained BERT-base model and fine-tuned it with the NLI dataset, and the model uses a mean pooling strategy for computing sentence representation.
- `roberta-base-nli-max-tokens` is a pre-trained Sentence-BERT model where we have taken a pre-trained RoBERTa-base model and fine-tuned it with the NLI dataset, and the model uses a max pooling strategy for computing sentence representation.
- `distilbert-base-nli-mean-token` is a pre-trained Sentence-BERT model where we have taken a pre-trained DistilBERT-base model and fine-tuned it with the NLI dataset, and the model uses a mean pooling strategy for computing sentence representation.

Thus, when we say the pre-trained Sentence-BERT model, it basically implies that we have taken a pre-trained BERT model and fine-tuned it using the Siamese/triplet network architecture. In the upcoming sections, we will learn how to use pre-trained Sentence-BERT models.

Computing sentence representation using Sentence-BERT

Let's see how to compute sentence representation using a pre-trained Sentence-BERT model. We can also access the complete code from the GitHub repository of the book. In order to run the code smoothly, clone the GitHub repository of the book and run the code using Google Colab. First, let's import the `SentenceTransformer` module from our `sentence_transformers` library:

```
from sentence_transformers import SentenceTransformer
```

Download and load the pre-trained Sentence-BERT:

```
model = SentenceTransformer('bert-base-nli-mean-tokens')
```

Define the sentence for which we need to compute the sentence representations:

```
sentence = 'paris is a beautiful city'
```

Compute the sentence representation using our pre-trained Sentence-BERT model with the `encode` function:

```
sentence_representation = model.encode(sentence)
```

Now, let's check the shape of our representation:

```
print(sentence_representation.shape)
```

The preceding code will print the following:

```
(768,)
```

As we can see, our sentence representation size is 768. In this way, we can use the pre-trained Sentence-BERT model and obtain the fixed-length sentence representation.

Computing sentence similarity

In this section, let's learn how to compute the semantic similarity between two sentences using the pre-trained Sentence-BERT model.

Import the necessary libraries:

```
import scipy
from sentence_transformers import SentenceTransformer, util
```

Download and load the pre-trained Sentence-BERT model:

```
model = SentenceTransformer('bert-base-nli-mean-tokens')
```

Define the sentence pair:

```
sentence1 = 'It was a great day'
sentence2 = 'Today was awesome'
```

Compute the sentence representation of the sentence pair:

```
sentence1_representation = model.encode(sentence1)
sentence2_representation = model.encode(sentence2)
```

Compute the cosine similarity between the two sentence representations:

```
cosine_sim = \
util.pytorch_cos_sim(sentence1_representation,sentence2_representation)
```

The preceding code will print the following:

```
[0.93]
```

From the preceding result, we can observe that the given sentence pair is 93% similar. In this way, we can use the pre-trained Sentence-BERT model for sentence similarity tasks.

Loading custom models

Apart from the pre-trained Sentence-BERT models available in the `sentence-transformers` library, we can also use our own models. Let's suppose we have a pre-trained ALBERT model. Now, let's see how to use this pre-trained ALBERT model to obtain the sentence representation.

First, let's import the necessary modules:

```
from sentence_transformers import models, SentenceTransformer
```

Now, we define our word embedding model, which will return the representation of every token in the given sentence. Let's use the pre-trained ALBERT as the word embedding model:

```
word_embedding_model = models.Transformer('albert-base-v2')
```

Next, we define the pooling model that computes the pooled representation of tokens. We learned that in Sentence-BERT, we use different strategies for obtaining the sentence representation, such as `[CLS]` tokens, mean pooling, or max pooling. Now, we set the pooling strategy we want to use for computing the sentence representation. As shown in the following code snippet, in this example, we have set `pooling_mode_mean_tokens = True`, which implies that we use mean pooling for computing fixed-length sentence representation:

```
pooling_model = \
models.Pooling(word_embedding_model.get_word_embedding_dimension(),
 pooling_mode_mean_tokens=True,
 pooling_mode_cls_token=False,
 pooling_mode_max_tokens=False)
```

That's it! Now, we define our Sentence-BERT with the word embedding and pooling models, as shown in the following code:

```
model = SentenceTransformer(modules=[word_embedding_model, pooling_model])
```

We can use this model and compute the sentence representation as shown:

```
model.encode('Transformers are awesome')
```

The preceding code will return a vector of shape 768 holding the representation of the given sentence. It basically computes the representation of every token in the given sentence and returns the pooled value as the sentence representation.

Finding a similar sentence with Sentence-BERT

In this section, let's explore how to find a similar sentence using Sentence-BERT. Suppose we have an e-commerce website and say in our master dictionary we have many order-related questions, such as *How to cancel my order?*, *Do you provide a refund?*, and so on. Now, when a new question comes in, our goal is to find the most related question in our master dictionary to the new question. Let's see how we can do this using Sentence-BERT.

First, let's import the necessary libraries:

```
from sentence_transformers import SentenceTransformer, util
import numpy as np
```

Download and load the pre-trained Sentence-BERT model:

```
model = SentenceTransformer('bert-base-nli-mean-tokens')
```

Define the master dictionary:

```
master_dict = [
 'How to cancel my order?',
 'Please let me know about the cancellation policy?',
 'Do you provide refund?',
 'what is the estimated delivery date of the product?',
 'why my order is missing?',
 'how do i report the delivery of the incorrect items?'
 ]
```

Define the input question:

```
inp_question = 'When is my product getting delivered?'
```

Compute the input question representation:

```
inp_question_representation = model.encode(inp_question,
  convert_to_tensor=True)
```

Compute the representation of all the questions in the master dictionary:

```
master_dict_representation = model.encode(master_dict,
  convert_to_tensor=True)
```

Now, compute the cosine similarity between the input question representation and the representation of all the questions in the master dictionary:

```
similarity = util.pytorch_cos_sim(inp_question_representation,
  master_dict_representation )
```

Print the most similar question:

```
print('The most similar question in the master dictionary to given input
  question is:',master_dict[np.argmax(similarity)])
```

The preceding code will print the following:

```
The most similar question in the master dictionary to given input question
is: What is the estimated delivery date of the product?
```

In this way, we can use the pre-trained Sentence-BERT for many interesting use cases. We can also fine-tune it for any downstream tasks. We learned how Sentence-BERT works and how to use it for computing sentence representation. Apart from applying Sentence-BERT for the English language, can we also apply it for other languages? Yes, and that's exactly what we will learn about in the next section.

Learning multilingual embeddings through knowledge distillation

In this section, let's understand how to make the monolingual sentence embedding multilingual through knowledge distillation. In the previous chapter, we learned how M-BERT, XLM, and XLM-R work and how they produce representations for different languages. In all these models, the vector space between languages is not aligned. That is, the representation of the same sentence in different languages will be mapped to different locations in the vector space. Now, we will see how to map similar sentences in different languages to the same location in the vector space.

In the previous section, we learned how Sentence-BERT works. We learned how Sentence-BERT generates the representation of a sentence. But how do we use the Sentence-BERT for different languages other than English? We can apply Sentence-BERT for different languages by making the monolingual sentence embedding generated by Sentence-BERT multilingual through knowledge distillation. To do this, we transfer the knowledge of Sentence-BERT to any multilingual model, say, XLM-R, and make the multilingual model generate embeddings just like pre-trained Sentence-BERT. Let's explore this in more detail.

We know that the XLM-R model generates embeddings for 100 different languages. Now, we take the pre-trained XLM-R model and teach the XLM-R model to generate sentence embeddings for different languages just like Sentence-BERT. We use the pre-trained Sentence-BERT as the teacher and the pre-trained XLM-R as the student model.

Say we have a source sentence in English and the corresponding target sentence in French: [*How are you, Comment ça va*]. First, we will feed the source sentence to the teacher (Sentence-BERT) and get the sentence representation. Next, we feed both the source and target sentences to the student (XLM-R) and get the sentence representations, as shown in the following figure:

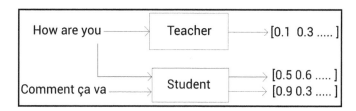

Figure 8.10 – Teacher-student architecture

Now, we have sentence representations generated by the teacher and student models. We can observe that the source sentence representations generated by the teacher and the student are different. We need to teach our student model (XLM-R) to generate representations similar to the teacher model. In order to do that, we compute the mean squared difference between the source sentence representation generated by the teacher and the source sentence representation generated by the student. Then, we train the student network to minimize the **mean squared error** (**MSE**).

As shown in the following figure, in order to make our student generate representations the same as the teacher, we compute the MSE between the source sentence representation returned by the teacher and the source sentence representation returned by the student:

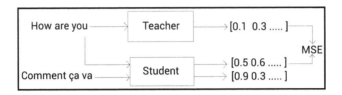

Figure 8.11 – Computing the MSE loss

We also need to compute the MSE between the source sentence representation returned by the teacher and the target sentence representation returned by the student. But why? The reason is that the target French sentence is the equivalent of the source English sentence. So, we need our target sentence representation to be the same as the source sentence representation returned by the teacher. So, we compute the MSE between the source sentence representation returned by the teacher and the target sentence representation returned by the student, as shown in the following figure:

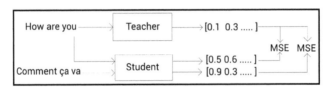

Figure 8.12 – Computing the MSE loss

After computing the MSE, we train our student network by minimizing it. By minimizing the MSE, our student network will learn how to generate embeddings the same as the teacher network. In this way, we can make our student (XLM-R) generate multilingual embeddings the same as how the teacher (Sentence-BERT) generates the monolingual embedding. Let's look at this in more detail in the next section.

Teacher-student architecture

Let's suppose we have parallel translated source-target sentence pairs as $[(s_1, t_1), (s_2, t_2), \ldots, (s_i, t_i), \ldots, (s_n, t_n)]$, where s_i is the original sentence in the source language and t_i is the translated sentence in the target languages. t_i can be in different languages as well. For example, (s_1, t_1) can be a source (English) and target (French) pair and (s_2, t_2) can be a source (English) and target (German) pair, and so on.

Let's denote the teacher model as M and the student model as $\hat{M}$. First, we feed the source sentence, s_i, to the teacher BERT, M, and obtain the source sentence representation, $M(s_i)$. Next, we feed both the source, s_i, and target, t_i, sentences to the student BERT, $\hat{M}$, and obtain the source, $\hat{M}(s_i)$, and target, $\hat{M}(t_i)$, sentence representations, as shown in the following figure:

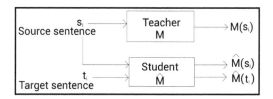

Figure 8.13 – Teacher-student architecture

Now, we compute the MSE between the source sentence, s_i, representation computed by the teacher, M, and student, $\hat{M}$, that is, the MSE between $M(s_i)$ and $\hat{M}(s_i)$.

We also compute the MSE between the source sentence, s_i, representation computed by the teacher, M, and target sentence, t_i, representation computed by the student, $\hat{M}$, that is, the MSE between $M(s_i)$ and $\hat{M}(t_i)$.

Next, we train the student network by minimizing the aforementioned two MSEs:

$$\frac{1}{B} \sum_i \left[(M(s_i) - \hat{M}(s_i))^2 + (M(s_i) - \hat{M}(t_i))^2 \right]$$

In the preceding equation, B denotes the batch size. The teacher-student architecture is shown in the following figure:

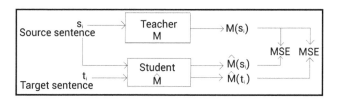

Figure 8.14 – Teacher-student architecture

In this way, we can train our student network to generate embeddings the same as the teacher network. Note that we can use any pre-trained model as a teacher and student.

Using the multilingual model

In the previous section, we learned how to make the monolingual model multilingual through knowledge distillation. In this section, let's learn how to use the pre-trained multilingual model. The researchers have made their pre-trained models publicly available with the `sentence-transformers` library. So, we can directly download the pre-trained model and use it for our task. The available pre-trained multilingual models are as follows:

- `distiluse-base-multilingual-cased`: This supports Arabic, Chinese, Dutch, English, French, German, Italian, Korean, Polish, Portuguese, Russian, Spanish, and Turkish languages.
- `xlm-r-base-en-ko-nli-ststb`: This supports Korean and English.
- `xlm-r-large-en-ko-nli-ststb`: This supports Korean and English.

Now, let's learn how to use these pre-trained models. Let's see how to compute the similarity between two sentences in a different language. First, let's import the `SentenceTransformer` module:

```
from sentence_transformers import SentenceTransformer, util
import scipy
```

Download and load the pre-trained multilingual model:

```
model = SentenceTransformer('distiluse-base-multilingual-cased')
```

Define the sentences:

```
eng_sentence = 'thank you very much'
fr_sentence = 'merci beaucoup'
```

Compute the embeddings:

```
eng_sentence_embedding = model.encode(eng_sentence)
fr_sentence_embedding = model.encode(fr_sentence)
```

Compute the similarity between the two sentence embeddings:

```
similarity = \
util.pytorch_cos_sim(eng_sentence_embedding, fr_sentence_embedding)
```

Print the result:

```
print('The similarity score is:', similarity)
```

The preceding code will print the following:

```
The similarity score is: [0.98400884]
```

In this way, we can use the pre-trained multilingual models. We can also fine-tune them for any downstream tasks. In the next section, let's explore several interesting domain-specific BERT models.

Domain-specific BERT

In the preceding chapters, we learned how BERT is pre-trained using the general Wikipedia corpus and how we can fine-tune and use it for downstream tasks. Instead of using the BERT that is pre-trained on the general Wikipedia corpus, we can also train BERT from scratch on a domain-specific corpus. This helps the BERT model to learn embeddings specific to a domain and it also helps in learning the domain-specific vocabulary that may not be present in the general Wikipedia corpus. In this section, we will look into two interesting domain-specific BERT models:

- ClinicalBERT
- BioBERT

We will learn how the preceding models are pre-trained and how we can fine-tune them for downstream tasks.

ClinicalBERT

ClinicalBERT is a clinical domain-specific BERT pre-trained on a large clinical corpus. The clinical notes or progress notes contain very useful information about the patient. They include a record of patient visits, their symptoms, diagnosis, daily activities, observations, treatment plans, results of radiology, and many more. Understanding the contextual representation of clinical notes is challenging since they follow their own grammatical structure, abbreviations, and jargon. So, we pre-train ClinicalBERT with many clinical documents to understand the contextual representation of the clinical text.

Okay, how is this ClinicalBERT useful? The representation learned by ClinicalBERT helps us to understand many clinical insights, a summary of clinical notes, the relationship between diseases and treatment measures, and much more. Once pre-trained, ClinicalBERT can be used for a variety of downstream tasks, such as readmission prediction, length of stay, mortality risk estimation, diagnosis prediction, and more.

Pre-training ClinicalBERT

ClinicalBERT is pre-trained using the MIMIC-III clinical notes. MIMIC-III is a large collection of health-related data from the Beth Israel Deaconess Medical Center. It includes a health-related dataset that observed over 40,000 patients who stayed in the ICU. ClinicalBERT is pre-trained using the masked language modeling and next sentence prediction tasks just like we pre-trained the BERT model, as shown in this figure:

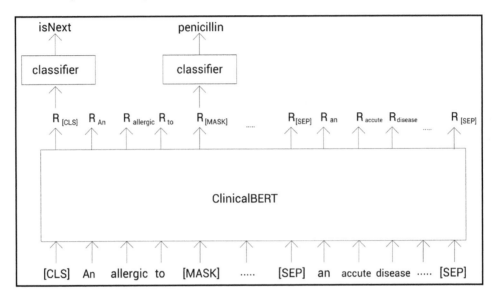

Figure 8.15 – Pre-training ClinicalBERT

As shown in the preceding figure, we feed two sentences with a masked word to our model and train the model to predict the masked word and also to predict whether the second sentence is the next sentence of the first sentence. After pre-training, we can use our pre-trained model for any downstream tasks. In the next section, we will look into how to fine-tune the pre-trained ClinicalBERT.

Fine-tuning ClinicalBERT

After pre-training, we can fine-tune ClinicalBERT for a variety of downstream tasks, such as re-admission prediction, length of stay, mortality risk estimation, diagnosis prediction, and many more.

Suppose we fine-tune the pre-trained ClinicalBERT for the re-admission prediction task. In the re-admission prediction task, the goal of our model is to predict the probability of a patient being re-admitted to the hospital within the next 30 days. As shown in the following figure, we feed the clinical notes to the pre-trained ClinicalBERT and it returns the representation of the clinical notes. Then, we take the representation of the [CLS] token and feed it to a classifier (feedforward + sigmoid activation function) and the classifier returns the probability of the patient being re-admitted within the next 30 days:

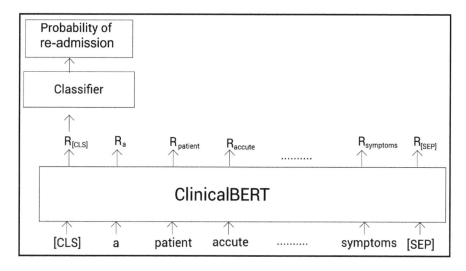

Figure 8.16 – Fine-tuning ClinicalBERT

Wait! We know that in the BERT model, the maximum token length is 512. How can we make predictions when the clinical notes of a patient consist of more tokens than 512? In that case, we can split the clinical notes (long sequence) into several subsequences. Now, we feed each subsequence to our model, and then make a prediction for all the subsequences separately. Then, at the end, we can compute the score with the following equation:

$$P(\text{readmit} = 1|h_{\text{patient}}) = \frac{P_{\max}^n + P_{\text{mean}}^n \, n/c}{1 + n/c}$$

In the preceding equation, the following applies:

- n denotes the number of subsequences.
- $P_{\max}^n$ denotes the maximum re-admission probability across all the subsequences.
- P_{mean}^n denotes the mean re-admission probability across all the subsequences.
- c is the scaling factor.

Let's understand the preceding equation step by step. Suppose we have n subsequences. Now, all these n subsequences will not contain useful information related to the re-admission prediction, right? Yes! There could be some subsequences that contain more information related to re-admission prediction and there could be some subsequences that contain no information related to re-admission prediction. Thus, not all subsequences are useful in making a prediction. So, we can just use the maximum probability across all the subsequences as our prediction. So, our equation becomes the following:

$$P(\text{readmit} = 1|h_{\text{patient}}) = P_{\text{max}}$$

Suppose a subsequence contains noise and say due to the noise it gets the maximum prediction probability. Then, in this case, simply taking the maximum probability as our final prediction will be incorrect. So, to avoid this, we will also include the mean probability across all the subsequences. So, our equation becomes the following:

$$P(\text{readmit} = 1|h_{\text{patient}}) = P_{\text{max}} + P_{\text{mean}}$$

Okay, when the patients have many clinical notes or longer clinical notes, then the number of subsequences, n, will be large. Then, in this case, there is a greater chance that we would obtain a noisy maximum probability, P_{max}^n. So, in this case, we should give more importance to the mean probability, P_{mean}^n. To give more importance to P_{mean}^n depending on n, we multiply P_{mean}^n by n/c, where c is the scaling factor. So, now our equation becomes the following:

$$P(\text{readmit} = 1|h_{\text{patient}}) = P_{\text{max}}^n + P_{\text{mean}}^n \, n/c$$

Next, to normalize the final score, we divide our score by $1 + n/c$, thus our final equation becomes the following:

$$P(\text{readmit} = 1|h_{\text{patient}}) = \frac{P_{\text{max}}^n + P_{\text{mean}}^n \, n/c}{1 + n/c}$$

The preceding equation gives us the probability of re-admission of a patient. In this way, we can leverage the pre-trained BERT and fine-tune it for other downstream tasks.

Extracting clinical word similarity

Now, let's empirically evaluate the representation learned by ClinicalBERT. In order to evaluate it, we will compute the representation of medical terms using ClinicalBERT. After computing the representation of medical terms, we plot them using **t-distributed stochastic neighbor embedding (t-SNE)**. The plot is shown in the following figure:

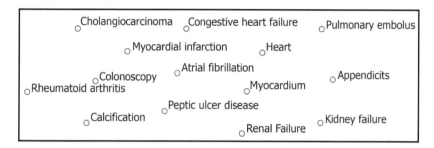

Figure 8.17 – Embeddings of ClinicalBERT

The preceding has been taken from the following paper: `https://arxiv.org/pdf/1904.05342.pdf`.

From the preceding figure, we can observe that medical conditions related to the heart, such as **Myocardial infarction**, **Congestive heart failure**, and **Heart**, are plotted close together and the medical terms related to the kidney, such as **Renal failure** and **Kidney failure**, are plotted together. This indicates that our ClinicalBERT's representation holds contextual information for the medical terms, which is why similar medical terms are plotted close together.

Now that we have learned how ClinicalBERT works, in the next section, we will look into BioBERT.

BioBERT

As the name suggests, BioBERT is a biomedical domain-specific BERT model pre-trained on a large biomedical corpus. Since BioBERT understands biomedical domain-specific representations, once pre-trained, BioBERT performs better than the vanilla BERT on biomedical texts. The architecture of BioBERT follows the same as the vanilla BERT model. After pre-training, we can fine-tune BioBERT for many biomedical domain-specific downstream tasks, such as biomedical question answering, biomedical named entity recognition, and more. We will learn more about this in the upcoming sections.

Pre-training the BioBERT model

BioBERT is pre-trained using biomedical domain-specific texts. We use the biomedical datasets from the following two sources:

- **PubMed**: This is a citation database. It includes more than 30 million citations for biomedical literature from life science journals, online books, and MEDLINE (an index of the biomedical journal, the National Library of Medicine).
- **PubMed Central** (**PMC**): This is a free online repository that includes articles that have been published in biomedical and life sciences journals.

BioBERT is pre-trained using PubMed abstracts and PMC full-text articles. The PubMed corpus consists of about 4.5 billion words and the PMC corpus consist of about 13.5 billion words. We know that the general BERT is pre-trained using a general domain corpus that is made up of the English Wikipedia and Toronto BookCorpus datasets, so before directly pre-training BioBERT, first, we initialize the weights of BioBERT with the general BERT model, and then we pre-train BioBERT with the biomedical domain-specific corpora.

We use the WordPiece tokenizer for tokenizing. The researchers used the original vocabulary that is used in the BERT-base model instead of using a new vocabulary from a biomedical corpus. This is because of the compatibility between the BioBERT and BERT models and the unseen words will also be represented and fine-tuned using the original BERT-base vocabulary. The researchers also observed that instead of using the uncased vocabulary, using the cased vocabulary results in a good performance in downstream tasks. The BioBERT model is pre-trained for 3 days on eight NVIDIA V100 GPUs.

The researchers also made the pre-trained BioBERT publicly available. So, we can download the pre-trained BioBERT and use it for our tasks. The pre-trained BioBERT can be downloaded from `https://github.com/naver/biobert-pre-trained`.

The pre-trained BioBERT model is available in different combinations:

- **BioBERT + PubMed** where the model is trained using the PubMed corpus
- **BioBERT + PMC** where the model is trained using the PMC corpus
- **BioBERT + PubMed + PMC** where the model is trained using both the PubMed and PMC corpora

In the next section, let's learn how to fine-tune the pre-trained BioBERT model.

Fine-tuning the BioBERT model

After pre-training the BioBERT model, we fine-tune it for downstream tasks. BioBERT outperforms the general BERT in downstream tasks in the biomedical domain. In this section, let's look at some of the downstream tasks where we fine-tune the pre-trained BioBERT model.

BioBERT for NER tasks

We know that in NER tasks, our goal is to classify the named entities into their respective predefined categories. Suppose we have predefined categories such as disease, drug, chemical, infection, and so on. Now, consider the sentence *An allergy to penicillin can cause an anaphylactic reaction.* In this sentence, *allergy* should be categorized as a disease, *penicillin* should be categorized as a drug, and *anaphylactic* should be categorized as a disease.

Now, let's learn how to fine-tune the pre-trained BioBERT for performing the NER task. First, we tokenize the sentence and add the [CLS] token at the beginning and the [SEP] token at the end. Then, we feed the tokens to the pre-trained BioBERT and obtain the representation of every token.

Next, we feed those token representations to a classifier (feedforward network + softmax function). Then, the classifier returns the category to which the named entity belongs to. This is shown in the following figure:

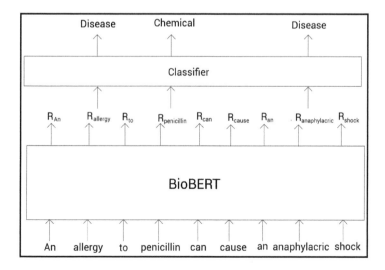

Figure 8.18 – Fine-tuning BioBERT for an NER task

Our initial results will not be accurate but over the course of several iterations, we will get good results by fine-tuning our model parameters.

Okay, but what dataset we can use for fine-tuning? For the disease-related entity, we can use the following datasets:

- **NCBI (National Center for Biotechnology Information)**
- **2010 i2b2/VA (informatics for integrating biology and bedside)**
- **BC5CDR (BioCreative 5 Chemical Disease Relation)**

For the drug/chemical-related entity, we can use the following datasets:

- **BC5CDR (BioCreative 5 Chemical Disease Relation)**
- **BC4CHEMD (BioCreative IV Chemical and Drug)**

For the gene-related entity, we can use the following datasets:

- **BC2GM (BioCreative II Gene Mention)**
- JNLPBA

For the species-related entity, we can use the following:

- **LINNAEUS (LINeage tracing by Nuclease-Activated Editing of Ubiquitous Sequences)**
- Species-800

We can also merge all these datasets and fine-tune our BioBERT model to classify the biomedical terms in the given text into the four different entities (disease, drug/chemical, gene, and species).

BioBERT for question answering

We can also fine-tune the pre-trained BioBERT for the biomedical question answering task. BioASQ (http://bioasq.org/) is popularly used for biomedical question answering dataset. The format of BioASQ is the same as SQuAD. We can fine-tune BioBERT for question answering just like how we fine-tuned the BERT model. After fine-tuning with BioASQ, we can use BioBERT for answering biomedical questions.

Apart from the aforementioned tasks, we can also fine-tune BioBERT for any other biomedical downstream tasks.

Thus, in this chapter, we have learned about Sentence-BERT and two interesting domain-specific BERT models. In the next chapter, let's learn about VideoBERT and BART.

Summary

We started off the chapter by understanding how Sentence-BERT works. We learned that in Sentence-BERT, we use mean or max pooling for computing the sentence representation. We also learned that Sentence-BERT is basically a pre-trained BERT model that is fine-tuned for computing sentence representation. For fine-tuning the pre-trained BERT model, Sentence-BERT uses a Siamese and triplet network architecture, which makes the fine-tuning faster and helps in obtaining accurate sentence embeddings.

Later, we learned how to use the `sentence-transformers` library. We learned how to compute sentence representation and also how to compute the semantic similarity between a sentence pair using `sentence-transformers`. Following this, we learned how to make monolingual embeddings multilingual using knowledge distillation. We learned how to make the student (XLM-R) generate multilingual embeddings the same as how the teacher (Sentence-BERT) generates the monolingual embedding.

Next, we explored domain-specific BERT models. We learned how the ClinicalBERT is pre-trained using the MIMIC-III clinical notes and how to fine-tune ClincalBERT for the re-admission prediction task. Then, at the end of the chapter, we learned about BioBERT and how to fine-tune it for downstream tasks. In the next chapter, we will understand how VideoBERT and BART work.

Questions

Let's assess our knowledge by answering the following questions:

1. Define Sentence-BERT.
2. What is the difference between max pooling and mean pooling?
3. What is ClinicalBERT?
4. What is the use of ClinicalBERT?
5. What is the dataset used for training ClinicalBERT?
6. How is the probability of re-admission computed using ClinicalBERT?
7. What is the dataset used for training BioBERT?

Further reading

For more information, refer to the following resources:

- *Sentence-BERT: Sentence Embeddings using Siamese BERT-Networks* by *Nils Reimers* and *Iryna Gurevych*, available at `https://arxiv.org/pdf/1908.10084.pdf`
- *Making Monolingual Sentence Embeddings Multilingual using Knowledge Distillation* by *Nils Reimers* and *Iryna Gurevych*, available at `https://arxiv.org/pdf/2004.09813.pdf`
- *ClinicalBERT: Modeling Clinical Notes and Predicting Hospital Readmission* by *Kexin Huang, Jaan Altosaar*, and *Rajesh Ranganath*, available at `https://arxiv.org/pdf/1904.05342.pdf`
- *BioBERT: a pre-trained biomedical language representation model for biomedical text mining* by *Jinhyuk Lee, Wonjin Yoon, Sungdong Kim, Donghyeon Kim, Sunkyu Kim, Chan Ho So*, and *Jaewoo Kang*, available at `https://arxiv.org/pdf/1901.08746.pdf`

9
Working with VideoBERT, BART, and More

Congratulations! We have made it to the final chapter. We have come a long way. We started off with understanding transformers, then we learned about BERT and several different variants of BERT in detail, from ALBERT to SentenceBERT. In this chapter, we will learn about two interesting models named VideoBERT and BART. We will also explore two popular BERT libraries known as **ktrain** and **bert-as-service**. We will start off the chapter by learning how VideoBERT works. We will look at how the VideoBERT model is pre-trained to learn the representation of language and video in a joint manner. Then, we will look into some of the applications of VideoBERT.

Moving on, we will learn what BART is and how it differs from the BERT model. We will understand the different noising techniques used in BART in detail. Then, we will see how to perform text summarization using the pre-trained BART model.

After that, we will learn about an interesting library called ktrain. We will explore how ktrain works and we will learn to use ktrain for sentiment analysis, document answering, and document summarization.

Following ktrain, we will learn about another popular BERT library called bert-as-service, which is used to obtain sentence representations. We will learn how to use bert-as-service to compute sentence and contextual word representations.

In this chapter, we will learn about the following topics:

- Learning language and video representations with VideoBERT
- Understanding BART
- ktrain
- bert-as-service

Learning language and video representations with VideoBERT

In this section, we will learn about yet another interesting variant of BERT called **VideoBERT**. As the name suggests, along with learning the representation of language, VideoBERT also learns the representation of video. It is the first model that learns the representation of both video and language in a joint manner.

Just as we used a pre-trained BERT model and fine-tuned it for downstream tasks, we can also use a pre-trained VideoBERT model and fine-tune it for many interesting downstream tasks. VideoBERT is used for tasks such as image caption generation, video captioning, predicting the next frames of a video, and more.

But how exactly is VideoBERT pre-trained to learn video and language representations? Let's find out in the next section.

Pre-training a VideoBERT model

We know that the BERT model is pre-trained using two tasks, called **masked language modeling** (**cloze task**) and **next sentence prediction**. Can we also pre-train VideoBERT using masked language modeling and next sentence prediction? Yes and no, respectively. We can pre-train VideoBERT using the cloze task but we cannot use next sentence prediction; instead, we use a new task called **linguistic-visual alignment**. Now, let's explore how exactly the VideoBERT model is pre-trained using the cloze task and linguistic-visual alignment.

Cloze task

First, let's see how VideoBERT is pre-trained using the cloze task. In order to pre-train VideoBERT, we use instructional videos such as cooking videos. But why instructional videos? Why can't we use any random videos? Let's understand this with an example. Consider a video where someone is teaching us how to cook. Say the speaker is saying, *"Cut lemon into slices."* As we hear the speaker saying *cut lemon into slices*, they will also visually show us how they are cutting the lemon into slices, right? This is shown in the following figure:

Figure 9.1 – Sample video

These sorts of instructional videos, where the speaker's statement and the corresponding visuals align with each other, are very useful for pre-training VideoBERT. In instructional videos, the speaker's statement and the corresponding visuals tend to match with one another, which helps us to learn the representations of the language and video in a joint fashion.

Okay, we have learned that instructional videos are useful for pre-training VideoBERT. What's next? How we can use video for training? First, we need to extract the language tokens (linguistic tokens) and visual tokens (video tokens) from the video. Let's see how to extract these tokens.

From the audio (speaker statements) used in a video, we can extract the linguistic tokens. We need to extract the audio from the video and convert the audio to text. In order to achieve this, we will leverage the **automatic speech recognition** (**ASR**) toolkit. By using ASR, we extract the audio used in the video and convert it into text. After converting the audio to text, we will tokenize the text, and this forms our language tokens.

Now, how to obtain the visual tokens? To obtain the visual tokens, we sample the image frames from the video at 20 fps (frames per second). Then, we convert the image frames into visual tokens with a duration of 1.5 seconds.

That's it. Now, we have language and visual tokens. What's next? How do we pre-train the VideoBERT model with these language and visual tokens? First, we combine the language and visual tokens. After combining them, we will have the language and visual tokens as they are shown in the following figure. We can observe that there is a [>] token in between the language and visual tokens. This is a special token used to combine the language and visual tokens:

Tokens = [Cut , lemon , into , slices , [>] ,   ,   ,   ]

Figure 9.2 – Input tokens

We know that we add the [CLS] token at the beginning of the first sentence and the [SEP] token at the end of every sentence. Now, we add the [CLS] token at the beginning of the language token and the [SEP] token only at the end of the visual tokens, which indicates that we treat the whole collection of language and visual tokens as a single sentence, as shown in *Figure 9.3*:

Figure 9.3 – Input tokens with CLS and SEP tokens

Now we randomly mask a few language and visual tokens as shown in the next figure:

Figure 9.4 – Masked input tokens

Next, we feed all the tokens to the VideoBERT model, which returns the representation of all the tokens. For instance, as shown in the following figure, we can observe that $R_{[CLS]}$ denotes the representation of [CLS] token, R_{Cut} denotes the representation of the token cut, and so on:

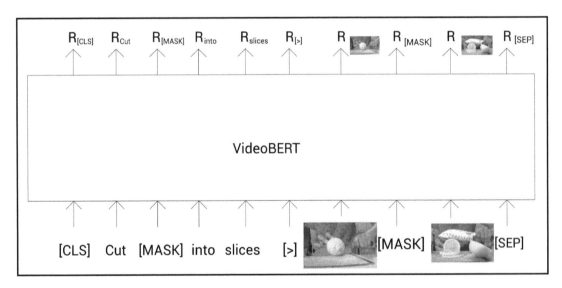

Figure 9.5 – VideoBERT returning the representation of all the tokens

Now, we feed the representation of the masked token returned by VideoBERT to a classifier (feedforward + softmax) and the classifier predicts the masked token as shown in the following figure:

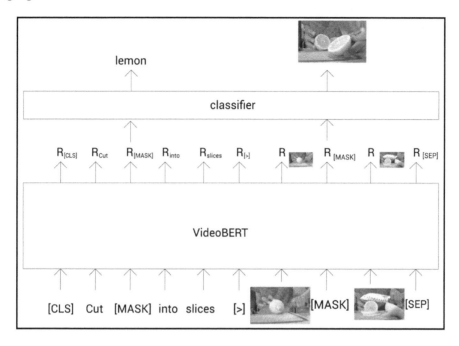

Figure 9.6 – Pre-training VideoBERT by predicting the masked tokens

In this way, we pre-train the VideoBERT model with a cloze task by predicting the masked linguistic and visual tokens.

Okay, now that we have learned how VideoBERT is pre-trained using the cloze task, in the next section, we will see how VideoBERT is pre-trained using linguistic-visual alignment.

Linguistic-visual alignment

Similar to the next sentence prediction task we learned about for BERT, linguistic-visual alignment is also a classification task. But here, we are not going to predict whether a sentence is the next sentence after another. Instead, we are going to predict whether the language and visual tokens are temporally aligned with each other. Okay, what does that mean? It means that we need to predict whether the text (the language tokens) matches with the video (the visual tokens).

Thus, the objective is to predict whether the language tokens (the linguistic sentence) is aligned with the visual tokens (the visual sentence). Okay, how can we do that? To achieve this, we will take the representation of the [CLS] token and feed it to a classifier that classifies whether the given language and visual tokens are temporally aligned or not aligned, as shown in the following figure:

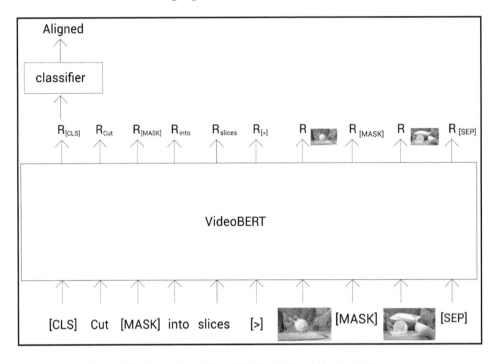

Figure 9.7 – Pre-training VideoBERT with linguistic-visual alignment

Similar to next sentence prediction, linguistic-visual alignment is a classification task, but here we use the representation of the [CLS] token to predict whether the language and visual tokens are aligned with each other, whereas in next sentence prediction, we used the [CLS] representation to predict whether a sentence was the next sentence after a given sentence.

We have learned how VideoBERT is pre-trained using the cloze task and linguistic-visual alignment in detail. In the next section, we will look at the final objective of pre-training VideoBERT.

The final pre-training objective

The VideoBERT model is pre-trained using the following three objectives, called **text-only**, **video-only**, and **text-video**:

- In the **text-only** method, we mask the language tokens and train the model to predict the masked language tokens. This makes the model better at understanding the language representation.
- In the **video-only** method, we mask the visual tokens and train the model to predict the masked visual tokens. This helps the model to better understand the video representation.
- In the **text-video** method, we mask the language and visual tokens and train the model to predict the masked language and visual tokens. We train the model for linguistic-visual alignment. This helps the model understand the relationship between the language and visual tokens.

The final pre-training objective of VideoBERT is the weighted combination of all of the three aforementioned methods. VideoBERT is pre-trained using the preceding objective for 2 days using 4 TPUs for 0.5 million iterations. We can use a pre-trained VideoBERT model and fine-tune it for downstream tasks.

Are you curious about the dataset used for pre-training VideoBERT? If you are, then check out the next section, where we see what dataset researchers have used to pre-train VideoBERT.

Data source and preprocessing

In order for VideoBERT to learn better language and video representations, we need a large number of videos. We have learned that we don't use random videos for pre-training; instead, we use instructional videos. How do we obtain instructional videos? Researchers have used instructional videos from YouTube to form their dataset. They filtered out YouTube videos related to cooking using the YouTube video annotation system. Out of these filtered videos, they only included videos whose duration was less than 15 minutes. In total, the number of videos is 312,000, which equals about 23,186 hours or 966 days.

Next, to convert the audio used in the video to text, researchers used the automatic speech recognition tool provided by the YouTube API. The YouTube API converts the audio to text and returns the text, along with timestamps. From this API, we will also get information about the language used in the video.

The API did not convert the audio to text for all the 312,000 videos; it converted only for 180,000 videos. Now, out of these 180,000 videos, only 120,000 videos are predicted to be in the English language. For the text-only and video-text objectives, the researchers used only those 120,000 videos that were in English. For the video-only objective, they used all 312,000 of the videos.

Okay, so how are the visual tokens obtained? We learned that to obtain visual tokens, we sample image frames from the video at 20 fps. Now, from these image frames, the researchers extracted the visual features using a pre-trained video convolutional neural network, and the visual features were tokenized using a hierarchical k-means algorithm.

We have learned how VideoBERT is pre-trained and what dataset is used to pre-train VideoBERT, but where exactly can we apply VideoBERT? What are its applications? Let's find that out in the next section.

Applications of VideoBERT

In this section, let's take a quick look into some of the interesting applications of VideoBERT.

Predicting the next visual tokens

By feeding a visual token to a VideoBERT model, it can predict the top three next visual tokens. For instance, as shown in the following figure, we can feed a visual token to the VideoBERT, and based on the given visual token, the model understands that we are baking a cake and predicts the top three future tokens:

Figure 9.8 – Predicting the next visual tokens using VideoBERT

This image has been taken from the paper here: https://arxiv.org/pdf/1904.01766.pdf.

Text-to-video generation

Given text as an input, VideoBERT can generate a corresponding visual token. For instance, as shown in the following figure, based on the given cooking instruction, our model generates the corresponding video:

Figure 9.9 – Text-to-video generation using VideoBERT

This image has been taken from this paper: `https://arxiv.org/pdf/1904.01766.pdf`.

Video captioning

Given a video, we can use VideoBERT to caption it. We just feed the video to the VideoBERT model and it returns the caption. A sample generated caption is shown in the following figure:

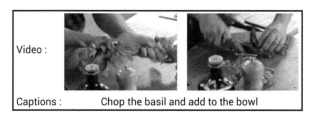

Figure 9.10 – Video caption generation using VideoBERT

Now that we have learned how the VideoBERT model works, in the next section, we will look at another interesting model called BART.

Understanding BART

BART is another interesting model introduced by Facebook AI. It is based on the transformer architecture. The BART model is essentially a denoising autoencoder. It is trained by reconstructing corrupted text.

Just like the BERT model, we can use the pre-trained BART model and fine-tune it for several downstream tasks. The BART model is best suited to text generation. It is also used for other tasks such as language translation and comprehension. The researchers have also shown that the performance of BART is equivalent to that of the RoBERTa model. But how exactly does BART work? What's special about BART? How does it differ from BERT? Let's find out the answers to all these questions in the next section.

Architecture of BART

BART is essentially a transformer model with an encoder and a decoder. We feed corrupted text to the encoder and the encoder learns the representation of the given text and sends the representation to the decoder. The decoder takes the representation produced by the encoder and reconstructs the original uncorrupted text.

The encoder of the BART model is bidirectional, meaning that it can read a sentence in both directions (left to right and right to left), but the decoder of the BART model is unidirectional and it reads a sentence only in the left-to-right direction. Thus, in BART, we have a bidirectional encoder (for both directions) and an autoregressive decoder (for a single direction).

The following figure shows the BART model. As we can see, we corrupt the original text (by masking few tokens) and feed it to the encoder. The encoder learns the representation of the given text and sends the representation to the decoder, which then reconstructs the original uncorrupted text:

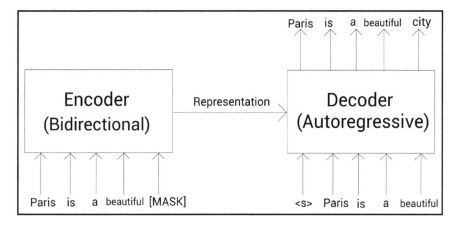

Figure 9.11 – BART model

The BART model is trained by minimizing the reconstruction loss, that is, a cross-entropy loss between the original text and the text produced by the decoder. Note that BART is different from the BERT model. In BERT, we just feed the masked tokens to the encoder and then feed the result of the encoder to the feedforward network, which predicts the masked tokens. But in BART, we feed the result of the encoder to the decoder, which generates/reconstructs the original sentence.

The researchers have experimented with two different configurations of the BART model:

- **BART-base**: 6 encoder and decoder layers
- **BART-large**: 12 encoder and decoder layers

We learned that we corrupt the text and feed it to the encoder of BART. But how exactly do we corrupt the text? Does corrupting only include masking few tokens? Not necessarily. The researchers have proposed several interesting noising techniques for corrupting the text; we will look into those techniques in the next section.

Noising techniques

The researchers introduced the following different noising techniques to corrupt the text:

- Token masking
- Token deletion
- Token infilling
- Sentence shuffling
- Document rotation

Let's take a closer look at each of these methods.

Token masking

In **token masking,** as the name suggests, we randomly mask a few tokens. That is, we randomly replace a few tokens with [MASK], just as we did in the BERT model. A simple example is shown in the following figure:

original	corrupted
Chelsea is my favorite football club	Chelsea is my favorite [MASK] club

Figure 9.12 – Token masking

Token deletion

In the token deletion method, we randomly delete some tokens. Token deletion is just like token masking, but instead of masking the tokens, we directly delete them. A simple example is shown here:

original	corrupted
Chelsea is my favorite football club	Chelsea is my favorite club

Figure 9.13 – Token deletion

Since here no [MASK] token is used and the tokens are deleted directly, our model finds the positions where the tokens are randomly deleted and predicts a new token in that position.

Token infilling

In the token infilling method, we mask the contiguous set of tokens with a single [MASK] token. Wait – is it similar to SpanBERT? No: in SpanBERT, if we were masking a contiguous set of four tokens, then we'd replace them with four [MASK] tokens. But here, we replace them with a single [MASK] token. Let's understand this with the following example:

original	corrupted
I loved the book so much and I have read it so many times	I loved [MASK] and I have read it so many times

Figure 9.14 – Token infilling

As we can see, we are masking the contiguous set of tokens (the, book, so, much) with a single [MASK] token.

Sentence shuffling

In sentence shuffling, as the name suggests, we randomly shuffle the order of sentences and feed them to the encoder. A small example is shown here:

original	corrupted
I completed my assignment by evening. Then I started playing a game. I played the game until 10 PM. Then I went to sleep.	I played the game until 10 PM. Then I started playing a game. I completed my assignment by evening. Then I went to sleep.

Figure 9.15 – Sentence shuffling

As we can see from the preceding table, we have shuffled the sentence order.

Document rotation

In the document rotation method, with a given document, we randomly select a particular word (token) in the document to be the start of the document. Then, all the words before the selected word will be appended to the end of the document. For example, as shown in the following figure, if we select the word **playing** as the starting word of the document, then all the words before this will be appended to the end of the document:

original	corrupted
I completed my assignment by evening. Then I started <u>playing</u> a game. I played the game until 10 PM. Then I went to sleep	Playing a game. I played the game until 10 PM. Then I went to sleep. I completed my assignment by evening Then I started

Figure 9.16 – Document rotation

We can use any of the aforementioned noising techniques to corrupt some text and pre-train BART to predict the corrupted text. After pre-training, we can fine-tune it for other downstream tasks. Suppose we were using a pre-trained BART model for a sentence classification task; in that case, we would feed an uncorrupted sentence to the encoder, and then use the representation from the final decoder for the classification task.

Comparing different pre-training objectives

In the previous section, we learned about the different noising techniques that are used to pre-train BART, but which one is best? The researchers have experimented with different noising techniques and fine-tuned BART on several datasets, and their results are shown in the following figure:

Noising technique	SQuAD 1.1 F1	MNLI Acc	ELI5 Acc	XSum PPL	ConvAI2 PPL	CNN/DM PPL
Token Masking	90.4	84.1	25.05	7.08	11.73	6.10
Token Deletion	90.4	84.1	24.61	6.90	11.46	5.87
Text Infiling	90.8	84.0	24.26	6.61	11.05	5.83
Document Rotation	77.2	75.3	53.69	17.14	19.87	10.59
Sentence Shuffling	58.4	81.5	41.87	10.93	16.67	7.89
Text Infilling + Sentence Shuffling	90.8	83.8	24.17	6.62	11.12	5.41

Figure 9.17: Comparing different noising techniques. Results as given in the BART paper: https://arxiv.org/pdf/1910.13461.pdf

Now that we have learned how the BART model is pre-trained, in the next section, let's see how to use a pre-trained BART model for text summarization.

Performing text summarization with BART

We can also access the complete code from the GitHub repository of the book. In order to run the code smoothly, clone the GitHub repository of the book and run the code using Google Colab. First, let's import `BartTokenizer` for tokenizing and `BartForConditionalGeneration` for text summarization from the `transformers` library:

```
from transformers import BartTokenizer, BartForConditionalGeneration
```

We will use the pre-trained BART-large model. `bart-large-cnn` is the pre-trained BART-large model for text summarization:

```
model = \
BartForConditionalGeneration.from_pretrained('facebook/bart-large-cnn')
tokenizer = BartTokenizer.from_pretrained('facebook/bart-large-cnn')
```

Now, define the text that we want to summarize:

```
text = """Machine learning (ML) is the study of computer algorithms that
improve automatically through experience.It is seen as a subset of
artificial intelligence. Machine learning algorithms build a mathematical
model based on sample data, known as training data, in order to make
predictions or decisions without being explicitly programmed to do
so.Machine learning algorithms are used in a wide variety of applications,
such as email filtering and computer vision, where it is difficult or
infeasible to develop conventional algorithms to perform the needed
tasks."""
```

Tokenize the text with the following code:

```
inputs = tokenizer([text], max_length=1024, return_tensors='pt')
```

Get the summary IDs, which are the IDs of the tokens generated by the model:

```
summary_ids = model.generate(inputs['input_ids'], num_beams=4,
                             max_length=100, early_stopping=True)
```

Now decode the summary IDs and get the corresponding token (word):

```
summary = ([tokenizer.decode(i, skip_special_tokens=True,
                             clean_up_tokenization_spaces=False) \
           for i in summary_ids])
```

That's it. Now, let's print the summary of our given text:

```
print(summary)
```

The preceding code will print the following:

```
Machine learning is the study of computer algorithms that improve
automatically through experience. It is a subset of artificial
intelligence. Machine learning algorithms are used in a wide variety of
applications, such as email filtering and computer vision, where it is
difficult or infeasible to develop conventional algorithm.
```

As we can see, we now have the summarized text. In this way, we can use BART for text summarization. Next, we will explore two interesting BERT libraries.

Exploring BERT libraries

In the previous chapter, we saw how to use Hugging Face's `transformers` library. In this section, let's explore the following two other popular libraries for BERT:

- ktrain
- bert-as-service

Understanding ktrain

ktrain is a low-code library for augmented machine learning that was developed by Arun S. Maiya. It is a lightweight wrapper for Keras that makes it easier for us to build, train, and deploy deep learning models. It also includes several pre-trained models that make tasks such as text classification, summarization, question answering, translation, regression, and more easier. It is implemented using `tf.keras`. It includes several interesting functionalities, such as a learning rate finder, a learning rate scheduler, and others.

With ktrain, you can build a model in 3-5 lines of code, which the author calls low-code machine learning. Let's see how we can use ktrain.

Before going forward, let's install the ktrain library. It can be installed via `pip` as shown here:

```
!pip install ktrain
```

Now that we have installed ktrain, in the upcoming sections, we will learn how to use the ktrain library for sentiment analysis, question answering, and summarization.

Sentiment analysis using ktrain

In this section, let's learn how to perform sentiment analysis using ktrain. We will use the Amazon product reviews dataset. The dataset can be downloaded from here: `http://jmcauley.ucsd.edu/data/amazon/`.

At the preceding URL, we can find the complete reviews data and also a small subset of data. In this exercise, we will use the subset of data containing the reviews of digital music. We can download digital music reviews from here: `http://snap.stanford.edu/data/amazon/productGraph/categoryFiles/reviews_Digital_Music_5.json.gz`. The downloaded digital music reviews will be in a compressed `gzip` format. So, after downloading, we will uncompress them and get the reviews in JSON format. Now, let's get started.

We can also access the complete code from the GitHub repository of the book. In order to run the code smoothly, clone the GitHub repository of the book and run the code using Google Colab.

First, load the necessary libraries:

```
import ktrain
from ktrain import text
import pandas as pd
```

Download and load digital music reviews:

```
!gdown https://drive.google.com/uc?id=1-8urBLVtFuuvAVHi0s000e7r0KPUgt9f
df = pd.read_json(r'reviews_Digital_Music_5.json',lines=True)
```

Let's have a look at a few rows of our dataset:

```
df.head()
```

The preceding code will print the following:

	reviewerID	asin	reviewerName	helpful	reviewText	overall	summary	unixReviewTime	reviewTime
0	A3EBHHCZO6V2A4	5555991584	Amaranth "music fan"	[3, 3]	It's hard to believe "Memory of Trees" came ou...	5	Enya's last great album	1158019200	09 12, 2006
1	AZPWAXJG9OJXV	5555991584	bethtexas	[0, 0]	A clasically-styled and introverted album, Mem...	5	Enya at her most elegant	991526400	06 3, 2001
2	A38IRL0X2T4DPF	5555991584	bob turnley	[2, 2]	I never thought Enya would reach the sublime h...	5	The best so far	1058140800	07 14, 2003
3	A22IK3I6U76GX0	5555991584	Calle	[1, 1]	This is the third review of an irish album I w...	5	Ireland produces good music.	957312000	05 3, 2000
4	A1AISPOIIHTHXX	5555991584	Cloud "..."	[1, 1]	Enya, despite being a successful recording art...	4	4.5; music to dream to	1200528000	01 17, 2008

Figure 9.18 – The first few rows of the dataset

We only need the review text and overall rating, so let's subset the dataset to get only the `reviewText` and `overall` columns, as shown in the following code:

```
df = df[['reviewText','overall']]
df.head()
```

The preceding code will print the following:

	reviewText	overall
0	It's hard to believe "Memory of Trees" came ou...	5
1	A clasically-styled and introverted album, Mem...	5
2	I never thought Enya would reach the sublime h...	5
3	This is the third review of an irish album I w...	5
4	Enya, despite being a successful recording art...	4

Figure 9.19 – Subset of the dataset with the reviewText and overall columns

We can see that we have ratings ranging from 1 to 5. Let's convert these ratings to sentiment by mapping ratings 1 to 3 to the `negative` class and 4 to 5 to the `positive` class:

```
sentiment = {1:'negative',2:'negative',3:'negative',
             4:'positive',5:'positive'}

df['sentiment'] = df['overall'].map(sentiment)
```

Now, let's subset the dataset for only the `reviewText` and `sentiment` columns, as shown in the following code:

```
df = df[['reviewText','sentiment']]
df.head()
```

The preceding code will print the following:

	reviewText	sentiment
0	It's hard to believe "Memory of Trees" came ou...	positive
1	A clasically-styled and introverted album, Mem...	positive
2	I never thought Enya would reach the sublime h...	positive
3	This is the third review of an irish album I w...	positive
4	Enya, despite being a successful recording art...	positive

Figure 9.20 – The first few rows of the dataset

From the preceding result, we can notice that we have review text matched to its corresponding sentiment.

The next step is creating the train and test sets. If our data is in a pandas DataFrame, we can use the `texts_from_df` function to create train and test sets, and if our data is in a folder, then we can use the `texts_from_folder` function.

Since our dataset is in a pandas DataFrame, we will use the `texts_from_df` function. The arguments of the function include the following:

- `train_df`: The DataFrame containing the reviews and their sentiment.
- `text_column`: The name of the column containing the reviews.
- `label_column`: The name of the column containing the label.
- `maxlen`: The maximum length of the review.
- `max_features`: The maximum number of words we use in vocabulary.
- `preprocess_mode`: This is used to preprocess the text. If we want to use normal tokenization then we set `preprocess_mode` to `standard`, and if we want to perform tokenization as we do in BERT, then we set `preprocess_mode` to `bert`.

In this exercise, we will set `maxlen` to `100` and `max_features` to `100000`. We will use `bert` for `preprocess_mode` since we are going to use BERT to perform the classification:

```
(x_train, y_train), (x_test, y_test), preproc = \
text.texts_from_df(train_df = df,
                   text_column = 'reviewText',
                   label_columns=['sentiment'],
                   maxlen=100,
                   max_features=100000,
```

```
                              preprocess_mode='bert',
                              val_pct=0.1)
```

The preceding code will print the following:

```
downloading pre-trained BERT model (uncased_L-12_H-768_A-12.zip)...
[██████████████████████████████████████████████████████████]
extracting pre-trained BERT model...
done.

cleanup downloaded zip...
done.

preprocessing train...
language: en
done.
Is Multi-Label? False
preprocessing test...
language: en
done.
```

From the preceding result, we can see that we are downloading the pre-trained BERT model. We can see that ktrain is also identifying whether our task is a binary or multi-class classification task.

The next step is to define our classifier. Before that, let's have a look at the classifiers offered by ktrain:

```
text.print_text_classifiers()
```

The preceding code will print the following:

```
fasttext: a fastText-like model [http://arxiv.org/pdf/1607.01759.pdf]
logreg: logistic regression using a trainable Embedding layer
nbsvm: NBSVM model [http://www.aclweb.org/anthology/P12-2018]
bigru: Bidirectional GRU with pre-trained fasttext word vectors
[https://fasttext.cc/docs/en/crawl-vectors.html]
standard_gru: simple 2-layer GRU with randomly initialized embeddings
bert: Bidirectional Encoder Representations from Transformers (BERT)
[https://arxiv.org/abs/1810.04805]
distilbert: distilled, smaller, and faster BERT from Hugging Face
[https://arxiv.org/abs/1910.01108]
```

From the preceding result, we can notice that kt rain provides a diverse set of classifiers, ranging from logistic regression and bidirectional GRU to the BERT model. In this tutorial, we will use the BERT model.

Now, let's define the model using the text_classifier function, which builds and returns a classifier. The following are the important arguments to the function:

- name: The name of the model we want to use; in this case, we use bert
- train_data: A tuple containing our train data, which is (x_train, y_train)
- preproc: An instance of our preprocessor
- metrics: The metrics with which we want to assess the performance of our model; in this example, we will use accuracy:

```
model = text.text_classifier(name='bert', train_data = (x_train,
                                                         y_train),
                             preproc=preproc, metrics=['accuracy'])
```

Next, we create an instance called learner, which is used to train our model. We will use the get_learner function to create the learner instance. The following are the important arguments to the function:

- model: The model that we defined in the previous step
- train_data: A tuple containing our training data
- val_data: A tuple containing our test data
- batch_size: The batch size that we want to use
- use_multiprocessing: A Boolean value indicating whether we want to use multiprocessing:

```
learner = ktrain.get_learner(model = model,
                             train_data=(x_train, y_train),
                             val_data=(x_test, y_test),
                             batch_size=32,
                             use_multiprocessing = True)
```

Now, we can finally train the model using the fit_onecycle function. The following are the important arguments to the function:

- lr: The learning rate
- epoch: The number of epochs we want to train for
- checkpoint_folder: The directory where we want to store the model weights:

```
learner.fit_onecycle(lr=2e-5, epochs=1,checkpoint_folder='output')
```

In this example, we are training only for one epoch for simplicity. The preceding code will print the following:

```
begin training using onecycle policy with max lr of 2e-05...
1820/1820 [==============================] - 1004s 551ms/step - loss:
0.3573 - accuracy: 0.8482 - val_loss: 0.2991 - val_accuracy: 0.8778
```

As we can see from the results, we have obtained 87% accuracy on the test set. That's it. Training a model using ktrain is this simple.

Now, we can use the trained model and make predictions using the get_predictor function. We need to pass our trained model and the instance of our preprocessor as shown here:

```
predictor = ktrain.get_predictor(learner.model, preproc)
```

Next, we can make a prediction with the predict function by passing the text:

```
predictor.predict('I loved the song')
```

The preceding code will print the following:

```
'positive'
```

As we can see, our model has identified that the given sentence is a positive sentence.

Building a document answering model

In this section, let's learn how to use ktrain to build a document answering model. We know that in document answering, we will have a set of documents and we use those documents to answer a question. Let's see how we can do this using ktrain.

First, let's import the necessary libraries:

```
from ktrain import text
import os
import shutil
```

In this exercise, we will use the BBC News dataset. The BBC News dataset consists of 2,225 documents containing news from 2004 to 2005. It includes news in these five categories: business, entertainment, politics, sports, and technology.

First, let's download the dataset:

```
!wget http://mlg.ucd.ie/files/datasets/bbc-fulltext.zip
```

Next, unzip the dataset:

```
!unzip bbc-fulltext.zip
```

Now, import the necessary libraries:

```
from ktrain import text
import os
```

Change directory to our BBC News folder:

```
os.chdir(os.getcwd() + '/bbc')
```

The first step is initializing the index directory. It is used to index all the documents. We don't need to create any new directories manually. We just need to pass the name of the index directory to the `intialize_index` function and the index directory will be created:

```
text.SimpleQA.initialize_index('index')
```

After initializing the index, we need to index the documents. Since we will have all the documents in the folder, we will use the `index_from_folder` function. The `index_from_folder` function takes the `folder_path` value for where we have all the documents and `index_dir` as parameters:

```
text.SimpleQA.index_from_folder(folder_path='entertainment',
                                index_dir='index')
```

The next step is creating an instance of the SimpleQA class as shown next. We need to pass the index directory as an argument:

```
qa = text.SimpleQA('index')
```

That's it. Now, we can use the `ask` function and retrieve answers from the documents for any question:

```
answers = qa.ask('who had a global hit with where is the love?')
```

Let's print the top five answers:

```
qa.display_answers(answers[:5])
```

The preceding code will print the following:

	Candidate Answer	Context	Confidence	Document Reference
0	the black eyed peas	the black eyed peas -who had a global hit with where is the love ?-picked up the prize for best pop act, beating anastacia, avril lavigne, robbie williams and britney spears.	0.994715	153.txt
1	but angels	some people will adopt their slightly snobby stances, but angels has hit home with a far larger audience than any other song.	0.002225	253.txt
2	huge robbie	i am a huge robbie fan and love that song.	0.001946	253.txt
3	out kast	out kast will add their awards to the four they won at the us mtv awards in august and three grammys in february.	0.000182	153.txt
4	u2	u2 stars enter rock hall of fame	0.000132	291.txt

Figure 9.21 – Answers returned by the model

As we can see, along with obtaining the candidate answer, we get other information, such as context, confidence, and document reference values.

Let's try with another question:

```
answers = qa.ask('who win at mtv europe awards?')
qa.display_answers(answers[:5])
```

The preceding code will print the following:

	Candidate Answer	Context	Confidence	Document Reference
0	out kast	out kast win at mtv europe awards	0.552339	153.txt
1	duo out kast	us hip hop duo out kast have capped a year of award glory with three prizes at the mtv europe music awards in rome.	0.274871	153.txt
2	was justin timberlake	last year ' s big winner at the mtv europe awards, held in edinburgh, scotland, was justin timberlake , who walked away with three trophies.	0.112146	153.txt
3	duo out kast	us rap duo out kast ' s trio of trophies at the mtv europe awards crowns a year of huge success for the band.	0.054767	132.txt
4	band franz ferdinand	scottish rock band franz ferdinand , who shot to prominence in 2004, have won two brit awards.	0.002645	236.txt

Figure 9.22 – Answers returned by the model

In this way, we can use `ktrain` for document answering use cases.

Document summarization

Let's explore how to use the ktrain library to perform document summarization. Let's extract content from Wikipedia for a topic of interest and then perform summarization using ktrain.

First, let's install the `wikipedia` library using `pip`:

```
!pip install wikipedia
```

After installing, import the `wikipedia` library:

```
import wikipedia
```

Specify the title of the Wikipedia page that we want to extract:

```
wiki = wikipedia.page('Pablo Picasso')
```

Extract the plain text content of the page:

```
doc = wiki.content
```

Let's see what we have extracted. Let's print only the first 1,000 words:

```
print(doc[:1000])
```

The preceding code will print the following:

```
Pablo Diego José Francisco de Paula Juan Nepomuceno María de los Remedios
Cipriano de la Santísima Trinidad Ruiz y Picasso (UK: , US: , Spanish:
['paβlo pi'kaso]; 25 October 1881 – 8 April 1973) was a Spanish painter,
sculptor, printmaker, ceramicist and theatre designer who spent most of his
adult life in France. Regarded as one of the most influential artists of
the 20th century, he is known for co-founding the Cubist movement, the
invention of constructed sculpture, the co-invention of collage, and for
the wide variety of styles that he helped develop and explore. Among his
most famous works are the proto-Cubist Les Demoiselles d'Avignon (1907),
and Guernica (1937), a dramatic portrayal of the bombing of Guernica by
German and Italian airforces during the Spanish Civil War.\nPicasso
demonstrated extraordinary artistic talent in his early years, painting in
a naturalistic manner through his childhood and adolescence. During the
first decade of the 20th century, his style changed as
```

Now, let's see how to summarize this using ktrain. Download and instantiate the text summarization model from the ktrain library:

```
from ktrain import text
ts = text.TransformerSummarizer()
```

Now, just call the `summarize` function and pass the document that we want to summarize:

```
ts.summarize(doc)
```

The preceding code will print the following:

```
Pablo Diego José Francisco de Paula Juan Nepomuceno María de los Remedios
Cipriano de la Santísima Trinidad Ruiz y Picasso (25 October 1881 — 8 April
1973) was a Spanish painter, sculptor, printmaker, ceramicist and theatre
designer. He is known for co-founding the Cubist movement, the invention of
constructed sculpture, the co-invention of collage, and for the wide
variety of styles that he helped develop and explore. Among his most famous
works are the proto-Cubist Les Demoiselles d'Avignon (1907), and Guernica
(1937), a dramatic portrayal.
```

As we can see, we have the summarized text. Now that we have learned how to use ktrain, let's explore another library called bert-as-service.

bert-as-service

bert-as-service is another widely used library for BERT. It is simple, scalable, and easy to use. Besides that, bert-as-service also has excellent documentation with clear details about how the library works. We can see the documentation here: `https://bert-as-service.readthedocs.io/en/latest/index.html`.

In this section, let's get a basic overview of how to use bert-as-service to obtain sentence representations.

Installing the library

`bert-as-service` can be installed directly using `pip`. As shown in the following code, we will install `bert-serving-client` and `bert-serving-server`:

```
!pip install bert-serving-client
!pip install -U bert-serving-server[http]
```

Next, let's explore how to use `bert-as-service` to obtain sentence representation.

Computing sentence representation

Let's compute the representation of two sentences using bert-as-service and find the similarity between the two sentences. First, we will download and unzip the pre-trained BERT model that we want to use. In this example, we use the pre-trained BERT-base uncased model. We can also try any other pre-trained BERT models:

```
!wget
https://storage.googleapis.com/bert_models/2018_10_18/uncased_L-12_H-768_A-12.zip
!unzip uncased_L-12_H-768_A-12.zip
```

Next, we will start the BERT server. While starting the BERT server, we also pass the pooling strategy that we want. That is, we learned that BERT returns the representation for each word in the sentence, and to obtain the representation of a complete sentence, we use a pooling method. So, we pass the pooling strategy that we want to use. In this example, we use the mean pooling strategy:

```
!nohup bert-serving-start -pooling_strategy REDUCE_MEAN \
-model_dir=./uncased_L-12_H-768_A-12 > out.file 2>&1 &
```

Next, import the BERT client:

```
from bert_serving.client import BertClient
```

Start the BERT client:

```
bc = BertClient()
```

Define the sentences for which we need to compute representation:

```
sentence1 = 'the weather is great today'
sentence2 = 'it looks like today the weather is pretty nice'
```

Compute the representation of the sentences using our BERT client:

```
sent_rep1 = bc.encode([sentence1])
sent_rep2 = bc.encode([sentence2])
```

Now let's check the size of the representation of the given two sentences:

```
print(sent_rep1.shape, sent_rep2.shape)
```

The preceding code will print the following:

```
(1, 768) (1, 768)
```

As we can see, the shape for both sentences is (1, 768). Next, we can compute the similarity between the vector representation of the given sentences:

```
from sklearn.metrics.pairwise import cosine_similarity
cosine_similarity(sent_rep1,sent_rep2)
```

The preceding code will print the following:

```
array([[0.8532591]], dtype=float32)
```

Thus, we can see that our given two sentences are 85% similar.

Computing contextual word representation

In the previous section, we learned how to use bert-as-service to obtain sentence representations. In this section, let's learn how to use bert-as-service to obtain a contextual word representation.

We know that BERT returns the representation of each word in a sentence and the representation of a word is based on the context of the words used in the sentence. To obtain the word representation, we set the pooling strategy to NONE while starting the BERT server. We also pass the maximum sequence length as an argument. Every sentence varies in length, right? So, we set the maximum sequence length to 20 as in the following code:

```
!nohup bert-serving-start –pooling_strategy NONE –max_seq_len=20 \
–model_dir=./uncased_L-12_H-768_A-12 > out.file 2>&1 &
```

Import the BERT client:

```
from bert_serving.client import BertClient
```

Define the sentence:

```
sentence = 'The weather is great today'
```

Next, compute the vector representation of the sentence:

```
vec = bc.encode([sentence])
```

Let's check the size of the vector:

```
print(vec.shape)
```

The preceding code will print this:

```
(1, 20, 768)
```

As you can see, unlike what we saw in the previous section, here the size of the given sentence is (1,20,768). This basically implies that we have a representation for each word in the given sentence. That is, we know that in the BERT model, we use the [CLS] token at the beginning and [SEP] token at the end of the sentence:

- **vec[0][0]**: Holds the representation of the [CLS] token
- **vec[0][1]**: Holds the representation of the first word in the sentence, "the"
- **vec[0][2]**: Holds the representation of the second word in the sentence, "weather"
- **vec[0][3]**: Holds the representation of the third word in the sentence, "is"
- **vec[0][4]**: Holds the representation of the fourth word in the sentence, "great"
- **vec[0][5]**: Holds the representation of the fifth word in the sentence, "today"
- **vec[0][6]**: Holds the representation of the [SEP] token
- **vec[0][7] to vec[0][20]**: Holds the representation of the padding tokens

In this way, we can use bert-as-service for various use cases.

BERT has revolutionized the world of NLP by achieving state-of-the-art results. Now that you understand how BERT and several popular variants of BERT work, you can start applying BERT in your projects. Learn and transform!

Summary

We started the chapter by learning how VideoBERT works. We learned how VideoBERT is pre-trained by predicting the masked language and visual tokens. We also learned that VideoBERT's final pre-training objective function is the weighted combination of text-only, video-only, and text-video methods. Later, we explored different applications of VideoBERT.

Then, we learned that BART is essentially a transformer model with an encoder and an decoder. We feed corrupted text to the encoder and the encoder learns the representation of the given text and sends the representation to the decoder. The decoder takes the representation produced by the encoder and reconstructs the original uncorrupted text. We also saw that BART uses a bidirectional encoder and a unidirectional decoder.

We also explored different noising techniques, such as token masking, token deletion, token infilling, sentence shuffling, and document rotation, in detail. Then, we learned how to perform text summarization using BART with Hugging Face's `transformers` library.

Moving on, we learned about the ktrain library. We explored how to perform sentiment analysis with the Amazon digital music reviews dataset and document answering with the BBC dataset, and we also saw how to perform document summarization. At the end of the chapter, we learned how to obtain sentence and contextual word representations using the bert-as-service library.

BERT is a major breakthrough and has paved the way for many recent developments in NLP. Now that you have completed reading this book, you can start building interesting applications using BERT.

Questions

Let's assess the knowledge gained in this chapter. Try answering the following questions:

1. What is the use of VideoBERT?
2. How is VideoBERT pre-trained?
3. How does linguistic-visual alignment differ from next sentence prediction?
4. Define the text-only training objective.
5. Define the video-only training objective.
6. What is BART?
7. Explain token masking and token deletion.

Further reading

For more information, refer to the following resources:

- *VideoBERT: A Joint Model for Video and Language Representation Learning* by Chen Sun, Austin Myers, Carl Vondrick, Kevin Murphy, Cordelia Schmid, available at `https://arxiv.org/pdf/1904.01766.pdf`
- *BART: Denoising Sequence-to-Sequence Pre-training for Natural Language Generation, Translation, and Comprehension* by Mike Lewis, Yinhan Liu, Naman Goyal, Marjan Ghazvininejad, Abdelrahman Mohamed, Omer Levy, Ves Stoyanov, Luke Zettlemoyer, available at `https://arxiv.org/pdf/1910.13461.pdf`
- *ktrain: A Low-Code Library for Augmented Machine Learning* by Arun S. Maiya, available at `https://arxiv.org/pdf/2004.10703.pdf`
- *BERT-as-a-service* documentation: `https://bert-as-service.readthedocs.io/en/latest/`

Assessments

The following are the answers to the questions given at the end of each chapter.

Chapter 1, A Primer on Transformers

1. The steps involved in the self-attention mechanism are given here:

   - First, we compute the dot product between the query matrix and the key matrix QK^T and get the similarity scores.
   - Next, we divide QK^T by the square root of the dimension of the key vector $\sqrt{d_k}$.
   - Then, we apply the softmax function to normalize the scores and obtain the score matrix $\text{softmax}(QK^T/\sqrt{d_k})$.
   - Finally, we compute the attention matrix Z by multiplying the score matrix with the value matrix V.

2. The self-attention mechanism is also called **scaled dot product attention**, since here we are computing the dot product (between the query and key vector) and scaling the values (with $\sqrt{d_k}$).

3. To create query, key, and value matrices, we introduce three new weight matrices called W^Q, W^K, W^V. We create the query , Q key K, and value V matrices, by multiplying the input matrix X by W^Q, W^K, and W^V, respectively.

4. If we were to pass the preceding input matrix directly to the transformer, it would not understand the word order. So, instead of feeding the input matrix directly to the transformer, we need to add some information indicating the word order (position of the words) so that our network can understand the meaning of the sentence. To do this, we introduce a technique called **positional encoding**. Positional encoding, as the name suggests, is an encoding that indicates the position of a word in a sentence (the word order).

5. The decoder consists of three sublayers: masked multi-head attention, multi-head attention, and the feedforward network.

6. The multi-head attention sublayer in each decoder receives two inputs; one is from the previous sublayer, masked multi-head attention, and the other is the encoder representation.

Chapter 2, Understanding the BERT Model

1. **BERT** stands for **B**idirectional **E**ncoder **R**epresentation from **T**ransformer. It is a state-of-the-art embedding model published by Google. BERT is a context-based embedding model, unlike other popular embedding models such as word2vec, which are context-free.

2. The BERT-base model consists of $L = 12$, $A = 12$, $H = 768$, and **110 million** parameters, and the BERT-large model consists of $L = 24$, $A = 16$, $H = 1024$, and **340 million** parameters.

3. The segment embedding is used to distinguish between the two given sentences. The segment embedding layer returns only either of the two embeddings E_A and E_B as the output. That is, if the input token belongs to sentence A, then the token will be mapped to the embedding E_A, and if the token belongs to sentence B, then it will be mapped to the embedding E_B.

4. BERT is pre-trained using two tasks, namely masked language modeling and next-sentence prediction.

5. In the masked language modeling task, in a given input sentence, we randomly mask 15% of the words and train the network to predict the masked words. To predict the masked words, our model reads the sentence in both directions and tries to predict the masked words.

6. In the 80-10-10% rule, 80% of the time, we replace the token (actual word) with the [MASK] token; 10% of the time, we replace the token (actual word) with a random token (random word); and 10% of the time, we don't make any changes.

7. Next-sentence prediction is a binary classification task. In this task, we feed two sentences to BERT and it has to predict whether the second sentence is the follow-up (next sentence) of the first sentence.

Chapter 3, Getting Hands-On with BERT

1. We can use the pre-trained model in the following two ways:

    - As a feature extractor by extracting embeddings
    - By fine-tuning the pre-trained BERT model on downstream tasks such as text classification, question-answering, and more

2. The [PAD] token is used to match the token length.

3. To make our model understand that the [PAD] token is added only to match the `tokens` length and that it is not part of the actual tokens, we use an attention mask. We set the attention mask value to 1 in all positions and 0 for the position where we have the [PAD] token.

4. Fine-tuning implies that we are not training BERT from scratch; instead, we are using the already-trained BERT and updating its weights according to our task.

5. For each token i, we compute the dot product between the representation of the token R_i and the start vector S. Next, we apply the softmax function to the dot product $S.R_i$ and obtain the probability: $P_i = \frac{e^{S.R_i}}{\sum_j e^{S.R_j}}$. Next, we compute the starting index by selecting the index of the token that has a high probability of being the starting token.

6. For each token i, we compute the dot product between the representation of the token R_i and the end vector E. Next, we apply the softmax function to the dot product $E.R_i$ and obtain the probability: $P_i = \frac{e^{E.R_i}}{\sum_j e^{E.R_j}}$. Next, we compute the ending index by selecting the index of the token that has a high probability of being the ending token.

7. First, we tokenize the sentence, add the [CLS] token at the beginning, and add the [SEP] token at the end. Then, we feed the tokens to the pre-trained BERT and obtain the representation of every token. Next, we feed those token representations to a classifier (the feedforward network and the softmax function). Then, the classifier returns the category to which the named entity belongs.

Chapter 4, BERT Variants I – ALBERT, RoBERTa, ELECTRA, SpanBERT

1. In the next-sentence prediction task, we train the model to predict whether a sentence pair belongs to the `isNext` or `notNext` class, whereas in the sentence order prediction task, we train the model to predict whether a sentence order in a given sentence pair is swapped or not.

2. ALBERT uses the following two techniques to reduce the number of parameters: cross-layer parameter sharing and factorized embedding layer parameterization.

3. In cross-layer parameter sharing, instead of learning the parameters of all the encoder layers, we only learn the parameters of the first encoder layer, and then we just share the parameters of the first encoder layer with all the other encoder layers.

4. In a shared feedforward network, we only share the parameters of the feedforward network of the first encoder layer with the feedforward networks of other encoder layers. In shared attention, we only share the parameters of the multi-head attention of the first encoder layer with the multi-head attention of other encoder layers.

5. RoBERTa is essentially BERT with the following changes in pre-training:

    - Use dynamic masking instead of static masking in MLM tasks.
    - Remove the next-sentence prediction task and train using only MLM tasks.
    - Train with large batch size.
    - Use byte-level BPE as a tokenizer.

6. The replaced token detection task is very similar to masked language modeling, but instead of masking a token with the [MASK] token, here we replace a token with a different token and train the model to classify whether the given tokens are actual or replaced tokens.

7. In SpanBERT, instead of masking the tokens at random positions, we mask the random contiguous span of tokens.

Chapter 5, BERT Variants II – Based on Knowledge Distillation

1. **Knowledge distillation** is a model compression technique in which a small model is trained to reproduce the behavior of a large pre-trained model. It is also referred to as teacher-student learning, where the large pre-trained model is the teacher and the small model is the student.

2. The output of the teacher network is called a **soft target**, and the prediction made by the student network is called a **soft prediction**.

3. In knowledge distillation, we compute the cross-entropy loss between the soft target and soft prediction and train the student network through backpropagation by minimizing the cross-entropy loss. The cross-entropy loss between the soft-target and soft-prediction is also known as the **distillation loss**.

4. The pre-trained BERT model has a large number of parameters and also high inference time, which makes it harder to use them on edge devices such as mobile phones. To solve this issue, we use DistilBERT, which was introduced by researchers at Hugging Face. DistilBERT is the smaller, faster, cheaper, and lighter version of BERT.

5. The loss function of DistilBERT is the sum of the following three losses: distillation loss, masked language modeling loss (student loss), and cosine embedding loss.

6. The transformer layer is basically the encoder layer. We know that in the encoder layer, we compute the attention matrix using multi-head attention, and the encoder layer returns the hidden state representation as output. In the transformer distillation, we transfer the knowledge from the attention matrix of the teacher to the student and we also transfer knowledge from the hidden state of the teacher to the student.

7. In prediction layer distillation, we transfer knowledge from the final output layer, which is logits produced by the teacher BERT, to the student BERT.

Chapter 6, Exploring BERTSUM for Text Summarization

1. In **extractive summarization**, we create a summary from a given text by just extracting the important sentences. In abstractive summarization, given a text, we will create a summary by re-expressing the given text using different words, holding only the essential meaning of the given text.

2. Interval segment embedding is used to distinguish between the multiple given sentences. With interval segment embedding, we map the tokens of the sentence occurring in the odd index to E_A and we map the tokens of the sentence occurring in the even index to E_B.

3. To perform abstractive summarization, we use the transformer model with encoder-decoder architecture. We feed the input text to the encoder and the encoder returns the representation of the given input text. In the encoder-decoder architecture, we use the pre-trained BERTSUM as an encoder. So, the pre-trained BERTSUM model will generate a meaningful representation and the decoder uses this representation and learn to generate the summary.

4. **ROUGE**, which stands for **Recall-Oriented Understudy for Gisting Evaluation**, is a set of metrics used to evaluate text summarization tasks.

5. ROUGE-N is an n-gram recall between a candidate summary (predicted summary) and a reference summary (actual summary).

6. The recall is defined as a ratio of the total number of overlapping n-grams between the candidate and reference summary to the total number of n-grams in the reference summary.

7. **ROUGE-L** is based on the **longest common subsequence** (**LCS**). The LCS between two sequences is the common subsequence with a maximum length. So, if the candidate and reference summary have an LCS, then we can say that our candidate summary matches the reference summary.

Chapter 7, Applying BERT to Other Languages

1. **Multilingual BERT**, or **M-BERT** for short, is used to obtain the representation of text in different languages and not just English.
2. Similar to BERT, M-BERT is also trained with masked language modeling and next-sentence prediction tasks, but instead of using only English language Wikipedia text, M-BERT is trained using Wikipedia text in 104 different languages.
3. M-BERT works better for languages that have a shared word order (SVO-SVO, SOV-SOV) than for languages that have different word order (SVO-SOV, SOV-SVO).
4. Mixing or alternating different languages in a conversation is called code-switching. In transliteration, instead of writing text in the source language script, we use the target language script.
5. The XLM model is pre-trained using casual language modeling, masked language modeling, and translation language modeling tasks.
6. **Translation language modeling** (TLM) is an interesting pre-training strategy. In casual language modeling and masked language modeling, we train our model on monolingual data, but in TLM, we train the model on cross-lingual data, that is, parallel data that consists of the same text in two different languages.
7. The researchers of FlauBERT have also introduced a new unified evaluation benchmark for downstream tasks called **FLUE**, which stands for French Language Understanding Evaluation. FLUE is similar to the GLUE benchmark but for the French language.

Chapter 8, Exploring Sentence- and Domain-Specific BERT

1. **Sentence-BERT** (**SBERT**) was introduced by the **Ubiquitous Knowledge Processing Lab** (**UKP-TUDA**). As the name suggests, SBERT is used to obtain fixed-length sentence representations. SBERT extends the pre-trained BERT model (or its variants) to obtain the sentence representation.

2. If we obtain a sentence representation by applying mean pooling to the representation of all the tokens, then essentially the sentence representation holds the meaning of all the words (tokens), and if we obtain a sentence representation by applying max pooling to the representation of all the tokens, then essentially the sentence representation holds the meaning of important words (tokens).

3. **ClinicalBERT** is the clinical domain-specific BERT pre-trained on a large clinical corpus. The clinical notes or progress notes contain very useful information about the patient. This includes a record of patient visits, their symptoms, diagnosis, daily activities, observations, treatment plans, results of radiology, and much more. Understanding the contextual representation of clinical notes is challenging since it follows its own grammatical structure, abbreviations, and jargon. So, we pre-train ClinicalBERT with many clinical documents to understand the contextual representation of the clinical text.

4. The representation learned by ClinicalBERT helps us to understand many clinical insights, the summaries of clinical notes, the relationship between diseases and treatment measures, and much more. Once pre-trained, ClinicalBERT can be used for a variety of downstream tasks, such as re-admission prediction, length-of-stay estimation, mortality risk estimation, diagnosis prediction, and more.

5. ClinicalBERT is pre-trained using the MIMIC-III clinical notes. MIMIC-III is a large collection of health-related data from the Beth Israel Deaconess Medical Center. It includes the health-related data of over 40,000 patients who stayed in ICU.

6. The probability of readmission is computed as follows:

$$P(\text{readmit} = 1 | h_{\text{patient}}) = \frac{P_{\text{max}}^n + P_{\text{mean}}^n \, n/c}{1 + n/c}$$

7. BioBERT is pre-trained using biomedical domain-specific texts. We use the biomedical dataset from the following two sources: PubMed and **PubMed Central (PMC)**.

Chapter 9, Working with VideoBERT, BART, and More

1. In VideoBERT, along with learning the representation of a language, we also learn the representation of the video. It is the first model to learn the representation of both video and language in a joint manner.

2. The VideoBERT model is pre-trained using two important tasks called **masked language modeling (cloze task)** and the **linguistic visual alignment task**.

3. Similar to the next-sentence prediction task we learned about for BERT, the linguistic visual alignment is also a classification task. But here, we will not predict whether a sentence is the next sentence. Instead, we predict whether the language and the visual tokens are temporally aligned with each other.

4. In the **text-only** method, we mask the language tokens and train the model to predict the masked language tokens. This makes the model better at understanding language representation.

5. In the **video-only** method, we mask the visual tokens and train the model to predict the masked visual tokens. This helps the model to better understand the video representation.

6. BART is essentially a transformer model with an encoder and a decoder. We feed the corrupted text to the encoder and the encoder learns the representation of the given text and sends the representation to the decoder. The decoder takes the representation produced by the encoder and reconstructs the original uncorrupted text.

7. In **token masking**, as the name suggests, we randomly mask a few tokens. That is, we randomly replace a few tokens with [MASK], just as we did in the BERT model. In the token deletion method, we randomly delete some tokens. That is, token deletion is just like token masking, but instead of masking the tokens, we directly delete the tokens.

Other Books You May Enjoy

If you enjoyed this book, you may be interested in these other books by Packt:

Hands-On Python Natural Language Processing

Aman Kedia, Mayank Rasu

ISBN: 978-1-83898-959-0

- Understand how NLP powers modern applications
- Explore key NLP techniques to build your natural language vocabulary
- Transform text data into mathematical data structures and learn how to improve text mining models
- Discover how various neural network architectures work with natural language data
- Get the hang of building sophisticated text processing models using machine learning and deep learning
- Check out state-of-the-art architectures that have revolutionized research in the NLP domain

The Applied AI and Natural Language Processing Workshop

Krishna Sankar, Jeffrey Jackovich, Ruze Richards

ISBN: 978-1-80107-130-7

- Grasp the fundamentals of AI, ML, and AWS
- Explore the AWS command line, its interface, and its applications
- Import and export data to Amazon S3
- Perform topic modeling on a set of documents to analyze common themes
- Develop a custom chatbot to get the latest stock market quotes
- Create a personal call center and connect it to the chatbot

Leave a review - let other readers know what you think

Please share your thoughts on this book with others by leaving a review on the site that you bought it from. If you purchased the book from Amazon, please leave us an honest review on this book's Amazon page. This is vital so that other potential readers can see and use your unbiased opinion to make purchasing decisions, we can understand what our customers think about our products, and our authors can see your feedback on the title that they have worked with Packt to create. It will only take a few minutes of your time, but is valuable to other potential customers, our authors, and Packt. Thank you!

Index

Efficiently Learning an Encoder that Classifies
    Token Replacements Accurately (ELECTRA)
    about 141
    efficient training methods, exploring 149
    replaced token detection task 141, 143, 144
ELECTRA model
    training 148
embeddings, extracting from pre-trained BERT
    model
    about 95, 96, 97, 98
    Hugging Face transformers, using 98
embeddings, from encoder layers
    extracting 104
    input, preprocessing 104
    obtaining 105, 106, 107
embeddings
    extracting, from encoder layers of BERT 102,
        103, 104
    extracting, with ALBERT 133, 134
encoder layers, of BERT
    embeddings, extracting from 102, 103, 104
encoder of transformer, self-attention mechanism
    about 21
    step 1 15, 16, 17
    step 2 17
    step 3 18
    step 4 19, 20
encoder of transformer, sublayers
    about 10
    feedforward network sublayer 28
    multi-head attention mechanism 22, 23, 24
    self-attention mechanism 11, 12, 14
encoder of transformer
    about 9, 10
    add and norm component 29
    working 30, 31
encoder-decoder attention layer. 42
extractive summarization
    about 194, 195
    with BERT 196, 198, 199, 200, 201

F

factorized embedding parameterization 130
FinBERT
    for Finnish 247

FlauBERT
    for French 237
    used, for obtaining representation of French
        sentence 238, 239
French Language Understanding Evaluation
    (FLUE) 239

G

Gaussian Error Linear Unit (GELU) 79
generalization
    across scripts 225
    across typological features 225, 226
German BERT 244

H

Hugging Face transformers 98

J

Japanese BERT 247

K

knowledge distillation
    about 158, 159, 160
    student network, training 161, 162, 163, 164
knowledge, transferring from BERT to neural
    networks
    about 182
    data augmentation method 186
    data augmentation method, masking method
        186
    data augmentation method, n-gram sampling
        method 187
    data augmentation method, POS-guided word
        replacement method 186
    data augmentation procedure 187, 188
    student network, training 185
    teacher-student architecture 183
    teacher-student architecture, student network
        183, 184, 185
    teacher-student architecture, teacher BERT 183
ktrain
    about 300
    used, for building document answering model
        306, 307, 308

transliteration 228

U

Ubiquitous Knowledge Processing Lab (UKP-TUDA) 256
UmBERTo
  for Italian 248

V

VideoBERT applications
  text-to-video generation 293
  video captioning 293
  visual tokens, predicting 292
VideoBERT model
  pre-training 286
  pre-training, data source used 291
  preprocessing 291
VideoBERT

applications 292
  used, for learning languages 286
  used, for video representations 286
vocabulary overlap 223, 224, 225

W

Whole Word Masking (WWM) 73, 74
WordPiece 89, 90
WordPiece tokenizer 67, 68
World Atlas of Language Structures (WALS) 226

X

XLM-R model
  about 235
  evaluating 236

Z

zero-shot 221

CPSIA information can be obtained
at www.ICGtesting.com
Printed in the USA
LVHW060610240422
716916LV00011B/98

9 781838 821593